Promoting and Marketing Events

This accessible book introduces students to the theories, concepts and skills required to promote an event successfully. To promote an event effectively it is essential to understand marketing, but it is also important to recognise that it is not just consumers who are the audience: other publics who may not necessarily attend can have a fundamental effect on the success of an event as well. Uniquely therefore, this book covers two related themes: marketing and public relations in an events context. This will offer events planners a comprehensive guide on how to promote events to a range of audiences, and on how to use this to manage an event's long-term reputation.

The book focuses on core marketing and PR current theory specifically relevant to the events industry and introduces topics such as marketing strategy, the consumer, marketing PR and how to use the Internet to promote events. It integrates a range of international case studies from small-scale events to mega-events to help show how theory can be applied in practice. It further includes inserts of interviews with practitioners in the field, to offer insight into the realities of event communication and to show how to overcome potential pitfalls. Learning outcomes, discussion questions and further reading suggestions are included to aid navigation throughout the book, spur critical thinking and further students' knowledge.

The book is essential reading for all students studying events management, and provides valuable reading for students, academics and practitioners interested in marketing and public relations in general.

Nigel Jackson is Programme Manager in Events Management at Plymouth University.

Promoting and Marketing Events

Theory and practice

Nigel Jackson

Routledge
Taylor & Francis Group

LONDON AND NEW YORK

First published 2013
by Routledge
2 Park Square, Milton Park, Abingdon, Oxon OX14 4RN

Simultaneously published in the USA and Canada
by Routledge
711 Third Avenue, New York, NY 10017

Routledge is an imprint of the Taylor & Francis Group, an informa business

British Library Cataloguing in Publication Data
A catalogue record for this book is available from the British Library

Library of Congress Cataloging in Publication Data
Jackson, Nigel A.
    Promoting and marketing events: theory and practice / Nigel Jackson. – 1st ed.
        p. cm.
    Includes bibliographical references and index.
    1. Special events – Marketing. 2. Special events – Public relations. I. Title.
    GT3405.J26 2013
    394.2 – dc23   2012034838

ISBN: 978-0-415-66732-6 (hbk)
ISBN: 978-0-415-66733-3 (pbk)
ISBN: 978-0-203-58316-6 (ebk)

Typeset in Sabon and Frutiger
by Keystroke, Station Road, Codsall, Wolverhampton

MIX
Paper from
responsible sources
FSC FSC® C013056
www.fsc.org

Printed and bound in Great Britain by
TJ International Ltd, Padstow, Cornwall

To those who support me every day, Team Jackson: Catherine, Eliot and Toby.

Contents

Figures and images

Figures

Images

Tables

Case studies

Case studies

Boxes

Preface

This book has been several years in gestation and has two main sources. During my career in the communications field I have used events within a marketing and public relations perspective. Many of the ideas highlighted in this book reflect the lessons I have learnt from an eclectic experience in the political, charity, commercial and agency fields. Of more direct relevance is a year-long module I have been delivering at Plymouth University for six years, 'Promoting Events'. Although structured very differently from my course, this book stems from discussions I have had with students, and from both their and my feeling that there was a gap for an up-to-date textbook which addressed both theory and practice. I always believe that it is important to get behind ideas, so a thread within the book is assessing a number of core theories which may help us better understand events management. These are supported by a range of examples and case studies which provide context, and remind us that every different event will need to establish its own rules and principles in how it communicates. Although clearly I teach in a UK university, most of the theory can be applied universally and much of the practical material draws from events globally. And while my main audience is students, I know from my own experience that ideas, concepts and doctrines can help practitioners. This is especially so in a young industry like events management. I hope that whether you are a student, lecturer, commentator or practitioner this book will be of value to you.

While businesses, communities and politicians have been hosting events for millennia, the study of events management as a discrete discipline is recent, arguably over the last twenty years or so. Understandably the focus has been on establishing the discipline in its own right in a broad sense. This might explain why most events management textbooks have a chapter or two on marketing and public relations. But there have been very few that specifically focus on event communication. Hoyle (2002 and 2012) is an excellent book which is innovative and forward thinking, and this introduction to the subject has been followed up more recently by Masterman and Wood (2006), which provides a very good introduction to promoting events. Some of the material is now becoming slightly dated in a period where events management has changed rapidly. A more practical approach from a US perspective is taken by Saget (2006), which is essentially a 'How to' guide. Similarly, Braggs (2006), looking at his experience in Australia, considers how events are used as a marketing tool. Thus, the student, lecturer and practitioner have had to rely to a large degree on generic marketing and public relations material. Yet the models, lessons and approaches of such generic texts may not easily apply to events management, or events may require unique solutions. This book aims to add to the material available by identifying those lessons which apply to events, and discarding those that do not. This is not a book on marketing and public relations *per se*, but marketing, public relations and communications applied to events management.

Acknowledgements

Obviously any errors are entirely my own, but there are a number of people without whose help this book would not have come to fruition and who I want to thank. Clearly the support and love, not forgetting regular sustenance, of my family has provided me with the right environment. All students on the 'Promoting Events' module have helped stimulate me with their enthusiasm, ideas and comments about communicating events in general. I would also like to record thanks to colleagues at Plymouth University who have offered their comments. I would particularly like to thank Steve Butts for thoughts on evolving events, Richard Parkman for advice on customer service, Wai Mun Lim for many discussions on the links between marketing and events, and Kristin Brophy for her ideas on research methods. Shannon Heaney helped provide insight as to how events use social networking sites, and Beth Clayton and Emily Goss were the coders for the data in Chapter 11. This content analysis of event websites would not have happened without seed corn funding from Plymouth University's Service and Enterprise Research Centre. Over a number of years I have enjoyed discussions on communication and persuasion theory with Darren Lilleker of Bournemouth University. I owe a big thank you to Julia Hidy, who went beyond what I could expect, and whom I hope will be a great source of information and inspiration to my students in years to come.

I would also like to say thank you to the anonymous referees whose comments helped shaped how students and lecturers might use the book. I owe a debt of gratitude to the editorial team at Routledge, Carol Barber, Emma Travis and Faye Leerink, who saw something in my original idea, and have helped a rough idea through to being published. I have been touched by the enthusiasm of those who have been interviewed to provide the case studies, and of those who kindly agreed to check examples. I am particularly grateful for the time they have taken to offer me their experience, ideas and to check my copy. Without them this book would have lacked real-world application.

On a personal note I would like to finish by wondering whether my adopted team, Plymouth Argyle Football Club, will ever play my boyhood heroes West Ham United in the Premier League.

I would also like to acknowledge the following for permission to the use illustrations: Figure 1.2 from Plymouth Business School Seminar Series; Figure 3.4 from Elsevier and Dr Martin Christopher; Figure 6.2 from Festival Awards Ltd; Figure 11.2 from Jackson, N. and Lilleker, D. (2009), 'Building and Architecture of Participation? Political Parties and Web 2.0 in Britain', *Journal of Information Technology and Politics*, 6 (3–4), pp.

Acknowledgements

232–50, Taylor & Francis (http://www.tandfonline.com); Picture 2.1 from the Campaign for Real Ale (CAMRA); Picture 8.1, the Dutch Dress event, from Bavaria Netherlands; Picture 8.2, Advertorial, from Julia Hidy (http://juliahidymarketing.com), *RIS News* (www.risnews. com) and Magstar Inc (www.magstarinc.com).

Chapter 1

Introduction – what is event marketing and public relations?

Introduction

This chapter will help set the scene for understanding both marketing and public relations within the milieu of promoting an event. First, we will set the context of events, and then look at the role they play within the communication process. We will then assess the literature on marketing and public relations within the events field. At the end of the chapter students will be able to:

- Evaluate the meaning of an event.
- Identify the drivers for current change in events management.
- Assess how communication plays a role within events management.
- Critique the current approaches to the promotion of events.

What is an event?

Former UK Prime Minister Harold Macmillan is supposed to have said in the 1960s that as a politician what he most feared was *'Events, my dear boy, events.'* By this he meant that things such as war, industrial conflict and political scandal made it difficult for him to direct government policy in the way he wanted. This apocryphal story highlights a problem for students of events management: namely, that the term 'event' can have many meanings, some of which have no direct bearing on your field of study. In addition to political science and history, the term 'event' also has meaning in mathematics and statistics, psychology and physics. In the natural sciences the term 'event' is more associated with rules of nature, but in the social sciences we are more interested in events which have something to say about the interactions between humans. We need to provide a meaning of the term 'event' that is relevant to events management within the behavioural context of social sciences.

The *Collins Concise Dictionary* (2001) defines an event as: *'Anything that takes place, especially something important; an incident.'* This broad definition means that historians can refer to past events, political scientists to current events and mathematicians can predict the probability of an event occurring. In order for this definition to be helpful, what we need to focus on is that an event is a happening within a physical space, rather than just happening to someone or something. The events you will organise happen to someone precisely because they happen within physical (or occasionally virtual) boundaries.

The events management literature provides a more detailed and tailored definition. For example, Getz (2005) suggests that events have two key traits: each is unique; and they are temporary. This definition, emphasising that each event is different and has a start, middle and end, resonates with several other similar approaches. The temporary nature of an event is emphasised by Silvers (2008: 7), who suggests that an event is: *'The gathering of people at a specified time and place for the purpose of celebration, commemoration, communication, education, reunion and/or leisure.'* Once this purpose has ended then so has the event. The characteristic of uniqueness of every event has led Yeoman *et al.* (2006) to suggest that there is no 'one size fits all' events management approach. This implies that in terms of communication, marketing and public relations the nature of each event will shape the appropriate options available to the event manager.

A different approach to defining an event stresses the role of the event manager. Thus, Van der Wagen (2007: 5) suggests that an event *'Is generally a complex social endeavour characterized by sophisticated planning with a fixed deadline, often involving numerous stakeholders.'* This definition stresses the importance of planning and organisation, but it goes much further and starts to highlight what an event is in marketing and promotional terms. An event implies that there is a range of stakeholders, such as the organisers, funders, participants, attendees, local residents and political actors. This definition reminds us that event management is not simply about ticking off what has to be done on a 'To do' list, but that the planning and communication aspects are integrated not separate. It also leads to what might ostensibly appear to be a philosophical question. Philosophers have asked the question: 'If a tree falls in a forest and no one hears it, has the tree actually fallen?' We might ask: 'If no one attends our event have we really organised an event?' This is not an abstract question, but lies at the core of promoting an event. Inherently, as event managers we should not just want to create an event, but to create a successful event, and to do so we need to communicate effectively with key audiences so that they will attend.

Definition box 1.1

Defining events

Events are essentially happenings constructed to bring together people for a defined period of time to achieve an identified purpose.

Looking at our event definitions, in terms of people this might include individual consumers, organisations, citizens, staff/volunteers and participants, amongst others. The type of events can be very broad, but could include meetings, rallies, training, open days, launches, sport, conventions and entertainment. A defined period might be just a few minutes as with a stunt like a flash mob, a day such as with a religious ceremony, or months as with the 1851 Great Exhibition in the Crystal Palace in Hyde Park, London. Events do not just happen spontaneously: they are thought about and planned, and so inherently seek to fulfil a function. The purpose could be, for example, commercial, social/cultural, economic, macro, micro, political or just purely hedonistic. Indeed, Bowdin *et al.* (2010) suggest that events represent milestones in our lives. Our definition of an event has clear implications on how it will be promoted (as we shall discuss in depth in Chapter 3). Unlike most tangible products an event is something which is consumed when it is produced: it can't be taken home and stored. This intangible nature influences what the consumer wants, what exact event is delivered and how the event manager promotes their event. What event consumers are effectively 'buying' is some form of experience. For example, the organisers of the Taste of the World Festival (www.tasteofthe worldfestival.com/) held in Los Angeles have to attract and then manage large crowds, every one of whom is a consumer looking to have a culinary experience.

Types of event

Given the huge number, and wide variety, of events organised each year it is helpful to identify shared characteristics across events so that they can be codified within typologies. Such typologies help us make greater sense of the proliferation of events, by identifying commonalities between apparently disparate activities. They also help practitioners identify and promote their specialist areas of expertise. Most textbooks suggest that we can identify two main approaches to constructing an events typology: by size; or the form of the event.

Bowdin *et al.* (2010) suggest that in terms of size we can identify four different types:

1 *Local or community event* – generally small and linked to a particular geography: for example, the Bretforton Silver Band Asparagus Auction, held at the Fleece Inn, Bretforton (www.thefleeceinn.co.uk/) in the heart of the world's best asparagus-growing area, the Vale of Evesham. Being probably the most high-profile part of the British Asparagus Festival Day in May, the auction brings thousands of people to a very small village. This is a many-faceted event, as it brings together the local community, attracts tourists and effectively launches a product each year.
2 *Major events* – these are capable of attracting significant numbers of visitors and media coverage, offering potentially positive economic benefits. Typically, this could be a sporting event such as American football's Super Bowl held in a different city every January. The Indian Premier League (IPL) 20:20 cricket competition takes place in March and April at nine cities throughout India, and attracts huge crowds and international television interest.
3 *Hallmark events* – they need not automatically be bigger than major events, but they are synonymous with a particular place, such as the Frankfurt Book Fair (www.book-fair.com/ en/) in Germany. Tracing its origins back some five hundred years, and in its current form since 1949, the Frankfurt Book Fair attracts more than 7,000 exhibitors from more than one hundred countries. More recently, the eco-friendly Burning Man Festival (http:// burningman.com/) has added a new element to hallmark events. Not only is it associated with a desert, Black Rock, Nevada, USA, but a temporary place is created – Black Rock City – and then taken down again at the end of the event.
4 *Mega-events* – these symbolic events are global and can influence the host country's economy. They tend to be either sporting or tourist in nature, such as the FIFA World Cup, IOC Olympics and the World Expo. Given that there are very few such mega-events, competition to be selected is fierce and is often a lengthy and expensive process. The bid team hope that winning will lead to positive social, economic and political impacts. Hosting such events is risky, but there is a perception that the benefits could be very significant.

This stressing of size implies that there is a hierarchy of events, with some being more important than others. Primarily, this is based upon their wider impact on society, the economy and politics. The smaller, and presumably less well-known, events may require greater relative levels of promotion to attract volunteers, participants or customers than the larger well known national and international events. This does not mean that hallmark and mega-events do not need promotion: rather, that it might focus on a wider range of stakeholders far beyond just paying customers, also including VIPs, sponsors, the media and possibly those who access an event from home via television, radio or the Internet. This typology of events implies that different marketing and public relations approaches, techniques and tools may be applicable for each classification. If size is a means of codifying events, then promotion is likely to emphasise this as part of an event's USP (unique selling point).

The second common way of codifying events is by form, whereby the focus is on the content or field of activity of an event. For example, Bowdin *et al.* (2010) identify just three types of event that can be categorised by form: cultural; sports; and business. This simple, imprecise and all-encompassing approach suggests that every event can be classified within one of these three categories. Thus, culture might include local community and religious events, sports would cover both amateur and professional, and business would be any event which helps an organisation (not just commercial) to achieve its goals. Form allows us to identify detailed activity, but Bowdin *et al.*'s categorisation is too sweeping in suggesting that all events can only be classified within one of these three approaches. Greater clarity of event types can be achieved by having more forms, so that, as Table 1.1 notes, both Getz (2008) and Raj *et al.* (2009) identify ten types of event.

There are clear similarities between both Getz and Raj *et al.*'s. typologies, as they reflect activities within individual, societal, business and political life. They are comprehensive lists, reflecting the fact that many event managers specialise in a particular type of event or market, though even here we might wonder where some events, such as stunts, fit in. These wider typologies suggest that while there may be commonalities of promotional approach applicable to all ten forms, we could also expect a level of promotional specialism reflecting the nature of an event, its purpose and its stakeholders' requirements. One promotional size does not fit all.

Table 1.1 Form of events

Getz (2008)	Raj et al. (2009)
Cultural celebrations	Religious events
Religious events	Cultural events
Political and state events	Musical events
Arts and entertainment	Sporting events
Business and trade events	Personal and private events
Education and scientific events	Political and governmental events
Sports events	Commercial and business events
Recreational events	Corporate events
Private events	Special events
Events at the margin	Leisure events

However, in Table 1.2, I suggest that we can go a stage further in our event typology, one that inherently links to the communication of those events: namely, their nature. Events can be understood and categorised not just by their size or form, but also by the interaction between the organiser and the attendee. We can identify three factors which can shape the nature of an event.

First, the source of the event idea can be initiated top-down, typically from the senior managers of an organisation. In most fields this approach is the norm, with senior managers discussing ideas and deciding on actions. But alternatively, occasionally an event idea and/or organisation can be driven from the bottom-up, as when the members of a large organisation, or even those not aligned to any formal organisational structure, come together in an *ad hoc* fashion. For example, the November 2010 student protest marches in London were organised nationally by the NUS (National Union of Students), but the decision to go ahead would in part have reflected pressure from individual student unions and students on NUS's executive body.

Second, what is the role of the audience of any event? Are they supposed to be essentially passive, merely taking in messages? Or are they an active component of the event? Spectators at a sporting event are, essentially, passive in that they do not take part in the actual contest (though they do help create the atmosphere), but the sport's participants are clearly active. Many events, especially sporting and entertainment based, may have both active and passive audiences, but some, such as marathons and triathlons, are primarily organised for the benefit of active participants and not spectators.

Third, communication to event stakeholders may be vertical or horizontal. It is worth noting that while vertical communication is often assumed to be only top-down communication, it also implies the potential for some two-way upwards communication, often in the form of feedback. Horizontal communication is where information flows between event actors: for example, the different departments of an event, such as marketing and finance, or groups of spectators as with online discussion forums. Where vertical communication may often be between manager and subordinate, horizontal is often between peers.

The nature of the event has an impact on its promotion, especially on how to communicate with, and between, audiences. Event managers may essentially consider the purpose of communication to be to help them achieve their aims by informing stakeholders of, and getting them to attend, an event. Outwith of formal event evaluation they may be tempted to view such communication as one-way top-down. This would certainly be the implication if events are assessed by size and form only. However, this third typology based on the nature of an event reminds us that communication between stakeholders of an event is not necessarily simply a vertical monologue. The astute event manager is flexible and willing to apply different promotional approaches, often encouraging dialogue, to different types of event.

Table 1.2 Nature of events

Factor	Response
Event origins	Top-down or bottom-up
Role of audience	Passive or active
Direction of communication	Vertical or horizontal

Developments in events management

Events do not remain static: rather, they reflect wider changes in society, the economy and politics, and so are gradually evolving. As a result we can identify trends in events management. For example, if society is hierarchical in nature, then events will be 'silos' which enable different social strata to defend and maintain their own discrete way of life. Alternatively, in a multicultural society events can play a role in helping different cultures interact. Cultural, economic and political factors will develop at differing rates across countries. Figure 1.1 outlines how such factors might shape the nature of events which exist at any one time. To understand the purpose and usage of events we need to understand the context within which they exist.

Current trends and developments in events management are usually identified through a combination of expert opinion and the study of empirical data. Looking to the future, even only from one to five years, is an inexact science and so there is no single consensus for what events and events management will look like as your career develops. We can, however, identify certain traits which different sources emphasise. Donald Getz (2009), who has given considerable thought to assessing where events management is going, has suggested that past events reflected an organic approach whereby they 'sprung' from communities. Such events had a social and cultural importance, whereas he suggests that the motive for events now is to meet commercial and strategic purposes. A slightly different emphasis is made by Raj *et al.* (2009), who suggest that events are moving away from primarily those that were religious and national ceremonies, which are collective in nature, towards events which reflect an individual's own lifestyle and economic interests. So the purpose of events is to meet individual needs in a consumer society rather than collective needs. Bowdin *et al.* (2010) bring together these two approaches by suggesting that events are becoming more important to individuals, groups and political actors. While community and collective-based events will continue to exist, the literature suggests that we should expect more and more events that meet personal individual and organisational needs, reflecting changes in society, commerce and where power resides.

These broad developments are having an impact on the nature and importance of marketing and public relations within events. Community and collective based events, such as country fairs, local art shows and village sporting activities, can often be promoted by word of mouth

Levels	Factors	Possible influence on events
Societal	Stratified society	Maintains differences between groups
	Flat society	Encourages different groups to share experiences
Economic	Booming economy	'Feel good' factor encourages people to spend money on attending events
	Faltering economy	Difficult for organisations to justify spending money on entertainment and having fun
Political	Liberal democracy	Businesses and organisations trusted to run events with limited political interference
	Authoritarian regimes	Awareness of the possible political effects of any event can lead to political interference and micromanaging

Figure 1.1 The impact on events of wider factors

through existing, and interconnected, social networks such as family, work and social strata. More individualistic and organisational events are often reaching an audience they don't know personally. This leads us to related consequences. The first is greater reliance on marketing and public relations to reach and persuade people to attend. The second, as Masterman and Wood (2006) suggest, is that events will play a more prominent role within marketing, and so they believe events will be more important for both consumers and organisations. Indeed, George P. Johnson's *Event View 2010* found that 32 per cent of respondents to their questionnaire consider event marketing a vital component of their marketing plan. The implication is that events, and consequently event promotion, is becoming increasingly important for consumers, citizens, governments and both commercial and non-commercial organisations.

While event fields and markets will be expanding differently, and some even contracting, in Figure 1.2 Lim and Jackson (2009) suggest that any growth in the provision of events is likely to be driven by any one of three factors. While they recognise that some events are organised as a commercial concern designed to make a profit, they focus on why other organisations might increasingly make use of events. They suggest that three industries, in particular, are shaping the growth of events. First, the hospitality industry, be it restaurants, hotels or venues, has turned to events as a means of encouraging new clientele or increasing existing clientele spend. For example, hotels which host events may increase occupancy, so that those who attend a Murder-Mystery Night may stay overnight at the hosting hotel. Second, the tourism industry, be it tourist boards, local authorities or trade associations, has turned to events as a means of

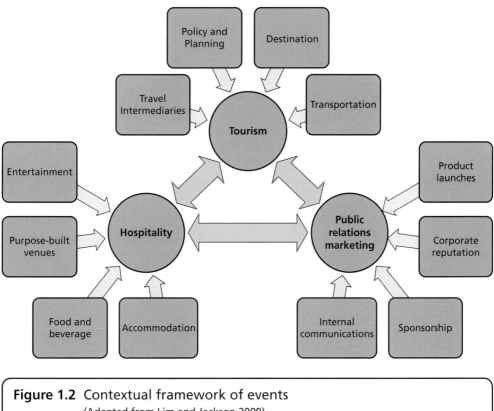

Figure 1.2 Contextual framework of events
(Adapted from Lim and Jackson 2009)

either attracting tourists or enhancing the stay of visitors. For example, Devine *et al.* (2010) assessed the value of ironman competitions as a tourist attraction aimed at participants, and Foley *et al.* (2009a) note that Singapore has sought to turn itself into an international events tourist location by hosting a range of sporting events such as golf, badminton, motor racing and marathons. Third, marketing and public relations practitioners appear to be turning to events as a means of achieving their objectives. One of the obvious manifestations of this is product launches, such as Apple's iPad at a press conference in January 2010 in San Francisco with a subsequent launch day in April 2010. Less obvious is how events can fit in with enhancing corporate reputation: for example, the British Phonographic Industry's (BPI) annual BRIT awards help promote the UK music industry. The career development of events management students will be largely shaped by how these three event fields evolve.

The link between events and communication

Leonard Hoyle (2002) draws an analogy between events and the film *Field of Dreams* starring Kevin Costner, where a mid-West farmer is persuaded to build a baseball diamond in his field of maize. The clincher is the phrase that pops into his head: *'If you build it they will come.'* Hoyle suggests that if you have the right product for the right market it can be promoted to encourage people to attend. I would suggest that this is not enough. The importance of promoting your event suggests that we should refine this to: *'If you build it, will they come and then will they return another day?'* Although some events are one-offs designed never to be repeated, this is not the expectation with most, so the event manager needs to encourage visitors to return the next time this or a similar event is held. This implies that the aim of communication for the event manager should be for the long term, and not just for the immediate event. The event manager is not in a position akin to selling 'snake oil', where all that matters is the individual sale: rather, a longer term relationship needs to be built.

For the event manager, communication can have two slightly different roles, shaping the relationship between the two:

● It is the means by which you market and promote your event.
● Some events are part of the marketing/promotion process.

It is important for the event manager to understand this duality. Sometimes marketing and public relations are the means by which you promote your event, and sometimes your event itself is part of someone else's (your client's or organisation's) wider promotional objectives. We noted above in Figure 1.2 that this is a key driver for why events exist. When you have a sponsor for your event you could be doing both: promoting your event but also being aware of what communication results your sponsor wants to achieve from your event. When assessing the concepts outlined in this book, it is important to know in which context an event is being used.

The bulk of this book will focus on the former aspect, namely how the event manager can get people to their event. However, we shall briefly introduce here the latter, namely how events are used by others. Such events have been referred to by Masterman and Wood (2006) as promotional events, and Johnson (2008) has used the term event marketing. Whatever they are called the primary purpose of such events is to promote a product, brand, organisation or idea to a specific audience. But more than this, as Masterman and Wood (2006) suggest, promotional events inherently encourage audience involvement. For example, *Cycle England* suggests that promotional events such as cycling festivals can encourage non-cyclists to try cycling. Similarly, as part of their global launch for 3D televisions, Samsung in July 2010 used figures from the 3D film *Monsters Versus Aliens* at a promotional event in Vietnam. We shall return to this concept in Chapter 3, where we look at experiential marketing, one of the latest trends in marketing. The key component of such events is that they add something which other marketing techniques cannot offer: they are experience based. It is for this reason that Emma Wood (undated) suggests that event marketing is not merely another form of promotion, but a new and different way of marketing because it can deal with individuals/small groups, can be customised, enhances interactivity, and can link to social responsibility. Promotional events are one answer to the question: 'Why organise an event?'

Book structure

There exists a consensus within the, admittedly limited, event marketing literature that Integrated Marketing Communications (IMC) is the appropriate approach, and that public relations is merely one portion of marketing (Hoyle 2002; Masterman and Wood 2006; Getz 2008; Raj *et al.* 2009; Hoyle 2012). Indeed, Sneath *et al.* (2005) go further and suggest that IMC also provides a means of evaluating the effectiveness of an event. As a general marketing practice, IMC came to prominence in the 1980s and 1990s as organisations sought to apply 'joined-up thinking' to their marketing. This approach reflected changes in the consumer landscape and the existence of new media systems (Kitchen and Schultz 2009). Pickton and Broderick (2001: 66) have defined IMC as the

> Bringing together of all marketing communications activities. To many IMC has become recognised as the process of integrating all elements of the promotional mi*x*.

At the core of IMC is that marketing communications techniques and tools are integrated within an event to deliver a coherent and consistent message to customers. In other words, all those involved in marketing are pulling in the same direction, so Raj *et al.* (2009) suggest that IMC harnesses synergy. Marketing is the glue that binds all external activities.

An alternative, and indeed opposing, approach to IMC is Integrated Communications (IC). This rejects the contention that marketing is the dominant partner and suggests in fact that public relations is the senior discipline, a view normally associated with James Grunig, the leading public relations commentator. Wightman (1999: 19) goes further and suggests that IMC is dead and defines IC as: '*Integrating the communications functions to communicate to all of an organization's stakeholders.*' The key difference then is that where marketing focuses on communicating with just customers, public relations focuses on all possible stakeholders (Gronstedt 1996; Grunig and Grunig 1998).

In terms of just marketing an event IMC is perfectly understandable and applicable, but I suggest that it is too narrow and this book will consider a broader horizon. However, this book does not support the view that public relations is or should be dominant, as suggested by IC. In some circumstances, such as product launches, IMC is entirely appropriate, but this book suggests that public relations is a discrete discipline in its own right which should be considered equal to marketing, with both working towards a greater good. Marketing and public relations work best when they are pulling together, working in an agreed direction, not when they appear to disagree on the key targets and who is in charge. The reason why only using the IMC model is too rigid an approach is that public relations is not a single concept. Rather, for event managers to be able to make the most out of public relations they should consider it to consist of two separate, but related, components: marketing public relations (MPR); and corporate

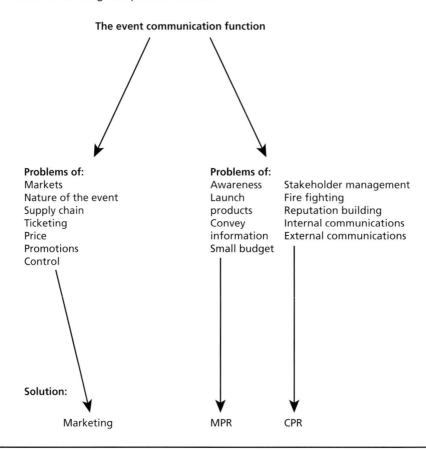

The event communication function

Problems of:
Markets
Nature of the event
Supply chain
Ticketing
Price
Promotions
Control

Problems of:
Awareness   Stakeholder management
Launch   Fire fighting
products   Reputation building
Convey   Internal communications
information   External communications
Small budget

Solution:

Marketing   MPR   CPR

Figure 1.3 The event communication process

public relations (CPR). MPR is used to support marketing activities and so is consistent with the IMC orthodoxy, but CPR is where public relations adds a completely different world view requiring a different approach. This book, therefore, rejects the narrowness of just a marketing approach: instead we assess events promotion by considering both marketing and public relations as two halves of the same whole, not separate. Similarly, the view that public relations alone should dominate the communication process is rejected, as different circumstances require different communication responses. Our approach is to consider the effective promotion of events to be a combination of both marketing and public relations techniques and approaches, within the remit of the communications function of an event.

Figure 1.3 suggests that the event communicator should think in terms of overall communications, thereby identifying what their specific problems are. Depending on the nature of each problem, and the best solution to it, this would direct them to the most appropriate approach and tools. In some circumstances this might weigh actions towards marketing and in others towards public relations, but whichever it is, ultimately it should be viewed within an overall communications function.

Universities around the world take two main approaches to teaching communications, marketing and public relations within events management degrees. First, some such as my own university teach all-year modules, and so probably cover between 16 and 24 topics, depending on the length of the academic year and the nature of assessments. Whilst such modules may or may not have greater depth, they are almost certainly going to have greater breadth and cover a much wider range of topics. Hence, communications, marketing and public relations are all likely to feature in the same module. Second, many other universities, especially in the USA, take a semester approach where there are shorter, more focused modules. Typically, these might cover between 8 and 12 topics, and so marketing and public relations are likely to be taught in separate modules. Indeed, some universities only teach one of these, usually a more marketing focused course, and some teach marketing and public relations modules in different years. This book has been structured in such a way that it can be taught either within an all-year module or shorter semester modules: lecturers and students can dip in and out as need be.

The book offers four chapters each on marketing and public relations. But before we start on these equal sections, we note that event managers are in the persuasion business, and Chapter 2 will outline the relevance of communication models and apply persuasion theories. This chapter lays down some important foundations which can be applied to both marketing and public relations. The first main section of the book, Chapters 3–6, will address event marketing. Chapter 3 will define marketing and identify its different components, techniques and tools. It will finish by assessing the application to events of three philosophical approaches to marketing: transactional; relationship; and experiential. Chapter 4 will define the meaning of strategy in general and explore how it can help the event marketer. It will consider positioning an event, and the construction of an event marketing plan. Chapter 5 outlines the marketing mix, first by introducing the traditional 4Ps approach and then the more service oriented 7Ps approach. Chapter 6 focuses on the consumer, market research, buying behaviour and segmentation, both of customers and participants. The concept of a consumer can be different for an event compared with other industries. The second main section, Chapters 7–10, will outline the role and importance of public relations. Chapter 7 will introduce why public relations is important for the event manager, define public relations and then adapt Jackson's (2010) public relations approaches model to understand the use of public relations in events. Chapter 8 defines MPR, and explains how it can be used to raise the visibility of an event. It will address all the tools used, such as sponsorship, stunts, guerrilla tactics and advertorials. Chapter 9 is more practitioner focused and will explain how an event manager can raise their profile to their key audiences through media relations. For instance, we will address how to employ some of the key tools, such as writing a press release and being interviewed. Chapter 10 switches to the strategic level by addressing the meaning and importance of corporate reputation, and the potential costs of losing it. The last substantive chapter, Chapter 11, will change style by looking at the use of both marketing and public relations together within one space: namely, how to promote an event online. This chapter will use some primary research data to assess how events use the Internet. It will address key conceptual issues, explore the use of various Internet modalities and evaluate how event communicators have used the Internet. The final chapter will provide a conclusion by drawing together the common themes of this book and outlining key lessons for event managers and events management students.

We finish this chapter with an unusual case study: Elfstedentocht in the Netherlands, which poses the almost unique problem of communicating for an event that rarely happens. This book addresses the material which would allow you to know what to do in whatever circumstances you find yourself.

CASE STUDY 1.1

Eleven Cities Tour (Elfstedentocht)

Imagine organising an event without actually knowing when it will happen, or even if it will happen at all. This is the situation the Royal Society of the Eleven Friesian Cities (www.elfstedentocht.nl/) finds itself in each year.

The association organises the 200km ice skating tour of eleven Frisian cities in the Netherlands, which takes place on the canals that runs between the cities if the ice is thick enough.

Each October the association selects the 16,000 of its 30,000 members who can participate. Only members of the association who have been so selected can participate. However, selection does not mean that participants will actually take part, for the event is rare, having been held only fifteen times in the twentieth century.

The ice needs to be at least 15cm in depth across the whole 200km. The last time it was held was in 1997, so in February 2012 when much of northern Europe had a severe winter front excitement grew. The organisers had to recruit 10,000 volunteers to marshal the event, had to decide if it was going to happen and if so on which day, and they had to deal with the media. The main news story in the Dutch media was the weather conditions, and what percentage chance there was of the Elfstedentocht taking place. A press conference from the organisers was broadcast live on national television. Hotel rooms in the area were booked just in case, and people voluntarily brushed snow off the canals to encourage the ice to reach the magical 15cm.

If the decision was made to go ahead, the event was likely to attract an estimated 2 million spectators along the course, with live television coverage. This event becomes almost a symbol of the soul of the Netherlands as a country.

In February 2012 the ice got to 12–13cm thick, with an estimated 63 per cent likelihood of the event happening, but two days later it was called off as the weather warmed up significantly. As the organisers said (https://twitter.com/11stvereniging): 'It's frustrating but safety comes first, the ice is just not thick enough.' They signed off by saying 'Thanks for the past few days. As long as the frost does not fully come back, we remain in the background. Hope to see you soon.'

Discussion questions

Events have many meanings, but we are essentially referring to some form of happening, be it physical or virtual. This chapter highlights that events communicators are faced with key issues:

1   How differently should you package a commercial as opposed to a culturally based event?
2   What is the impact on the event communicator of whether you are marketing your own event, or someone is using you to meet their marketing objectives?

3 Why is it not enough to say if we build it they will come?
4 Why does it matter how an event uses marketing and public relations, and what is the relationship between the two?

Further information

Other sources which might help you consider the issues outlined in this chapter include:

Journals

Tsai, S.-p. (2005) 'Integrated Marketing as a Management of Holistic Consumer Experience', *Business Horizons*, 48: 431–41 – explains IMC as an approach.

Websites

http://www.eventia.org.uk/ – event trade body that provides a range of material.
http://www.meetpie.com/ – source of information on the meetings industry.
http://www.mpiweb.org/Home – global association for meetings professionals.
http://www.eventmagazine.co.uk/ – UK trade magazine.
http://www.event-management-uk.co.uk/ – list of event management websites.

Chapter 2

Communication and persuasion within events

Introduction

Event managers are in the communication and persuasion business. This chapter will first explain why communication and persuasion theory are relevant for an event manager. We will then look at communications theory, drawing on empirical research from journalism, media studies and political science. The last section, persuasion, is heavily influenced by work within the field of psychology, addressing both cognitive (thought process) and heuristic (peripheral cues) factors. For an event manager to be effective they need to get their message across. By the end of this chapter students will be able to:

● Understand the importance of communication to event managers.
● Assess the relevance of key communication theories.
● Evaluate key models of the persuasion process.
● Assess the applicability of persuasion strategies.

The importance of communication and persuasion

Two of the core skills that event managers require are to communicate effectively by reaching their key audiences, and then to persuade them to act in the desired way. We can identify at least four areas beyond overt promotional activities where communication and persuasion theory may play a key role.

First, as Van der Wagen (2007) notes, an important part of an event manager's job is to get staff and teams to work together. One important aspect of this is internal communication: for example, informing different staff teams what is happening, and what is expected of them. So an event manager who recognises the means to good communication, is likely to give a clearer, more structured and effective briefing to temporary staff who turn up on the day.

Second, an effective communicator is able to negotiate better terms and prices with suppliers and contractors for their event. As Fowler (1996) and Kennedy (2003) note, negotiation helps two or more sides resolve their differences by finding some common ground through compromise. Persuasion theory can help an event manager get a better deal, perhaps in the form of a discount or preferential payment terms. This is underpinned by Unt's (1999) observation that communication is a vital component of effective negotiation.

Third, communication plays a key role operationally, in terms of how on the day of the event the individual departments and teams communicate to one another, health and safety, crowd management and logistical issues. For example, Fruin (1984) suggests that communication is one of the techniques required for effective crowd management. By this Fruin means both the systems in place to communicate messages, and what is actually said to staff, participants and attendees.

Fourth, impression management (Goffman 1959; Leary and Kowalski 1990), a component of persuasion, can play a key role in the personal and career development of event managers, by enhancing the impression they give of themselves to their superiors. Additionally, personal development is an area which Allen (2004) suggests is often overlooked by event managers, but persuasion theory can help you progress in your career. As well as 'selling' your event, you need also to be able to 'sell' yourself.

This suggests that there are at least five areas of an event manager's role where communication and persuasion are present. The most obvious, and the one this book focuses on, is the promotional process, but it also exists within the managerial, logistical and personal development aspects of event management. We can also possibly add a sixth: namely, getting an event off the ground in the first place. The event manager will need to persuade colleagues, managers, funders, other organisations, external stakeholders, sometimes venues and possibly participants that they have a good idea. This internal persuasion stage is required before an event has any chance of becoming a reality and thereby requiring that public and external promotion takes place.

Figure 2.1 shows that an event communicator's activities are shaped by the needs of how they communicate and persuade. In order to get people to attend, the communicator needs to understand, for example, how advertising can best be persuasive or how to negotiate costs down to keep prices affordable. While this chapter will introduce a range of theoretical material, communication and persuasion are not abstract concepts for event communicators.

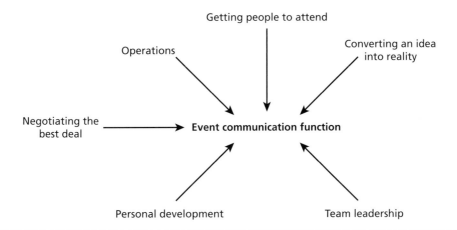

Figure 2.1 The role of communication and persuasion for an event

What is communication?

Definition box 2.1

Defining communication

Communication is the means by which information and opinion about an event are transferred from one person to another. It may be in the form of words, pictures, aurally or combine all of these. Communication is used to inform event stakeholders, change their attitudes and ultimately to encourage a change in behaviour, i.e. attend the event. Communication can be both deliberate and unintended.

As noted in the previous chapter, events need to be promoted to external audiences so people attend, but they also have a duality of purpose in that they themselves can be tools for achieving communication objectives. More specifically, Getz (2008: 152) notes that: *'Events can be considered communication tools or artefacts.'* Events are a means of getting across a message, which as Getz notes need not be just organisational, but they can have personal meanings to the receiver. For example, in different cultures certain birthdays such as the ages 13, 21 and 40 may have significant meaning by denoting adolescence, adulthood and middle age. There are, then, three possible levels to communication and events. An event organiser will want to communicate that an event is happening, for example, in the form of marketing communications. The event itself may be used to communicate a message about a product or organisation, as with promotional events (Masterman and Wood 2006). Lastly, events may be a means of communicating personal messages about an individual or group, so that as Getz (2008) notes they hold ritualistic meaning. Communication is ubiquitous: without it the event will not function effectively.

Event managers may use communication in a number of ways. Probably the first question to address is whether communication will be primarily mediated, unmediated or a combination of both. Mediated communication is indirect, using a third party to interpret and pass on a message. This approach was first identified by Lazarsfeld *et al.* (1944) when they assessed the use of the media during the 1940 US Presidential election. Once mass communication media, especially television, dominated political and economic discourse from the 1950s and 1960s, most organisations relied on mediated communication for external affairs. Indeed, some commentators believe that we now live in a mediated society, so that we see reality via what is projected by the media. This suggests there is a link between our everyday experiences, and what we see, hear and read in the media. For example, London 2012 was experienced worldwide by more people through television and the Internet, than actually attended a session. The dominance of mass communications, in how we receive information, has resulted in media management dominating external communications. The strength of mediated communications is that it offers third-party endorsement, typically through journalists, so a message appears more credible. The weakness is that the media may ignore your event, stress what you consider to be the less important messages or give it the sort of negative publicity you do not want. The alternative is direct communication from the event organiser straight to their key audiences, perhaps in the form of flyers, direct mail and meetings. This should minimise the opportunities for misunderstanding or for outside factors to 'distort' (Kotler 2005), or interrupt, the meaning of the message. The weakness of this approach is that the receiver may think 'You would say that', and so there might be a lack of credibility. However, increasingly this divide between strategies is being broken down, with Jackson and Lilleker (2004) referring to media agents who will use both.

Communication may be slightly more complex than just being simply direct or indirect. Figure 2.2 suggests there can be different lengths to the communication chain. Direct communication would normally be considered short, but indirect can be of different lengths. A medium chain would have only one gatekeeper – perhaps a parent, the media or employer. The long chain might use one gatekeeper, say the media, as a means to get to another, and parents in order to get to the final intended recipient, in this case children.

Historically we can see how new technologies are used to reach audiences. Norris (2000) developed the idea of three different ages of communication: pre-modern; modern; and post-modern. Table 2.1 adapts this model to explain the type of events which might use each form of communication. Pre-modern events, relying primarily on personal contacts and word of mouth, tend to be more localised and community based events. Mass communication encourages larger events aimed at bigger mass audiences. If the event manager is going to the expense of advertising, then they probably need to produce as big an event as possible to cover their costs. Post-modern communication based on more targeted one-to-one communication leads to more specialised events. Interestingly, as noted by Sheth and Parvatiyar (1995), such direct communication removes the middle person from the process, and so encourages a return of some of the communication channels of the pre-modern era based around personal contact. Changes in communication can shape the nature of those events that are provided.

We can also identify differences in the direction of communications. The first obvious difference is whether communication is designed to be one-way (monologue) or two-way (dialogue). With one-way communication the message is designed to inform the receiver, so it might be to tell them that an event is happening. Two-way communication allows for some

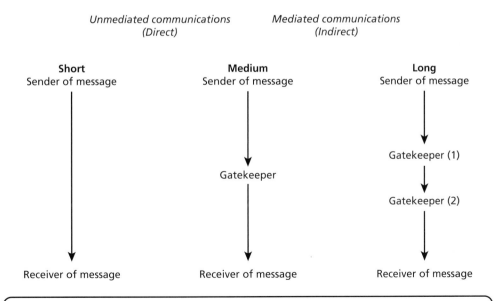

Figure 2.2 The nature of the communication chain

Table 2.1 The developing use of communication

Type	Era of dominance	Characteristics	Promotional techniques	Type of event
Pre-modern	Nineteenth century through to 1930s	Personal meetings, public meetings and personal contacts	Word of mouth Flyers/posters	Traditional community events Rallies/marches and public meetings
Modern	Dominated from 1930s (radio) and 1960s (television)	Mass media communications	Advertising	Popular mass-attendee events, often attracting the lowest common denominator
Post-modern	Some Westernised countries have started to challenge the dominance of modern communications since the 1990s	Wider range of communication channels used, of a more personalised nature	Internet Direct mail Text messaging Word of mouth	More niche and specialist events

(Adapted from Norris 2000)

form of feedback, so that the receiver of the message can offer a response, be it in writing, orally or through body language. For example, many training courses and conferences have formal evaluation sheets which ask delegates of their experience of the event. A second aspect is whether communication is vertical, horizontal or both. Vertical communication is up and down between different levels of an organisation. It can be one-way, typically top-down, or it can be, less commonly, also bottom-up. This is necessary when clear, unambiguous information must be communicated between different levels of an event. Horizontal communication tends to be between the same levels within an event, such as different event departments or spectators, and so inherently implies two-way communication. It is appropriate when ideas need to be developed between different organisers, or when event attendees share their experiences. This sharing of experiences can actually have an impact on the nature of the event. For example, the followers of many professional sports clubs add to their experience by engaging with online forums, so that supporters of the English football club Liverpool may log on to www.redandwhitekop.com to discuss their team. Vertical and horizontal communication are not necessarily in competition. In some circumstances one is more appropriate than the other, and in different circumstances they complement one another, meeting different audience needs.

Communication theory

Linear communication models

The first communication models were not based on empirical data; rather, they relied on assumptions made about the communication process. The propagandistic role of the Committee on Public Information by the US Government during World War I led the American political scientist Harold Lasswell to construct a neat and simple formula: Who Says What to Whom in Which Channel with What Effect? (Lasswell 1927) Similarly, in the 1920s and 1930s a number of left-wing intellectuals associated with the Frankfurt School in Europe concluded that the rise of fascism was due to a 'silver bullet' (Bottomore 1984; Strinati 2004). They suggested that the masses ingested information via a metaphorical 'hypodermic needle', where the intended message is directly received, understood and wholly accepted by the receiver. This was their explanation of why the German people accepted the Nazis. Mass media, then in the form of newspapers and radio, had an immediate effect on their readers and listeners. For example, reports suggest that CBS's airing in news format of the H.G. Wells story *War of the Worlds* led some people to believe that Martians really had landed in America (Weinstock 2001). However, Bernstein (1984) noted the existence of 'noise', which can take many forms, such as being unable to actually hear, not understanding the visual signs or words and the receiver not concentrating because of their interest in other things.

Such criticisms were addressed in models constructed by Shannon and Weaver (1948) and Schramm (1954), which effectively added a feedback loop into the process. This meant that the receiver was offered the ability to provide some form of feedback directly, indirectly or through body language which the sender of the message used to help them revise the message. Whilst these models, especially Shannon and Weaver's basic model, are still presented in textbooks, by the 1950s empirical data largely undermined them. The research on US Presidential elections found that newspapers did not directly affect the attitudes and behaviour of the receiver: rather, the process was more subtle (Lazarsfeld *et al.* 1944; Berelson *et al.* 1954). The basic linear models may offer us a simple means of understanding the communication process to get people to attend our event.

Mass media effects

Mass media effects theories seek to identify what is the impact of the media, and how it might affect people in different ways. The event manager who accepts some form of media effects theory will recognise the importance to them of media management: if the media does have an effect, then we want to influence the media. The research noted above on US Presidential elections suggested that the effect of the media was selective. The first variation was the two-step flow, which implied that the media did not act as a direct hypodermic needle injecting a message, but rather that the impact was through 'opinion leaders'. As Figure 2.3 shows, opinion leaders were of the same social standing as their peers, but on each particular issue or topic

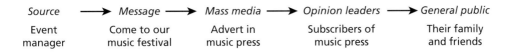

Figure 2.3 The application of the two-step flow model

their opinion was considered to have more weight because of their prior interest in that topic. Given that many events have a social aspect, most spectators do not want to attend alone but want friends and colleagues to come with them. Knowledge of this model may help event managers. For example, one of my students has an interest in darts, and in persuading her friends who were not so interested to attend the 888.com Premier League Darts in March 2011 at the Westpoint Arena, Exeter, UK she was acting as an opinion leader. Such opinion leaders can increase attendance at events by bringing along their friends and family.

The two-step model was refined to the multi-step when John Robinson (1976) noted that information is filtered through a series of opinion formers. This suggested that there exist a number of relays from a source to a large audience. Robinson believed that this could also be because of their different social position, as opinion formers might be considered experts in their field of interest. Figure 2.4 shows how multi-step flow may apply to an event. Rogers' (1962) work on the diffusion of ideas, new products and technologies and why some are adopted and others are not, is, within the marketing field, an example of the multi-step flow. Using the Robinson definition, bloggists become opinion formers such as www.eventmanager blog.com, by being read and linked to by other bloggists; the quantity and quality of linkage to a blogger's site creates a kind of social status (Clark 2001). Similarly, tweeters may play the same role, so that @amyclarke_uk as a member of the Royal Shakespeare Company's (RSC's) marketing team regularly tweets on the Arts, and so influences opinion. The views of such opinion formers may be an effective way of attracting attention to an event. As a consequence communication theory can help event managers identify who their target audiences should be – not just those who might attend our event, but also crucially those who may influence others to attend.

In the late 1980s and early 1990s countercultures around the world began to organise what became referred to as raves. In the UK they did so in part because of dissatisfaction with existing nightclubs and changes in local authority policies, but also to create a sense of exclusivity and belonging. Typically, they were held in isolated farmers' fields or abandoned industrial units. Attendees would hear about them at the last moment by word of mouth, by mobile phone, and

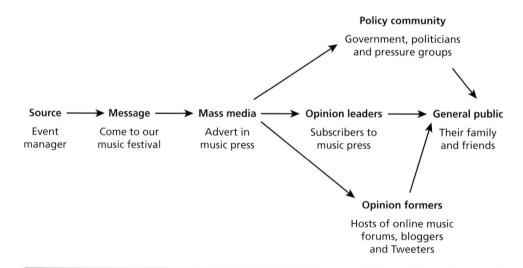

Figure 2.4 The application of the multi-step flow model

be directed to drive to a place, where they were told to go somewhere else, and this 'cloak and dagger' process might be repeated several times to throw off the authorities, until eventually they arrived at the site. The resultant high-level press interest claiming that such raves encouraged drug taking led to action by the policy community (the Government), and the police attempted to stop these 'illegal raves' happening and the organisers were often brought before the courts. Arguably the key role was played by some of the popular press who 'demonised' these events, which led to changes in public policy.

There are two variants of agenda setting which can have an impact on events promotion. First, Tichenor *et al.*'s (1970) knowledge gap hypothesis suggests that different socio-economic groups use different sources of information. They also suggest that those in higher socio-economic classes gather and retain more information, and so are easier to reach than lower socio-economic groups. For example, for a local event those in higher socio-economic groups are more likely to read a local newspaper. Second, Ball-Rokeach and DeFleur's (1976) dependency model suggests that we do not depend on all media equally. If a medium meets a wide range of your needs, then you are likely to be more dependent on it. In addition, in periods of high social instability we are more reliant on the media for information. This means that the effect of any media will vary depending on the audience, the circumstances and the prior relationship between that media and the audience.

The importance of the medium

The above theories generally assume a uniformity of effect for each medium. However, there is evidence that different media might be more applicable depending on the task at hand. Daft and Lengel (1986) suggested that the richness of a medium affects the ability of the receiver to understand the meaning of a message. Where complex information has to be conveyed, or a response is required, then rich media are required. When simple information is provided, such as when an event is happening, then less rich media should be used. The channel by which we communicate may influence the impact of that message.

Since Daft and Lengel constructed their Media Richness model, the use of communications has moved on significantly. There has been greater use of direct mail, and the widespread use

Table 2.2 The order of richness

1986	2012
1 Face to face	1 Face to face
2 Telephone	2 Social networks (such as Facebook)
3 Personal document (letters and memos)	3 Telephone
4 Impersonal written documents	4 Email
5 Numeric documents (statistical reports)	5 Personal documents
6	6 SMS
7	7 Websites
8	8 Impersonal written documents
9	9 Numeric document

(Adapted from Daft and Lengel 1986)

of the Internet in many countries has fundamentally changed how people communicate directly. In addition, the use of mobile phones, many with Internet access, has further enhanced such personal communication. As a result, the receiver no longer needs to be in a single physical location to secure the message. Table 2.2 identifies how the order of channels in richness has moved on since 1986. These technological developments make it easier for the event manager to engage media-rich conversations with target audiences.

The York Food and Drink Festival uses richness of media for reaching diverse audiences, be they exhibitors or attendees, but also depending on the purpose of the communication. Much of what they communicate is essentially informational and does not require media richness, but when trying to engage with exhibitors they need richer channels.

CASE STUDY 2.1

Using different channels

York Food and Drink Festival (www.yorkfoodfestival.com) is a not-for-profit organisation, providing a 10-day city-wide event to promote local and regional food and drink, that attracts 150,000 visitors (footfall count is 440,000, which is up one-third on the footfall count of the previous and following weeks). It aims to transform food culture in York and North Yorkshire by promoting local food production. It does this by educating minds and palates in a variety of non-threatening and fun ways, which include taste workshops, cookery workshops, lunches, dinners and demonstrations.

As a not-for-profit organisation the appropriate communication channels chosen are influenced by cost. There is small promotional budget as funds raised must cover the cost of putting on the event. The event is organised by two people for most of the year, and then from May to July extra staff are taken on, especially two who are responsible for handling ticketing. The main communication channel to them is verbal via regular face–to-face meetings. In addition, there are six directors, including the two main organisers and four others. They meet three times a year, and between these, depending on the issue, communication is by email or phone.

The key external audience is the market traders, whose fees (for booking stands) pay for the event to be run. Communication to them is mostly via email, partly because there are approximately 120 of them, but also because the organisers need a written record of what they have booked. A lot of the information is on the website, so an email is sent to traders telling them that they can book online. The organisers do use the telephone, but not as much as the website. Traders apply via the website, and receive a reply by email. During the festival, the organisers will meet informally with the traders face to face.

In terms of attendees, the festival targets first Friends, who pay a small fee. They receive discounted tickets, free events directed at them and they get information before the wider public. They sign up to receive regular emails, and they will also be informed before the wider public that information is up on the website for them to book.

The information for the 150 events within the festival will be available to the public at large via the website: details of daily programmes, workshops, food tasting and wine tasting are on the website. They also send out a generic leaflet promoting the event, which outlines what is on on certain days, and details any themes running through the festival. This is distributed in places where members of the public might find it, such as train stations, schools, bus stops, dentists' and doctors' surgeries.

The event has been going for sixteen years and has had a website from the outset, but it has grown in use. Because it is cheaper than printed material and can be updated more frequently, the website has transformed how the festival communicates. The website is the main communication channel, followed by email.

Since 2011 the organisers have used Twitter and social media, and got involved in ZappApps. They are now looking at using Apps and greater use of social media because people access them increasingly through their telephones.

From the receiver's perspective

The majority of research and models have focused primarily on communication from the sender's perspective, yet a clever communicator would also have an understanding of what their audience wants to hear, and through what form of delivery. The best-known reception theory is 'uses and gratifications' (Blumler and Katz 1974). As its name suggests this focuses on the receiver's views at two levels: the motivation for receiving information (uses); and the impact of receiving that information (gratification). The research suggests users are essentially motivated for two main reasons. First, audiences are active participants who specifically wish to find out information about a topic (Blumler and Katz 1974). Second, audiences access media to meet their own needs (Katz 1987). For example, someone interested in jazz music will specially seek out information about music in general, but especially jazz. However, if they are not interested in such music, then it is difficult, though not impossible, to get them interested.

In terms of the gratifications of receiving a message, Baskin and Aronoff (1992) suggest five main benefits: entertainment; information; a diversion; social relationships; personal identity and values. The research on online uses and gratifications suggests that two key main motivations for visiting a website, joining a social network, or subscribing to an e-newsletter are entertainment and information (Ferguson and Perse 2000; Papachrissi and Rubin 2000). Attendees to events may well be influenced by motivations such as the need to be entertained, to escape everyday life and because they say something about a person's social status or views. For example, attendance at a luxury event could be be evidence of conspicuous consumption, so as Veblen (1899) suggests, people will attend because it enhances their status. Events may be able to directly meet a range of gratifications.

Event promoters need to be able to reach and then persuade key audiences to attend your event. Understanding and applying a variety of aspects of communication theory will help you reach your key target audiences through appropriate channels. However, communication theory alone will not necessarily help you change their behaviour. Shaw (1979) suggests that while the media is all-pervasive it is not automatically persuasive. We need, therefore, to mix our knowledge of how to communicate with our choice of theory on how to persuade.

What is persuasion?

This section assumes that you can be more persuasive, and introduces some concepts that may help. Most persuasion models originate from psychology, and are based on the need for cognition (thinking). Persuasion involves the use of words, symbols, images, moods and emphasis to encourage the receiver of a message to agree with the desired action from the sender's perspective. It can be interpersonal, relying on rich media such as meetings, or mediated through mass persuasion, such as advertising and media relations. There is, as Stiff and Mongeau (2003) note, no single definition of persuasion, but Table 2.3 highlights some common traits.

However, we must differentiate persuasion from manipulation. Where persuasion seeks mutual understanding and/or fulfilment of needs, or at least some element of this, as Jowett and O'Donnell (2006) note manipulation is about control. Manipulation is designed to meet only the needs of the message sender, who takes on the role of a propagandist offering only one interpretation of the truth. Where persuasion can be a positive force, a means to achieve a goal (Benoit and Benoit 2008), manipulation and coercion occurs when the techniques of persuasion are misused. Persuasion is about two or more people benefiting, whereas the long-term beneficiary of manipulation is the manipulator (Lakhani 2005). In dictatorships events can be manipulative, where people are 'bussed in' to chant how wonderful life is under their leader, so offering an image which might be contrary to majority international opinion. However, it is difficult to see how, in a liberal-democratic society, where there is some assumption of freedom of action, you as an individual can be manipulated or coerced into attending an event.

Persuasion is essentially how and why individuals make decisions, and often reflects two elements coming together: namely, the head and the heart. The head assesses messages rationally and objectively, and the heart offers a more emotional and subjective response. Thaler and

---

Table 2.3 Traits of persuasion

Trait	Source
Persuasion has to be successful, it is not just the intention	O'Keefe (2002)
The persuadee has a measure of freedom as to whether they are persuaded or not	O'Keefe (2002) Perloff (2008)
Attitudes are created, reinforced or changed	Benoit and Benoit (2008) Brock and Green (2005)
Changes in attitudes lead to changes in behaviour	Perloff (2008)
Relies on a message being communicated	Jowett and O'Donnell (2006) Perloff (2008)

Sunstein (2008) have likened this to be akin to whether an individual makes decisions like the cartoon character Homer Simpson, or the fictional Vulcan *Star Trek* character Spock. They suggest that the vast majority of people are like Homer Simpson in that they are impulsive, and so the heart rules personal decision making. For the minority, like Spock, decisions are the result of careful rational argument, and the head is dominant. In all likelihood most decisions reflect a combination of both head and heart.

The process of persuasion

Two models, in particular, encapsulate this debate about the role of the head and heart in explaining the process of persuasion: the Elaboration Likelihood Model (ELM); and the Heuristic model.

Petty and Cacioppo's (1986) ELM suggests that individual attributes are not always processed in a thoughtful manner. So, elaboration is the extent to which a person thinks about issue-relevant information. The likelihood of elaboration is affected by

- The level of motivation (involvement with the message).
- The ability (cognitive and situational) to process the arguments.

The ability to persuade is a function of whether (the likelihood that) the receiver will think about (elaborate on) the information they receive. The two alternative routes to the process of understanding how individuals are persuaded are:

Central Route to Persuasion:

- Higher involvement with an event.
- Attention focused on event related material.
- Deep thoughts (elaboration) about the event, its attributes and consequences.

Peripheral Route to Persuasion:

- Lower involvement with an event.
- Attention focused on non-event information.
- Shallow thoughts on non-event information.

The nature of the route affects the sort of message the event manager should use. Those using the central route are persuaded by the event-related arguments. For those in the peripheral route, persuasion depends on non-event relevant cues. ELM is situational where, for example, a person might have high elaboration likelihood for rock festivals, but they may be low for bluegrass festivals.

ELM is a cognitive model which involves careful scrutiny of a message through systematic processes. Heuristic processing, however, involves very little effort by the receiver – emphasis is not on the message but on peripheral cues (Chaiken *et al.* 1996). Heuristics are simple rules that allow you to evaluate a message without having to scrutinise it, which explains why so many advertisers use celebrity endorsement. Chaiken (1982) suggests we are 'minimalist information processors'; so that decisions are made on the basis of simple rules that require no or little information processing. Such simple rules include the credibility of the sources, whether we like the source or not, and sometimes their physical attractiveness.

Heuristics are shortcuts designed to help us, so that we do not need to expend a lot of energy making decisions. This approach to persuasion might include the use of images, emotions or symbols to persuade. For example, a charity hosting a fundraising black tie Christmas dinner will often call upon a high-profile 'celebrity' associated with the charity, perhaps a patron, who gives credibility to the event because they are 'liked' by attendees. Moods are short cuts, so if you feel good you must like it, which is precisely the message which most music, sports and entertainment based events are promoting. Heuristics are appropriate for events where attendees have fairly low involvement, as may be typical with many entertainment based events.

Attitudes and behaviour

The orthodox view is that in order to change behaviour, such as getting people to decide to attend your event, you need first to change their attitudes towards your event. As a concept each person's attitudes are built up over a period of time, and so they evolve and change. Perloff (2008: 59) defined an attitude as:

> A learned, global evaluation of an object (person, place or issue) that influences thought and action. . . It is a predisposition, a tendency, a state of readiness that guides and steers behaviour in certain predictable, though not always rational, ways.

Our attitudes are based on both facts (what we know to be true) and our values (what we believe is right). Therefore, as Benoit and Benoit (2008) suggest, the combination of both cognition and experience shapes our actual behaviour.

Campaigners and governments who have tried to change behaviour with regard to smoking, health, diet, driving within speed limits, sexual activity and drinking alcohol have considered the importance of influencing individual attitudes. Two models in particular have been used to explain how attitudes can be changed to influence behaviour. The first is the theory of reasoned action (TRA), and the second is the theory of planned behaviour (TPB).

Fishbein and Ajzen (1975) suggested that any intended behaviour is the result of two factors: attitude to behaviour and subjective norms. Therefore, we create in our heads a debate – the attitude to the behaviour is governed by the norms we possess (built upon our values/beliefs) and these create an intention. The attitudes formed will be external, as will the norms to an extent, though both are accessed and processed in a way specific to the context and the individual.

Ajzen (1985) identified a limitation to TRA, and developed the Theory of Planned Behaviour (TPB). TPB extends TRA by strengthening the association between intention and behaviour. What differentiates TPB from TRA is 'perceived behavioural control': Can we actually do what we want to do? In effect, can we comply? This might explain why we say one thing and do another. Where TRA has two main components, TPB has three:

● Attitude to behaviour.
● Subjective norms.
● Perceived control of behaviour.

These three factors determine not just intended behaviour, but more importantly actual behaviour: why we actually take the decisions we do. Actions not just words are important.

Research conducted by Cunningham and Kwon (2003) found that TPB applied to attendance at sports events, especially the influence of social norms. This led them to conclude that sports events organisers need to encourage a social atmosphere both before and after the game.

Changing behaviour directly

While the orthodox view is that a persuader has to change a persuadee's attitudes (their view of your event) before changing their behaviour (whether they attend), some models suggest behaviour can be changed directly. Robert Cialdini's (2007) six principles of persuasion suggest that, by understanding how we comply with a request, behaviour can be influenced by:

- *Reciprocation* – more likely to say yes if you have done something for them – so pay in kind what you have received.
- *Consistency* – we want to appear consistent and rational in our beliefs, statements and actions.
- *Social Validation* – one fundamental way that we decide what to do in a situation is to look at what others are doing or have done there.
- *Liking* – people prefer to say yes to those people they like or are similar to them.
- *Authority* – we tend to defer to the counsel of authority figures and experts to help us to decide how to behave.
- *Scarcity* – items and opportunities become more desirable if they are less available.

Cialdini provides a framework for gaining compliance from consumers, which could shape an event's communications strategy.

Helping event managers communicate more persuasively

Event managers can be more persuasive, and there is a fairly simple framework to follow. Over two millennia ago Aristotle, referring to rhetoric, identified three key factors:

- *Ethos* – the speaker.
- *Logos* – the message.
- *Pathos* – the audience.

More recently Perloff (2008) has interpreted this to mean:

- The source of the message.
- The message.
- The personality of the message receiver.

We will consider each of these three components in turn to see how your promotional messages can be more impactful.

Source credibility

Aristotle suggested that the most important factor in persuasion was the speaker, and as Whalen (1996) notes this is the factor which can be most controlled by the persuader. We can identify three characteristics of credibility:

- *Expertise* – a perception that the communicator has special skills or know-how.
- *Trustworthiness* – refers to the communicator's perceived honesty, character and safety.
- *Goodwill* – that you have the listener's interests at heart and understand their problems/point of view.

This approach to persuasion is very common with business-to-business events. For example, training companies stress the expertise of themselves as specialists in the subject matter of training being offered, emphasise the style of their trainers and use testimonials from past clients to underline that they meet their needs.

When the message covers for the receiver relatively unimportant issues, as is likely with most events, social attractiveness can be influential. We can identify three components of this:

- *Likability* – Chaiken (1980) found that waiters can deliberately get a bigger tip through simple techniques such as writing thank you on the back of the bill, drawing a smiley face on the back of the bill and squatting down next to diners.
- *Similarity* – people who are like us, perhaps in age, interests or social background.
- *Physical attractiveness* – we may associate an event with positive images such as good-looking people or celebrities.

Social attractiveness may be persuasive if a person is using the peripheral route, but very unlikely for those using the central route.

The message

Having identified and reached your audience, and selected the right spokesperson, there are a number of tricks the event manager can use to make their message more persuasive. This is not just a case of good writing skills and clear images: there exists research on assessing how to organise and present the message. Perloff (2008) has suggested that the three core components of a message to address are how it is structured, the content and the precise use of symbols and words.

The research considering how to organise and prepare your arguments has assessed whether the sender of the message should recognise that another view exists (Allen 1998), and whether you should explicitly draw conclusions (O'Keefe 2002). Both Allen (1998) and O'Keefe (2002) suggested that recognising the opposite side is the best approach, provided you refute and not just mention opponents' arguments. In terms of the conclusion, O'Keefe (2002) found that an explicit conclusion is more persuasive. Therefore, you need to explain clearly what is expected of the receiver of your message, and why they should attend your event and not another.

The content can be very rational in approach, emotional or a mix of both. The former would use evidence such as factual assertions, quantitative information, eyewitness statements, testimonials, and opinions from credible sources. For example, the Pride London website www.londonpride.org addresses very serious issues such as how to tackle homophobia with the application of rational arguments, as well as encouraging people to attend the event. The more emotive approach is based on personal narratives, such as case studies of individual experiences, to inspire and motivate. For example, The Chocolate Festival (www.festival chocolate.co.uk/) uses interviews with leading chefs to present the pleasurable experience attendees will be rewarded with. Probably the most persuasive messages are those that combine rational quantitative data, with emotional qualitative evidence.

Language can be persuasive, so how and not just what we say can be powerful. While most of the time speed of speech has limited effect, those who are slightly quicker can be seen as experts who cannot wait to say their stuff if the audience has limited interest/knowledge in the topic (Smith and Shaffer 1995). No matter how you might be feeling inside, it is possible to present an image of a powerful speech which implies confidence and certainty of message. Lastly, the intensity of language can help create powerful images: for example, the use of metaphors, graphic descriptions/images and the use of words with meaning (Perloff 2008).

Cialdini found (Goldstein *et al.* 2008) that to get hotel guests to re-use towels, the statistically most powerful message was to point out that most guests in this room re-used their towels. This created a powerful social norm that people were less likely to ignore. Given that events are intangibles that you cannot usually physically show your audience, visual and contextual tricks are used to reinforce the message.

You will also be aware of the possible impact of nonverbal communication, and while your own gestures are best analysed after you have been filmed being interviewed, Simons (2001: 104–8) provides a good framework for understanding how nonverbal communication works. He suggests that there are four ways in which nonverbal communication works, which helps an event manager understand how to get their message across:

- *Vocalics* – the auditory channel, such as speed and volume of voice and how you articulate.
- *Kinesics* – the visual channel including posture, body movements, gestures, eye behaviour and facial expressions.
- *Proxemics* – how space and spatial relationships communicate, which is very important for international and multicultural events because cultures differ in what they are comfortable with.
- *Haptics* – the tactile channel, for example how important to first impressions is a good solid handshake.

What this means for the event communicator is that people like to be communicated with in a range of different ways – through sound, visual images, spatially and by touch. Focusing on just one limits how many people you reach. The best approach is to think how your communication campaign can use all four.

The receiver

The receiver, the third component of Aristotle's framework, addresses the question of whether some people are more persuadable than others. Researchers have sought to ascertain whether some people are more susceptible to persuasive communication than others. Stiff and Mongeau (2003) reviewed the possible factors and identified self-esteem, intelligence, gender, need for cognition (to think) and dogmatism. By and large there is little statistically significant data to suggest that some people are more susceptible to being persuaded. The one specific situation where there is evidence is that women are more persuadable in group pressure situations, where they are more likely than men to yield to the group position (see O'Keefe 2002). On the whole it is the source credibility and message which is likely to be the most persuasive, rather than the nature of the message receiver.

Aristotle was writing at a time when rhetoric was highly valued and so believed that of the three factors the source was the most important. There is a sense that in the modern world most focus is on the construction of the message. Figure 2.5 suggests that the order in which the event communicator should address the process of persuasion is to focus on the audience to start, and so applies the lessons of reception theory, such as uses and gratifications. Having identified the needs and interests of the audience, we should then look at who or what is the best way of reaching them, and only then should we craft our message. This approach suggests that persuasion requires a different approach to that implied by most communication theory, which starts with the sender and what they want to say.

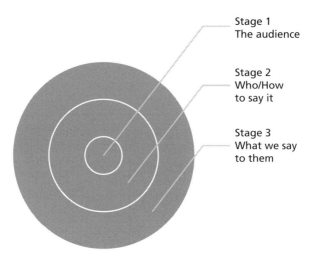

Stage 1
The audience

Stage 2
Who/How
to say it

Stage 3
What we say
to them

Figure 2.5 The stages of persuasion

Communication and persuasion

Practical checklist

- Identify why you need to communicate.
- Assume you are a media agent – consider both direct and indirect communication.
- Target opinion leaders – they bring their friends.
- Target opinion formers – they influence others.
- Communication is not just what you want to say – find out what your receivers want.
- Focus on content to persuade those interested in your field.
- Use peripheral cues, such as celebrity endorsement to persuade those not interested in your field.
- Identify the social norms which influence your audience's views.
- Choose the correct credible spokesperson in all communications for your event.
- Carefully craft your message so that it is unambiguous, easy to follow and has a clear instruction of what you want the receiver to do (and why).
- Mix and match your communication techniques using sound, pictures, space and touch.

Although we have separated them, understanding and applying communication and persuasion theory are closely interlinked. In the case study the Great British Beer Festival, we can see evidence of what this event's organisers think about who to communicate with, how best to do so and the persuasive impact of the atmosphere and mood of the event on the day.

CASE STUDY 2.2

The Great British Beer Festival – communicating with and persuading your audience

The Great British Beer Festival is Britain's biggest beer festival and brings together a wide range of approximately 1,000 different real ales, ciders, perries and international beers. Organised by CAMRA (the Campaign for Real Ale – http://www.camra.org.uk/) the Great British Beer Festival (http://gbbf.org.uk/home) is usually held in London during the summer, at one of the major exhibition centres such as Earls Court or London Olympia.

The Great Britain Beer Festival (GBBF) deliberately sets out to be more like a pub than an exhibition. One key audience CAMRA wants to attend are breweries, who have their own branded bars. To attract these CAMRA writes to those that have attended in previous years with a contract for them to sign. If space remains, other breweries are contacted, typically 8–20 each year depending on where the event is being hosted.

The event seeks to attract the attention of CAMRA members, experienced real-ale drinkers and people who have never tried real ale before. The marketing campaigns include advertisements in Greater London newspapers/radio, London Underground and London pub washrooms, and posters, beer mats and leaflets delivered to Greater London pubs. Geographically these campaigns are concentrated mainly on South East England, around London, as around 75 per cent who attend are from this area. To get people to attend the organisers:

- Use different colour beers to appeal to a variety of different drinkers.
- Ensure the booking details are prominent and social media links have been included in recent years.
- Sometimes use a slogan/headlines to get across that there will be a large range of beers and ciders to choose from.
- In 2012 the GBBF used famous images of London to appeal to those who were visiting the capital for the Olympics.

The main message to the brewery bars is functional: that this gives them a great chance to market their brands to more than 60,000 visitors. For visitors, the message is more emotional suggesting they come and have 'fun and enjoy a range of beers.'

GBBF has its own microsite – www.gbbf.org – that reflects the branding of the show and includes the lists of beers, entertainment, and pictures from past events and competitions. The purpose of the pictures on the website is to show visitors what the event is like. It is a social event that is fun, and the images try to reflect that message.

The source of messages is important for CAMRA, so all major press statements are from the CEO, and usually an MP who has been campaigning for pubs/beer throughout the year is asked to open the festival and make a speech.

To encourage visitors to join CAMRA they are offered a superb membership package and a copy of the *Good Beer Guide* (current RRP £15.99). Banners, beer mats, pump clip crowners and flags reinforce the message. CAMRA also promotes current campaigns as a way of encouraging people to sign up. As a result of all of these techniques, normally about 1,500 people sign up.

Psychology plays a key role in the layout of the event. For example, as more than 60,000 people attend the event, a lot of thought has to go into where the seating is to be placed, so that there is plenty of space for people to move around the festival to get to the different bars. The very nature of real ale also means that the beer has to remain still and settle for perhaps 24–48 hours and therefore it has to be in a safe, closed-off area. This usually means a lot of space is taken up by the beer stillages behind the bars.

In recent times the CAMRA membership stand and merchandise/bookshop has been placed in the centre of the hall to create a type of CAMRA village. Similarly, the branded brewery bars are usually close by to give a nice colourful look, and the food is also usually placed near each other.

To work out which campaigns/channels are most persuasive the organisers use a range of techniques:

- A source code box when people order tickets, asking them about where they heard of GBBF.
- CAMRA runs a number of competitions with codes on them from different materials. People enter the codes to stand a chance of winning prizes once they have bought a ticket. This helps identify where some of the attendees have heard about the festival.
- A visitor's survey in the GBBF programme asks, 'Where did you hear about GBBF?'.
- The organisers also track sales peaks against when different adverts appear.

CAMRA is conscious that in order to attract breweries and individuals it needs to present persuasive arguments, and then offer a quality of event that meets the offer made.

The picture opposite shows the importance of careful layout to how the organisers of The Great British Beer Festival seek to use persuasion. Picture courtesy of CAMRA.

Image 2.1 The Great British Beer Festival

Discussion questions

Event managers do not necessarily assume that core to their role is an understanding of how people communicate, and how we can persuade stakeholders. This chapter highlights that event communicators are faced with key issues:

1 What might be the consequences of not communicating effectively, or of the receiver misinterpreting the message?
2 Identify three key lessons for how you can be an effective communicator?
3 What are the strengths and limitations of understanding the process of persuasion?
4 In what ways do different stakeholders require different persuasion strategies?

Further information

Other sources which might help you consider the issues outlined in this chapter include:

Books

Berger, C., Roloff, M. and Roskos-Ewoldsen, D. (2009) *The Handbook of Communication Science*, Thousand Oaks, CA: Sage – detailed discussion of relevant theories.
Borg, J. (2007) *Persuasion: The Art of Influencing People*, Harlow: Pearson Education – popular easy-to-follow book that applies persuasion to real life.
Fletcher, W. (2008) *Powers of Persuasion: The Inside Story of British Advertising*, Oxford: Oxford University Press – applies persuasion to a key channel.
Fogg, B.J. (2003) *Persuasive Technology: Using Computers to Change What We Think and Do*, London: Morgan Kaufmann – the major source of online persuasion.
West, R. and Turner, L. (2010) *Introducing Communication Theory*, Boston, MA: McGraw-Hill – detailed discussion of relevant theories.

Websites

www.mindhacks.com – provides a psychological perspective.
www.influenceatwork.com – access to Robert Cialdini's research.
http://captology.stanford.edu/resources – online persuasion.

Chapter 3

Marketing your event

Introduction

This chapter will assess the historical development and meaning of marketing *per se* before we address what marketing specifically means in an event context. Marketing is a very broad discipline and we shall briefly address all the main areas that encompass marketing because marketers need the breadth of all these areas; and they will probably also have a far greater depth of knowledge of some. We will finish the chapter by anchoring the detailed practice within a wider conceptual discussion. By the end of this chapter, students will be able to:

● Define marketing.
● Evaluate the role of marketing within event planning.
● Assess the key components of event marketing.
● Evaluate the most appropriate marketing philosophies for marketing each event.

What is marketing?

In pre-industrial societies marketing meant going to market, whether to buy or sell. While this process involved several of the core components we would today recognise, such as an exchange taking place, what we understand to be modern marketing is a direct result of the Industrial Revolution. Mass production of goods, growing consumerism and the growth of global markets created new, and larger, problems which had to be solved through the development of unique skills and processes. By the first third of the twentieth century we could identify a discrete discipline, with practitioners in companies who fulfilled a marketing function.

Marketing is now a core management function of most organisations. Initially, it was considered to be the preserve of commercial companies who had products to sell, but an article by Kotler and Levy (1969) reflected growing practical behaviour whereby conceptually marketing could apply equally to those who did not have a traditional product to sell. Thus marketing was applied by non-commercial organisations, such as governments, charities, pressure groups and public bodies. While money may or may not have changed hands they had something to sell, and an exchange process took place.

Those organisations, be they commercial or not, which are large enough to have separate departments, will usually have a marketing department of some form. In small organisations (say fewer than 20 people) the marketing function will still be performed, but the person(s) conducting it may not have a marketing title. This means that for a medium or large event there will probably be a specialist marketer, but for a small or volunteer-led event this will probably not be the case. Whichever the situation, someone will be marketing the event.

Modern marketing can be viewed as moving through at least four stages, referred to as separate marketing orientations, reflecting different problems and solutions that emerged as technology, marketing skills and consumer behaviour developed. These four stages, generally but not exclusively representing particular timeframes in advanced industrial societies are:

- *Production oriented* – from the nineteenth century, where the focus is getting the products produced, and then distributed for sale. The key marketing question is how to get the products produced and then to market. The assumption is that they will then almost automatically be bought.
- *Product oriented* – from the 1930s, where the focus was on the features of the product. The assumption is that consumers purchase based on the quality, features and distinctiveness of a product. The key marketing question is how to design and make either new products or improved versions of existing products.
- *Selling orientation* – from the 1950s, where the focus was on how the product is sold. The assumption is that what matters is not so much the actual features of the product, but how it is presented and sold to the potential consumer. The key marketing question is how to promote a product. This stage was accompanied by the rapid growth of the advertising industry.
- *Marketing orientation* – from the 1960s, where the focus was on first understanding, and then meeting, the wants and needs of consumers. The assumption is that it is not enough for the company to sell what it wants to produce: rather, the emphasis is on what consumers want to buy. The key marketing question is to identify, through both quantitative and qualitative research, what products consumers want and how they want to purchase them.

It is often assumed that the fourth orientation is the most effective and appropriate. However, as we shall note at the end of this chapter, it is being challenged by a new concept based on building long-term relationships, implying a societal orientation to marketing.

It is crucial for us to know what we actually mean by marketing because of its importance to the functioning of any event (and to the parent organisation and partners of that event). However, given its long history and the variety of organisations and situations in which marketing is used, we do not have a single agreed definition. Marketing has not remained static: the organisations, industries, and societies in which it has been applied have evolved. Each situation presents its own unique problems, and how marketing has responded shapes our understanding of the term. However, it is important to have some guidance as to what event managers mean by marketing, otherwise there would be no consistency in activity from one event to the next.

Textbooks have tended to look to practitioners themselves to give an initial steer to what marketing means. So a well used definition is provided by the UK's Chartered Institute of Marketing (CIM – the trade body for marketing), which stated in 2001 that: '*Marketing is the management process responsible for identifying, anticipating and satisfying consumers' requirements efficiently and profitably.*' This definition suggests three core components to marketing. First, it is a management process, so that there is a deliberate attempt by the event manager to control both the event itself and whatever information and image the potential sponsors, participants and consumers are given about it. Second, the marketing process is viewed through the eyes of the consumer. Third, the first two are pointless if the marketer cannot make some profit, be it money or some other non-pecuniary value, from the event. This requires an assessment of how much the potential customer will pay, and how much it will cost to produce the event.

The CIM revised and expanded this definition in 2007 to suggest that marketing was

> The strategic function that creates value by stimulating, facilitating and fulfilling customer demand. It does this by building brands, nurturing innovation, developing relationships, creating good customer service and communicating benefits.

Although this adds precise information on how marketing will achieve its goals, it is still essentially the same as the earlier definition. The one key difference is that it does recognise the importance of building relationships, and opens the door to a new set of interpretations of marketing.

Another well used definition is provided by the American Marketing Association (AMA – the US marketing trade body), which suggested in 2008 that marketing is: '*The activity, set of institutions and processes for creating, communicating, delivering and exchanging offerings that have value for customers, clients, partners and society at large.*' This definition includes the three key points of marketing being a planned process, that the consumer is central to the process and it has to be worth the marketers while. In addition, it makes clear that what is being bought and sold is not just 'hard' products, but also 'soft' services such as events and ideas such as concerns about the environment.

These definitions emphasise two main characteristics to marketing. First, the centrality of the consumer – so marketing needs to identify the target market. Second, they stress the importance of devising a means, normally in the form of the marketing mix, to satisfy their markets. As a result they reflect a particular type of marketing, which we will address at the end of this chapter: namely, transactional marketing. This approach to marketing stresses the importance of the sale.

An alternative approach – relationship marketing – stresses the importance of relationships, and this shapes the meaning of marketing. For example, Gronroos (1997: 327) suggested that

> Marketing is to establish and enhance relationships with customers and other partners, at a profit, so that the objectives of the parties involved are met. This is achieved by mutual exchange and fulfillment of promises.

This approach to marketing stresses that long-term profitability is dependent upon building relationships with event attendees.

Although different definitions exist, we can identify core characteristics of marketing; what differs is how different approaches define and apply them. The core characteristics we can identify are:

- The importance of meeting the consumers' wants and needs.
- There is an exchange process.
- Something of value is exchanged.
- There must be something in it for the organisation.
- Inherently, marketing involves some form of communication.

Pulling these definitions together Figure 3.1 suggests that the core to marketing is a triangle centred on a fulcrum of the consumer, with a marketing mix for how consumer needs can be met, and a communications mix for how this offer will reach consumers.

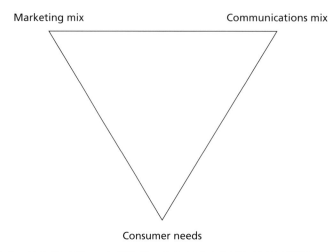

Figure 3.1 The marketing triangle

Events marketing

Definition box 3.1

Defining event marketing

At one level, events marketing is about making your event attractive to staff, volunteers, sponsors, participants, the media and attendees. It addresses all of the detail which makes up the event experience, both that which the attendee sees, and that which they are not necessarily aware of. It is therefore broad ranging. Events marketing is also a tool used by marketers for how they can reach audiences, promote products and enhance their brands.

Wood (2009) suggests that general marketing theory does not align with events marketing practice. The logic of this is twofold. First, marketing an event requires a revision of the marketing mix, a point we shall return to in Chapter 5. Second, non-event marketers may use events in a different way to other marketing tools. Indeed, there is evidence that non-event marketers are increasingly adopting events marketing. The 2009 *Global Event View Report* produced by George P. Johnson and the MPI Foundation, found that events marketing was the most popular marketing discipline for increased budget allocation.

Hall (1997: 136) provides a definition of marketing which is couched in event terms. He notes that

> Marketing is that function of event management that can keep in touch with the event's participants and visitors, read their needs and motivations, develop products that meet

their needs, and build a communication programme which expresses the event's purpose and objectives.

This definition adds to the broader definitions given earlier. It suggests that the consumer of an event may include not just those who pay to attend. Those who are part of the event as participants, such as artistes and players, are also a target market.

In non-event marketing, the marketer can concentrate on what their organisation wishes to achieve. Event marketers, however, may have to take into account an element not present in most other product and service marketing: namely, the concerns of other organisation's marketing needs. In particular, Hoyle (2002) notes event marketers have to think not just about their own marketing aims and objectives, but also those of any sponsors.

As noted earlier there is a duality for event marketers which shapes the purpose of the event, which in turn influences the nature of event marketing. For an event that seeks to make money for the promoters, then marketing is simply about achieving this goal. But for events with less overt direct commercial purposes, such as promotional events, the marketing reflects different purposes. For example, Saget (2006: 3) suggests that: '*Event marketing is all about facilitating, easing, opening, accelerating and shortening the sales cycle.*' Event marketing can be flexible, and its meaning is shaped by the purpose of an event.

We have covered a lot of dry theory but this case study from an events management agency highlights what they actually do.

CASE STUDY 3.1

The meaning of events marketing

London based independent events and marketing specialist Charlie Apple Events (www.charlieapple.co.uk) suggests that central to events marketing is reaching the target audience who would be interested in attending the event, ensuring they know when it is, what it is, how much it is, how long it lasts, and getting them to tell others they may be connected to and who would be interested. The key is always to reach your target audience, whether that is the attendees to the event or, in the case of exhibitions, reaching the exhibitors themselves.

For their clients, events marketing offers a captive audience: there are attendees who have taken a big step to be interested in the product/service offering, so they are already half way through the marketing process. Director Tracy Francis notes: 'It is face to face. You are obviously hoping for a sale but also perhaps a lifelong customer (depending on the product) and they are likely to mention you to others when saying, "I went to a . . . seminar/workshop/exhibition the other day. . ." – they may even tweet about it and so the viral marketing works for you too – provided you have a good product/service – if you don't, the bad word is likely to spread twice as fast!'

Events marketing is differentiated from other forms of marketing because it is measurable, whereas many other forms of marketing are not. With events, you can quite clearly measure tangibles, such as how many people booked and/or attended your event, or how many exhibition stalls or advertising spaces in your event catalogue you sold. The methods used to market the event may differ slightly according to budget, but the principles are the same.

Assessing developments in events marketing, Tracy considers that: 'Social media has become and will continue to be the most effective (by both cost and result) trend. The future is also being shaped by the fact that we have witnessed a reduction in the number of events, combined with the advent of virtual events.'

The components of marketing

As we note in the introduction to this chapter, marketing covers a range of functions. We shall familiarise ourselves with them here (Table 3.1) and explore some of them in more depth in later chapters. These activities cover the broad thrust of marketing, and as noted above you may personally only specialise in some of them, but they will all need to be addressed by your event(s) at some point. Marketing requires both depth and breadth of subject understanding and experience.

Market research

The purpose of market research is to find out information about actual or potential markets. This could be some general perspective such as basic consumer behaviour, or it could be very specifically related to what attendees think about an event. The former identifies whether there exists a possible market for a new event, and the latter provides feedback to help improve existing events. Research can be prior to, during and after the event, to help the event manager make better marketing decisions. Important decisions should be influenced by empirical data.

As noted in Figure 3.2, there are two main types of marketing research: secondary (desk) and primary (field). Depending on what you are trying to find out, the purpose and your budget, either or both may be suitable, but if you do both you should always start with the secondary research first. There is a range of secondary sources you could consider; some may be free, some others you pay for. If you were trying to find out if there is a potential market for a new event, foe example, then trade magazines such as *Event* in the UK and *Special Events* in the USA may include reports on markets. However, if your event is a large one entering a new market you may have to pay to access data from a sector report from agencies such as Plimsoll, Key Note and Euromonitor.

Collecting, analysing and applying data allows the event marketer to respond quickly to changing consumer trends. There are two main types of research: quantitative and qualitative. The former is based on statistical information, and so tends to use questionnaires to generate large numbers of responses. Thus you might ask consumers to evaluate the event experience possibly on a Likert scale of 1–5. The latter seeks to identify 'richness' of data and tries to find out in more depth respondents' motivations, use and impact of attending an event. Methods include small focus groups (say up to 10 people) or one-to-one interviews. Both quantitative and qualitative data can be used to help identify new markets and assess current events.

Table 3.1 The components of marketing practice

Marketing activity	Core event marketing purpose
Market research	Evaluating whether to put on an event. Identifying potential markets. Assessing what customers think of events. Assessing the importance of both macro and micro environmental factors on an event.
Marketing management	Identify what customers want, and how to achieve it with an event by creating a marketing strategy. Position an event *vis-à-vis* competitors. Construct, implement and revise a marketing plan.
Supply chain management	Identify how consumers will 'consume' the event – distribution/ticketing. Manage venue, suppliers (technical and participants) and equipment. Manage e-commerce.
Brand management	Identify the corporate message an event wishes to portray. Develop mission statement, event logo and corporate image. Dovetail sponsors' objectives within overall brand image.
Marketing communication	Provide external communication both direct and indirect to potential consumers in the form of promotional activities. Generate sales leads. Utilise the Internet to communicate marketing information.
Internal marketing	Communicate with staff and volunteers using face-to-face, print and Internet based methods.
Consumers relations	Construct mechanisms to identify consumers' needs. Develop standards and systems for meeting those needs. Manage corporate hospitality and VIPs.
Market and marketing evaluation	Construct evaluation mechanisms. Assess whether, how and why the event met its (and those of partner bodies') objectives. Learn, and suggest lessons for improvement.

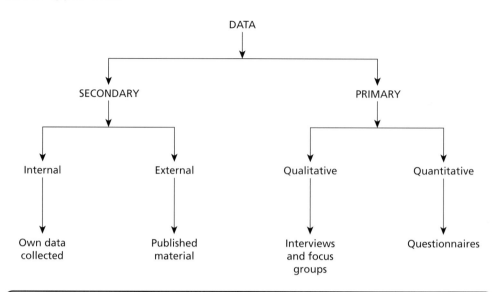

Figure 3.2 Marketing research classification

Marketing management

Nearly all the definitions of marketing make an implicit or explicit reference to a planned management of the process. The event marketer seeks to construct both long-term strategies and implement immediate courses of action. The event marketer manages the marketing process in three different timeframes. First, the long-term timeframe, such as where the host organisation or event wishes to be in a few years' time. Second, the medium-term timeframe, which addresses the planning issues for the next event, typically a year ahead. Third, the short-term timeframe, which is concerned with managing the immediate issues faced on a day-to-day basis.

Marketing management often takes place at two related but separate levels: corporate and event specific. The corporate level addresses broad questions, such as: What are the overall aims of the organisation? What markets does it wish to be in? How are resources to be allocated? What are the organisational structure and organisational culture to be? It is essentially strategic, long term and general in nature. The event specific level is shaped by the corporate strategy, but focuses on more specific questions such as identifying and reaching precise target markets, budgets and marketing plans. It is partially strategic, but primarily tactical, medium and short term, and detailed in nature.

Supply chain management

Kotler and Keller (2006: 26) identify the supply chain as follows:

> Whereas marketing channels connect the marketer to the target buyers, the supply chain describes a longer channel stretching from raw materials to components to final products that are carried to final buyers.

In traditional marketing the importance of the supply chain is that the producer and consumer are rarely in the same place at the same time. However, event marketing is different to marketing most other products as the supply chain is, in effect, the venue. For events, the supply chain is almost uniquely a geographical concept where production and consumption happen at the same time and in the same place. This means that the event producer is likely to retain a larger part of the value of the price.

Irrespective of the fact that the event supply chain is different from most other products, there is a common management issue for all marketers. The event marketer, like all marketers, has to address both the *backwards* and *forwards* facing links in the supply chain. The *backwards* facing links are the supply of the raw components of the event, such as participants, volunteers and equipment suppliers. The *forwards* facing links are the direct supply links to the consumer, such as ticketing. The event marketer has a supply chain, but it is usually different and simpler than that faced by other marketers.

Brand management

The brand is a product's or range of products' identity, and so aims to bring a product alive by creating a three-dimensional personality. The physical components of a brand can include a product's name, and words or symbols (logos) that are associated with it and which are designed to present it in a positive, distinctive and memorable way. In addition to such physical factors, de Chernatony and McDonald (1992) suggest that branding is also about a consumer's psychological perception of, and affinity with, a brand. The brand often tries to present a set of values about the product, range of products, or sometimes the company. In essence, therefore, a brand shapes the relationship a consumer has with a product. By trying to construct a narrative that says something about our event, we are also influencing what attendance at our event says about the consumer.

Although sometimes amorphous and difficult to pin down, brands are widely considered to be a major asset for any organisation, product or event. To the consumer the brand represents what they think and feel about the product or range of products. It is therefore a key means of attracting new consumers and then maintaining their loyalty. Brand management requires the event marketer to address three key issues:

- *Positioning* – where is the brand to be positioned in the market.
- *Strategies* – should there be an individual brand, family brand or co-brands.
- *Communication* – how to raise awareness of the brand and what it stands for.

Events branding raises some specific questions. Do you brand one single event individually, or a series of connected events? If you have sponsors, you need to consider their brand. A strong brand image will help an event through occasional difficult times.

Plymouth Summer Festival has very successfully used and branded events to encourage tourism. Most of the events already existed as separate entities; now they have been re-packaged as a whole.

CASE STUDY 3.2

The Plymouth Summer Festival

The counties of Devon and Cornwall are known as tourist destinations, but the most populated city in the two counties was not necessarily considered a major tourist attraction, despite its obvious link through the Pilgrim Fathers to America. Plymouth as a city has always hosted a range of events, but in 2007 the Plymouth City Centre Company, Plymouth Chamber of Commerce and Plymouth City Council decided to bring together disparate events under one banner: the Plymouth Summer Festival. The existing programme included maritime, music, Arts and street events. This was the application of strategic branding designed to promote the unique identify of Plymouth, as a means of attracting people within and beyond the south-west of England to visit Plymouth.

Funding was provided by the City Development Company, the South West of England Regional Development Agency, English Partnerships and the private sector. The brand of the Plymouth Summer Festival was not originally based on creating new events: rather, it brought together existing events. Instead the money was spent on the marketing of the events through a new logo, dedicated website, brochures, banners and flags and advertising and public relations campaigns.

In its first year the summer festival ran from late May through to the end of August, and comprised twenty-three events, which included pop concerts, the National Fireworks Championship, Plymouth Flavour Fest and the finish of the Fastnet Race. This first year was deemed a financial success, and now in its sixth year the Plymouth Summer Festival has evolved significantly. Ostensibly the festival runs from early May to September, though some years major events such as the British Art Show 2011 stretch these dates. More importantly, it has grown significantly in numbers and quality, attracting in 2011 major worldwide sporting events such as the America's Cup.

As a branding tool the Plymouth Summer Festival is now an important part of the tourist landscape, packaging and providing coherence to what might otherwise appear as disparate tourist related activities. The legacy of this brand is that it has now been joined by a Plymouth Winter Festival.

Marketing communication

As Chapters 4–6 are effectively about marketing communications we will be brief here. Organisations need to communicate with a range of different audiences, often promoting a tailored message, sometimes through different channels. Marketing communications is not a 'one size fits all' approach, so that Chris Fill (2009: 16), probably the best-known academic commentator in the field, suggests that it is:

A management process through which an organization engages with its various audiences. Through an understanding of an audience's preferred communication environments, organizations seek to develop and present messages for its identified stakeholder groups, before evaluating and acting upon any responses. By conveying messages that are of significant value, audiences are encouraged to offer attitudinal, emotional and behavioural responses.

Therefore, this process utilises a variety of tools, media and messages, to make the correct fit between the audience and the communications mix used to reach them.

Sometimes referred to as the communications mix, marketing communications is where the event promotes itself. De Pelsmacker *et al.* (2004: 3) suggest that where other parts of the marketing mix lay the foundation, it is the marketing communications which ultimately determines how successful an event is.

Internal marketing

Communicating to internal audiences is an area which many marketing textbooks largely ignore, reflecting the fact that marketers have a tendency to focus on 'hard' factors such as processes, tasks and results. Marketers are less likely to stress the 'soft' aspects, such as managing people. Yet, most events management textbooks give a very high priority to internal communications with staff, volunteers and suppliers. This reflects the fact that the interaction between internal and external audiences is a core part of shaping the final event experience. Internal audiences are of central importance to the event marketer, precisely because they will influence external audience experience of an event.

Internal marketing is essentially how an organisation communicates to its internal audiences. For events, this includes not just full-time paid staff, but often part-time staff, volunteers and suppliers. There are two main internal marketing methods:

● *Written* – in the form of memos, emails, newsletters and the Intranet. These tend to be short documents.
● *Verbal* – in the form of face-to-face meetings, which can be one to one, team level or organisational. They can also be regular or infrequent; the latter tend to be when something has or is about to go wrong. This approach may necessitate events be organised, such as road shows or an away day.

Edge Creative (http://www.edgecreative.net) is a New Zealand based event and change management company which specialises in designing and organising events and programmes designed to enhance internal communications and accelerate transformation. Its approach is based on the premise that internal audiences are important, but are often overlooked. It uses events to manage one-off problems such as organisational change, and also perennial issues of improving staff performance. The type of events it uses to address internal communications have included team celebrations, sales and marketing conferences, road shows and interactive workshops designed to shift staff attitudes and behaviour. The ultimate aim of such events is to help deliver long-term organisational cultural change.

Consumer relations

Until the 1980s mass marketing communication dominated and the focus was on reaching as many potential consumers as possible. With new technological developments, however, marketing could access and analyse more detailed information on customer behaviour, which allowed for more targeted marketing. Conceptually this has been presented as Customer

Relationship Marketing (CRM), which is: *'The process of managing detailed information about individual customers and carefully managing all customer "touch points" to maximise customer loyalty'* (Kotler and Keller 2006: 151). The overall aim is to find a way of using consumer information to maximise consumer value over a lifetime.

According to Soloman *et al.* (2009) CRM helps an organisation to identify profitable consumers and then develop relationships with them, to mutual benefit. By using all available data, the consumer offer can be more tailored, and this led to Peppers and Rogers (1993) suggesting that one-to-one marketing was possible. CRM, therefore, relies upon the collection of data and sending out the appropriate message, both of which are underpinned by good consumer service. Rather than focusing on the traditional target of market share, CRM focuses on share of consumer: How much of their spending activities can we capture? CRM will then often promote the cross-selling of other products produced by the same organisation, something event organisers do not always do.

Market and marketing evaluation

In many textbooks, evaluation is the last stage of a linear process, but this is far too inflexible. Rather, it should occur throughout as a circular process, so that the event marketer can respond to developments and change their approach. Indeed, the first part of planning should be to ask what lessons have been learnt from past events. Such evaluation requires a set of benchmarks to measure where we currently are, and whether action is required. For example, in the short term these could include sales leads, media coverage, website click-throughs, sales and cash flow. In the longer term they could include wider market trends and developments. At the end of an event one should measured whether the objectives were met.

There exists a variety of means for conducting event marketing evaluation. One option is the use of marketing metrics. These are ways of measuring the value of activity. Such measurements could include amount of media coverage, website hits and advertising effectiveness. Essentially this is a means of testing Return on Investment (ROI). Figure 3.3 offers a simple way of calculating this. Another way is a marketing audit, which assesses to what extent the organisation is matching its capabilities to its moving environment. It therefore focuses on the impact of both internal and external factors of event marketing. Whichever system and tools you apply, you need to construct internal mechanisms for assessing how successful your marketing activities have been.

Changes in marketing practice

Marketing practice has not remained static: what is appropriate for one industry or one period of time is not necessarily appropriate for another. Where early marketing theory implied one size fits all, in a more complex and global economy this is no longer the case. What we can

> **BENEFITS   minus   COSTS = RETURN (pecuniary and non-pecuniary)**

Figure 3.3 Calculating return on investment (ROI)

identify, however, are broad principles which may guide marketing practice. Such commonality of principles can be classified within three main marketing approaches: transactional; relational; and experiential. And the last of these is very explicitly driven by the experience, use and growth, of events.

Transactional marketing

Sometimes referred to as a 'one-night' stand, this is the traditional approach to marketing and can be traced back to the 1940s and 1950s (McCarthy 1960; Borden 1964). There are two key elements to transactional (or transient) marketing. First, it focuses on securing the individual sale now. Each individual sale is transient, so that once a product is sold, the marketer has to start all over again to sell to the same person at a later stage. As a consequence the timeframe is short to medium. The only purpose of interaction with the consumer is an immediate sale (Webster 1992). Second, it is based upon the traditional 4Ps approach to marketing: product; price; place; and promotion (McCarthy 1960) (see Chapter 5). The emphasis is on brand, market share and product. Thus when you see a marketer or a commentator referring to the marketing mix, this implies using a transactional approach.

The focus of transactional marketing is an exchange between the producer and the consumer (Sheth and Parvatiyar 1995). This means that there is both a beginning and an end to any contact (Rao and Perry 2002). Transactional marketers need to constantly attract new consumers (Wang *et al.* 2000; Lindgreen *et al.* 2004). The definitions we used earlier in this chapter from the Chartered Institute of Marketing and the American Marketing Association are both consistent with this approach.

Communication within this approach is essentially one-way, from producer/retailer to consumer, and is primarily top-down (O'Malley *et al.* 1999). This means that such communication is solely designed to be persuasive and does not seek to encourage any dialogue or feedback. The role of the consumer is to passively receive a marketing message. Transactional marketing primarily relies upon mass communication channels such as television, radio and newspapers to reach a very broad audience. Therefore, marketers rely upon paid advertising or media relations to reach large, generally untargeted audiences.

There exist two views about the efficacy of the transactional approach. One suggests that this approach was relevant up to the 1970s, but is irrelevant to current market and consumer conditions. Another version suggests that transactional marketing is only applicable to manufacturing and consumer markets. Both viewpoints imply that transactional marketing is not appropriate for events.

Relationship marketing

Sometimes referred to as a 'marriage', relationship marketing is a more recent development that Berry (1983) claimed to have coined. It traces its origins to the 1970s and was a direct alternative approach to transactional marketing. The proponents of relationship marketing suggest that the business environment has changed, reflecting different problems and opportunities. In particular, the means of communication is such that databases enable more tailored messages to be sent to highly profiled target audiences. With technological change, marketers do not have to rely on mass communication channels.

Relationship marketing reflects limitations in transactional marketing. The growth of relationship marketing has in particular been associated with service industries, such as events. But this paradigm shift (Gronroos 1997) reflects more than the experiences and needs of specific industries. The clear difference from transactional marketing is that the timeframe is longer term. What matters is not necessarily the immediate sale, but the life-time relationship a consumer has with an organisation. Consequently, Sheth and Parvatiyar (1995) suggest that such an exchange mechanism exists for a long time. The inherent idea is that a relational exchange is, as Morgan and Hunt (1994) suggest, more profitable in the long term. Moreover, whereas with transactional marketing there is a beginning and an end, this is not the case with relationship marketing.

Relationship marketing implies a completely different way of dealing with, and responding to, consumers. One of the most influential pieces of empirical research on this approach was conducted by Reichheld and Sasser (1990). They found that recruiting new consumers, as was the norm under transactional marketing, was five times more expensive in effort than retaining an existing consumer. This is not an argument for not recruiting new consumers: rather, it led to a growing awareness that cultivating an existing client base could be more profitable in terms of finite resources spent. Relationship marketing stresses retention of existing consumers rather than the recruitment of new ones. This suggests that the marketer needs to collect, monitor and use data collected on consumers in order to better meet their needs. Such data, combined with offering something which provides added value, can create the necessary loyalty required (Berry 1983). Indeed, McKenna (1985), when he suggests that personal relationships can be more successful than price alone in developing the required loyalty, suggests that relationship marketing implies a new business model.

Whereas transactional marketing communication is based on reaching the greatest number of potential consumers primarily via indirect communication channels, with relationship marketing communication is direct. Because the audience is often segmented into small groups, a targeted message can be sent to each. In addition, communication usually implies some form of interaction and dialogue with consumers over a long period of time. In part, the very act of encouraging interaction may have intrinsic value, but more importantly it allows the marketer to use feedback to deliver more products which meet the needs of consumers. Because relationship marketing has often, though not exclusively, been associated with service industries there is a general assumption that marketing communication will apply the 7Ps (Booms and Bitner 1981) (see Chapter 5).

One model which can help explain how relationship marketing might work is Christopher *et al.*'s (2002) loyalty ladder (Figure 3.4). Individuals might start off as prospective consumers, become purchasers and then move up the 'rungs' of the ladder to eventually become partners. This implies a shift of focus from a customer recruitment (transactional) to a customer retention (relationship) approach. A potential consumer might hear about an event, attend it once and then become a regular attendee, potentially championing it to their friends. Within relationship marketing the consumer may undertake a journey with the event. Worldwide events agency *experient* (http://www.experient-inc.com) noted (2008) that to use relationship marketing to secure attendees at an event required integration of activities, especially the use of databases.

Braggs (2006) suggests that events are a tactical means of achieving relationship management. So where above we have considered how discrete events can build relationships with their stakeholders, Braggs is suggesting that marketers should use events as a means of enhancing their relationships with key audiences. In particular, corporate hospitality offers a means of building such relationships with consumers over a long period of time. He suggests that staging small made-to-measure events for each audience is an effective relationship marketing approach. Relationship management through corporate hospitality is a means of building brand awareness with key audiences.

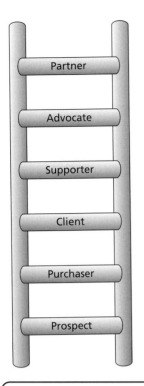

Partner: someone who has the relationship of a partner with you

Advocate: someone who actively recommends you to others, who does your marketing for you

Supporter: someone who likes your organisation, but only supports you passively

Client: someone who has done business with you on a repeat basis but may be negative, or at best neutral, towards your organisation

Purchaser: someone who has done business just once with your organisation

Prospect: someone whom you believe may be persuaded to do business with you

Figure 3.4 The loyalty ladder
(Adapted from Christopher *et al.* 2002)

Experiential marketing

This approach is heavily influenced by Pine and Gilmore's (1998) concept of an experiential economy. They suggested that consumer expectations have changed, that companies now need to market not just their products/services, but also to offer the consumer an experience. This inherently makes a clear link with events as part of that experience. The link was even closer, furthermore, in that they implied that metaphorically the market place was a theatrical stage involving actors, scripts and audience participation. In such an experiential economy entertainment can become part of marketing.

The term experiential marketing, 'friends with benefits', has developed since the late-1990s from the experience economy school of thought and is closely associated with Schmitt (1999). Experiential marketing was, he argued, a response to three developments: the growth of IT; the growing importance of brand; and the ubiquity of communication. Experiential marketing assumes that the consumer is not solely a rational decision maker concerned with just functional features and benefits, but also is an emotional being who is also concerned with pleasurable experiences. For example, Drew Westen (2007) suggested, in his idea of the 'political brain', that during election campaigns emotional factors can be the final arbiter in which candidate a voter finally decides to support. He suggests that rational factors alone, such as policy stances, do not always in the final account sway a voter. Experiential marketing implies that consumers can also be hedonists.

Schmitt (1999) suggests that consumers want a brand or product to connect with them not just through its features, but also through an experience. The consumer is not just a passive receiver of the product, as in transactional marketing, or engaged in dialogue as with relationship marketing, but is taking an active part in a public place. The focus is on the consumer experience, not consumer satisfaction. As a result, Holbrook (1999) suggests that consumers personally connect to a product through an experience. Leighton (2007) found that heritage sites such as museums, stately homes and tourist attractions used experiential marketing through the use of multimedia, actors and sights and sounds to encourage visitor engagement. She noted that this strategy was driven by the need to gain competitive advantage. Marketer and consumer share the same experience at the same time.

Schmitt (1999) identified four characteristics of experiential marketing:

- Focus on customer experiences.
- Consumption as a holistic experience, so a broader measurement given to products.
- Customers can be both rational and emotional.
- Methods and tools are eclectic.

One example of an experiential marketing campaign was provided by Blazinstar Experiential (www.blazinstar.co.uk), who were commissioned to create a live brand experience to build an emotional connection between young professionals and the 3 Mobile brand's latest campaign 'Social Notworking'. A 'Social Notworking' dome toured around three of London's most prestigious squares: Soho, Leicester and Golden. Consumers passing by were invited to use HP laptops with 3 Mobile's internet dongles, and have their photos taken in a customised, branded 3 Mobile photo booth. Participants had three photos taken against a 3 Mobile backdrop, and received an instant printout along with instructions on how to access their photos online through the 'Social Notworking' Facebook site. Additionally, people were able to experience a demonstration of the new Skype S2, and make free phone calls to their friends and family members anywhere around the world. The installation enabled consumers to interact with a range of 3 Mobile products, and access social networking sites that they use frequently more easily and conveniently such as Facebook and LinkedIn. After the campaign there was a 21 per cent increase in consumers who associated 3G with social networking.

It is not sufficient just to offer an event: as Wood (2009) notes, the event must provide the appropriate level of challenge for the audience so that they can 'immerse' themselves in the experience. This means that different audiences may experience the same event differently depending on their skills and interests. Experiential marketers often focus on live events where the target audience can see a product and experience it themselves. Experiential marketing segments audiences by grouping them according to values, enjoyment, personality and social group (Tsaur *et al.* 2006). In the Arts Petkus (2004) found that such segmentation should be based upon different audiences seeking different experiences. Success in experiential marketing is determined by whether a company can deliver memorable experiences.

Communication within experiential marketing is not via the media or traditional direct media such as direct mail: rather, it is essentially via physical events (Heitzler *et al.* 2008). An event, be it pre- or post-product launch, becomes the means by which a brand's personality is conveyed to the target audience. Where relationship marketing uses a range of offline and online channels to build relationships, experiential marketing primarily uses offline media, in the form of events, to build relationships. Both seek to build relationships: the key difference is not the purpose but how they go about building those relationships.

Events can help non-event marketers reach and build relationships with their key audiences. It could be just a product launch, and so a tactical one-off. However, some authors believe that the real value of events is as a strategic tool to build long-term relationships (Russell 2007; Crowther 2010). As a result Moor (2003) suggests that experiential marketing reflects a new marketing mix. The assumption is normally that experiential marketing only applies to B2C (Business to Consumer) markets, but Rinallo *et al.* (2010) found that the approach has some relevance to B2B (Business to Business) markets. They found at a trade fair that experience plays a role, but it does so not for individual products and stands, but for the whole event. This implies a level of universality which may not apply to transactional and relationship marketing.

The dance craze Zumba is a participatory activity, and the case study below shows how an event was used to reach, inform and mobilise Zumba trainers.

CASE STUDY 3.3

The Party In Pink™ Zumbathon®

In October 2011, Zumba® brought the charity fitness concert to Alexandra Palace to raise money for Breakthrough Breast Cancer via the Party In Pink™ Zumbathon® campaign. Zumba® sought to re-launch the Party In Pink™ campaign globally and asked experience marketing agency George P. Johnson to deliver this first ever charity fitness concert for 3,500 Zumba® enthusiasts. The inaugural event was a phenomenal success and raised over £130,000 for Breakthrough Breast Cancer.

Kevin Jackson, VP of Business Development at George P. Johnson (GPJ), suggests that traditional marketing is 'interruption' marketing, all about the sender of the message and what they are doing. It is 'look at me' marketing. Experience marketing, on the other hand, is about creating a holistic and mutually beneficial relationship between a brand and its consumers. Experience marketing reflects a change in the world, especially reflecting how we communicate online, so that increasingly internal and external markets want a relationship with brands when they want it. Experience marketing is a reaction to one-way marketing, based on creating a relationship between an individual and the brand.

Zumba®'s audience is women between the age of 25 and 45 who are active consumers and advocates of the brand, and for these women Zumba® is more than a fitness programme – it is a movement and a way of life. The charity Zumbathon® campaign provided a platform for UK based Zumba® fans to connect with the brand in a shared purpose for a greater cause. Active participation was central in the establishment of value and a long-lasting bond and the experience needed to seamlessly execute this at every touchpoint.

GPJ created a communally oriented environment with the objective of keeping attendees connected and motivated. The event opened with a high-octane performance style workout led by Colombian creator Beto and twelve Zumba® instructors. Following the mass fitness workout was an electric performance from International R&B artist Wyclef Jean. GPJ produced a phenomenal experience using a rock 'n' roll production crew who created a music based show. The stage was circular so that all members of the audience could see the performances – the Zumba® dancers and talent constantly moved around the stage to create a 360 degree performance that everyone could feel a part of. In addition to the fitness class turned dance party, the event included a large Zumba® pop-up store that also featured co-sponsors 505 Games and Fitness First. British celebrities, including Gail Porter, Rachel Stevens and Amy Childs were also on hand to offer support and encouragement.

As a brand, Zumba® presents both a rational and emotional message that it can do some good and make a difference through fitness and fun. It aims to get people to connect to the brand by enjoying themselves. For Zumba® this event is part of a long-term relationship building strategy, with a training event for 6,000 instructors at Excel London in February 2012.

Table 3.2 Comparing marketing approaches

Approach	Purpose	Audience	Communication	Style
Transactional	Short-term sales	Any of all possible Passive	Mass communication One-way	Scattergun
Relationship	Longer term relationship through loyalty	Existing consumers Interactive	Direct Dialogue	Rifle shot
Experiential	Longer term relationships by experiencing the brand	Segmented by values, personality and social group Active	Event led Emotional messages	Explosive (reaches all who are close to it)

Table 3.2 compares the three approaches in terms of why and how they are used. This enables event marketers to choose the appropriate approach for what they want to achieve, their resources, market and type of event.

The event marketer's role

Practical checklist

- Allocate individuals or teams to the marketing function.
- Agree what you mean by marketing – it will have practical implications on what you will do and how.
- Identify what your consumers want, not what you want.
- Consider how others can use your event for their purposes – collaboration may be possible.
- Create systems to easily collect data – for example, a sheet for asking telephone callers how they heard about the event.
- Work out whether you need to specialise in one form or have a basic knowledge in them all.
- Identify which marketing approach, or combination of approaches, is right for you.
- Get involved in all aspects of the event that affect the event experience.

There is, potentially, an assumption that the responsibility of the event marketer is very narrow, whereas in fact the opposite is the case. Whichever aspects of your event may have an impact on how consumers interact with it, are within your remit. This might lead to some uncomfortable internal discussions over your role, but stand firm. Case study 3.4 with a marketing practitioner explains just how broad the job of an event marketer is.

CASE STUDY 3.4

The remit of the event marketer

One of my guest lecturers, Lesley Shorrocks of SIGMA Marketing (www.sigma-marketing.co.uk), always says: *'You can have the best-organised event, but if no one turns up there is no point.'* Lesley has since its inception in 1992 been responsible for the marketing of Music of the Night. This is a joint civilian–military event, held biannually at the home of 29 Regiment of the Royal Marines in The Citadel, an imposing seventeenth-century building near the harbour in Plymouth. Long experience of the event, and analysis of empirical data of customer buying behaviour, means that Lesley knows who her main audience is in terms of age, social class and geography. Having identified her target market Lesley is able to devise the appropriate promotional messages, using the correct channels to reach her target audiences. However, this is not job done: Lesley knows that marketing is more than just getting the message out, and she plays a key role in the actual organisation of the event. Marketing involves also understanding and shaping all the aspects of the event which affect the customer's experience. For example, this includes the actual content of the music played and what the finale is, as feedback makes clear that attendees want certain things to be present every time. This behavioural pattern of wanting the familiar also occurs at other events, so that the BBC's Proms series at the huge Royal Albert Hall in London, which ends with the Last Night of the Proms televised live, has the same main components every year. In addition to the content, Lesley is involved in how the box office functions, the stewarding, management of volunteers and the handling of VIPs. In short, marketing should involve anything which affects the customer (and often staff and participant) experience of that event.

The event marketer should get involved in event planning from the outset. Event marketing strategy and planning cannot be divorced from overall event planning: they must be integrated. They are, in essence, two sides of the same coin. This means, as Lesley suggests above, that the event marketer must be involved from the beginning in a wide range of event activities, often ones which others are not initially sure they have a right to be involved with. For a new event, the marketer should play a central role, through market research, to determine whether what appears to be a good idea on paper can actually become an event because there is evidence that there is a market for it. The marketer will also usually play a key role in determining the content and feel of the event, revenue generation and evaluation. Where the event manager tends to focus on the practicalities of putting the event on, the event marketer is also concerned with the possible effect of these practicalities on participants and customers. The event marketer acts as a conduit between what the event organisers want to achieve, and what participants and customers want.

Discussion questions

Event marketing is much more than selecting which tools and techniques you use. This chapter highlights that event marketers are faced with key issues:

1 What is the practical impact of our definitions(s) of marketing?
2 How does the event marketer persuade other event organisers that they are not 'treading on their toes' unnecessarily but that marketing has a very wide scope centred on consumer service?
3 As the event marketer, do you specialise and buy-in expertise, or do you attempt to cover all marketing functions?
4 What are the similarities and differences between the three approaches, and what bearing does this have on which one(s) you choose for your event?

Further information

Other sources which might help you consider the issues outlined in this chapter include:

Books

Brunt, P. (1997) *Market Research in Travel and Tourism*, Oxford: Butterworth-Heinemann – detailed assessment of how to use research.

Carlsen, J. (2006) 'The Economics and Evaluation of Festivals and Events', *In* I. Yeoman, M. Robertson, J. Ali-Knight, S. Drummond, U. McMahon-Beattie (eds) *Festival and Events Management: An International Arts and Culture Perspective*, Oxford: Butterworth Heinemann: 246–59 – assesses the economic value of events.

Articles

Gronroos, C. (2006) 'On Defining Marketing: Finding a New Roadmap for Marketing', *Marketing Theory*, 6 (4): 395–417 – part of the Nordic School and so one of the leading relationship marketing sources.

Rafiq, M. and Ahmed, P. (1993) 'The Scope of Internal Marketing: Defining the Boundary between Marketing and Human Resource Management', *Journal of Marketing Management*, 9 (3): 219–32 – one of a few sources on this oft-overlooked topic.

Websites

http://www.nswevents.com/NSW – a good 'what's on' guide.

http://www.eventmarketing.com/ – US based trade body and think tank that looks at how events use marketing.

http://www.academyofmarketing.org/event-marketing-sig/event-marketing-sig.html – educational specialists in event marketing.

http://marketing-expert.blogspot.com/ – general blog on marketing.

http://www.marketingresearch.org/ – US based trade association.

Chapter 4

The importance of a marketing strategy

Introduction

The other chapters in this section focus on specific operational details of marketing an event. This chapter puts such practical detail into context by setting up the importance of marketing management. This chapter will first address strategy in general, then the relationship between events and strategy and constructing a marketing strategy. Last it will address how to write a marketing plan. While the detail is important to event marketers, we also need to consider wider operational issues. Marketing strategy is about setting the scene for an event from both an internal and external perspective.

By the end of this chapter, students should be able to:

- Identify the importance to an event manger of strategy in general.
- Assess the components of a strategic approach.
- Evaluate the importance of events to a strategic approach.
- Identify and assess the components of a marketing strategy.
- Construct a marketing plan.

The meaning of strategy

For many traditional permanent organisations, strategy has been a key buzz word for some twenty years or more. It is assumed that the long-term survival and health of an organisation heavily depends upon a clear strategic approach. There is an implication that if something is not 'strategic' it has a lesser value, that it is *ad hoc*, partial and undirected. Very often there is an implied qualitative difference between strategy and tactics, with the former being considered more important and therefore the preserve of senior managers. Indeed, if you read any business management magazines you will frequently find something written about strategy, and how important it is. As a result many organisations spend a lot of time, money and effort in getting it right. However, many events are organised in a different, more temporary way implying a focus on tactics rather than strategy. Events can be what Toffler (1990) referred to as a 'pulsating organisation', where the number of staff is not constant but reflects the different stages of the event, so they expand and contract. This implies that as a one-off, an event does not warrant a strategy, that tactics are alone required to put on the event.

Strategy is generally viewed as concerned with an organisation as a whole. This raises issues for a one-off event, where technically there may be no difference between the event and the organisation. If an event is unlikely to be organised again, or if the organisers create only this event, why is strategy relevant? Strategy is also about broad principles and frameworks for operating, which direct future decisions, and it is these principles for how an event organiser perceives the event in a wider context, at the very least, which justify the importance of strategy for any event, be it one-off or part of a wider portfolio.

The historical meaning of strategy was very specific: the word comes from the Greek *strategos* meaning military leader, derived from *stratos* meaning army and *ago* meaning leading. In particular it implies the plans of action required to meet a goal. One of the best known ancient texts on strategy is *The Art of War*, written in the sixth century BC by Sun Tze (translated by Giles, Sun Tzu 2010). A famous general, he clearly identified the importance of strategy to military success, and his approach is embodied by the phrase: 'It is best to win without fighting.' Sun Tzu suggested a clear link between the strategy and a detailed plan of action. Since ancient Greek times the meaning of strategy has been gradually broadened. In the sixteenth century, Machiavelli's *The Prince* associated strategy with politics. While the link to the military and to politics still remains, more commonly in modern society strategy has a much broader meaning, and is now often associated with the proposed activities of commercial and non-commercial organisations.

The word strategy implies that an organisation or individual tries to influence the direction they take. Robbins and Coulter (2009: 179) suggest that

> Strategies are the plans for how the organisation will do whatever its in business to do, how it will compete successfully, and how it will attract and satisfy its customers in order to achieve its goals.

This makes a very clear link with the business world, and so suggests that marketing is an important part of strategy. They see the purpose of strategy to be gaining competitive advantage, and to do so an event needs to understand its consumers.

Strategy implies that a range of different timeframes needs to be taken into account, rather than just immediate pressing matters. Johnson and Scholes's definition of strategy makes clear this importance of a longer timeframe to planning activities (Johnson and Scholes 2002: 10):

> Strategy is the direction and scope of an organisation over the long term which achieves advantages through its configuration of resources within a changing environment and to fulfil stakeholder expectations.

Strategy involves looking towards, and preparing for, the future.

A simple way of understanding strategy is to consider it a way of seeing the 'big picture'. The answer to a number of questions will shape your strategy: 'What you want to achieve from your event(s)? What resources do you have to achieve this;? and What is happening outside the event that may affect your ability to be successful?' As a result, we can consider strategy as the overall direction of an organisation, event or series of events. It is worth noting that different events organised by the same organisation may require different strategies.

While there may not necessarily be one agreed definition of strategy, we can identify some characteristics which we normally expect to be components of a strategic approach:

The importance of a marketing strategy

- Sets the overall direction of an organisation.
- Focuses on the long-term, not immediate day-to-day issues.
- The purpose is to gain competitive advantage.
- Is dependent upon an organisation's resources.
- May necessitate change in an organisation's resources, structures and culture.
- Codifies, in plans, an organisation's values, structure and culture.
- Considers the potential impact on the organisation of the wider environment.

We can identify some key terms which are relevant to understanding and developing a strategy. The mission, often in the form of a mission statement or vision, states the overall purpose of the organisation. It should help you focus on your event: for example, 'To hold a golf day to raise money for a named charity.' Goals (sometimes referred to as aims) offer a bit more clarity to the mission, and as a general statement of purpose indicate the overall direction required to achieve the mission. Goals, of which there would normally be only one or two, state your ideal outcome for the event: for example: 'To make a lot of money' or 'For everyone to have a great time.' Objectives are the means of achieving goals, and they need to be measurable. Many events will use the mnemonic SMART to help construct their objectives, so that they are: Specific, Measurable, Achievable, Realistic and Timed. Objectives are precise: for example, depending on the event, they could include the number of attendees required, the amount of money you wish to raise or sales leads generated. Strategy, then, is the means by which the specific objectives will be achieved, and hence help achieve the overall goals and mission. EventScotland (http://www.eventscotland.org/scotland-the-perfect-stage/the-national-events-strategy) identified a strategy to bring events to Scotland, and so stressed a distinct cultural heritage such as the friendliness of the people, the natural landscape and impressive architecture. Without tactics, strategy is merely an intention: it needs a plan of implementation. Tactics could include

Figure 4.1 The stages of event strategy development

the promotional material, theme, venue and clear signage on the day. Finally, but not chronologically last, is evaluation. For some this might be fairly informal in form of a 'wash-up' where the main protagonists discuss the event; or it could be much more formal, involving feedback and the assessment of whether the objectives were being met. Figure 4.1 shows how a strategy is developed, and suggests that evaluation is not the end of the process.

For high-profile big events, constructing a strategy can be very complex and multi-layered, as our case study of the Wimbledon Championships demonstrates. It is quite clear from this case study how the message(s) follow the strategy set.

CASE STUDY 4.1

The development of strategy and the Wimbledon Championships

The Wimbledon Championships (http://www.wimbledon.com) is held each year over a two-week period in June and July. The Championships, one of the four tennis 'majors', is one of best-known global sporting events and celebrated its 125th year in 2011 having started in 1877. The Championships is owned and run by The All England Lawn Tennis Club, and it represents the core marketing element of the brand.

The All England Lawn Tennis Club introduced in 1993 its Long Term Plan, which was concluded in 2011. It was designed to transform the infrastructure of the event, by enhancing facilities for spectators, players, officials and the media. This involved significant building of new facilities, and upgrading existing ones to make The Championships the world's premier tennis championships played on grass. Now that this plan has been completed, and a new chairman has been elected, the All England Lawn Tennis Club is looking at where they wish to be in 2020.

The process of developing the strategy for each championship starts with the professional staff, who around September/October analyse the departmental reports of what happened that year. There is then a series of meetings that address all the various elements of the events, such as catering, spectators and players. A series of recommendations is then made, which are put to various sub-committees that look after the operational aspects of The Championships. These then make recommendations to the full Committee of Management of nineteen members (12 from the Club and 7 from the Lawn Tennis Association). This committee, with the advice of the professional staff, acts as the steering group for devising the strategy of the next year's championships. Decisions are then communicated to the various departments for implementation, with regular formal and informal meetings to assess how well the strategic direction is being applied.

The ethos, mission and guiding principle of The Championships, Wimbledon, is Tradition with Innovation. This suggests that heritage is important, that the championships are where they are now because of where they have been over the past 125 years. At the same time they are not afraid of being forward thinking, so that they consider how they need to develop and change to remain a major sporting global brand.

The overall goals of The Championships are to run the event safely, effectively and in a way that leads to the greatest enjoyment by the greatest number of people. Essentially, the organisers seek to create an atmosphere which is both purposeful and entertaining. The means by which this is achieved is to focus on the needs of the players, spectators and the media. If the players are happy in terms of fair schedules and available facilities then the quality of the tennis will be higher, which enhances the enjoyment of those watching both at The Championships and on television. This is turn improves the television experience. The organisers seek to give people a fantastic experience, so they want to come again next year.

Given its global attraction, strategically The Championships has sought to create equal understanding around the world. For instance, a lot of work has been undertaken, first in Japan, then India, Brazil and Europe, to raise its profile. To try and enhance the experience of global audiences, key strategic decisions are taken. For example, after forty-three years with NBC in 2011 The Championships changed its television contract to ESPN, so that the American audience could watch games live, and not just recorded highlights.

The All England Tennis Club is always looking to improve the experience for the next year, and so evaluation is important. A number of surveys are conducted with players, spectators and specific questionnaires for those in a queue. This can lead to what might appear very minor issues being addressed: for example, if the Referees Department found that players were unhappy with a type of pasta in the players' lounge, they would look at changing it for the next year so that it made for a better experience.

Whilst the strategy has until 2011 been to work on building and improving the playing facilities, the future is likely to focus on the players' facilities, such as restaurants and where they rest.

There are a number of different ways of assessing strategy, with one popular framework being presented by Chaffee (1985) who identified three approaches:

1 *Linear* – strategy is seen as sequential planning, where the aim is achieving objectives or goals step by step. It assumes a very passive and predictable view of the organisation's environment. As a consequence this approach is based upon a belief that:

● Decisions made at the top will be implemented.
● The organisation or event exists within a predictable environment.
● Managers have timely access to the appropriate information so they can act rationally.

If any or all of these three assumptions are not supported, then the linear approach to strategy may not work.

2 *Adaptive* – strategy is a way that organisations respond to their environment and how it changes. It requires very regular SWOT (Strengths, Weaknesses, Opportunities, Threats) analysis. This approach views the environment as less predictable. Unlike the linear approach the organisation or event seeks to adapt to the environment, rather than seeking to impose its will on it. It is likely that an organisation or event will have a phased strategy, and one which will evolve depending on what happens in each phase. The adaptive approach, therefore, is much more likely to take into account, and give weighting towards, external factors such as political and economic instability. This approach emphasises the importance of actors in the strategic process, such as competitors, governments and consumers. It could be argued that this approach is particularly relevant during challenging economic and political times.

3 *Interpretive* – strategy is based on an organisation or event's world view or interpretation of its environment. Therefore, their culture and values are important to how they respond to the environment. It is important within this approach that all people in an organisation or event need to agree the strategy.

Chaffee (1985) suggests that organisations often go through these approaches, beginning with linear and ending up with interpretive. Essentially the strategic approach an event or organisation follows is based upon their world view, how pliable it is and their role in a wider context. Events are not a largely predictive environment. This is partly because something will go wrong that cannot necessarily be controlled, but more importantly because the nature of events, the events market and the competition are constantly evolving. The vast majority of events, therefore, need to take an adaptive or interpretive approach to strategy.

The original understanding of strategy suggested that it was only the preserve of the head of an organisation, but nowadays we can identify at least three different levels of strategy. First, there is corporate strategy. This is normally the level assumed by senior decision makers when talking about strategy, and involves decisions that affect the whole of the organisation. So it is directional, and sets the tone. Second is the business or competitive strategy level, which considers how an organisation/event should compete in particular markets, and as a result it is often marketing led. It affects various (though not all) business units within the organisation/event. Third, is the operational or functional level of strategy, which is concerned with the various functions of the organisation/event – marketing, finance, research and development, operations – which contribute to the success of the previous two strategic levels. The assumption behind these three approaches is that senior decision makers can take a dispassionate view of each department and its value to the collective whole.

This typology suggests a hierarchical approach to strategy. If we take the scenario of an organisation using an event as a strategic tool, then the decision to use events is likely to be the preserve of senior managers. The decision to organise a particular event, or attend say an exhibition in order to meet clear objectives, is likely to be in the remit of the second tier of management. The strategic decisions about actually delivering the event presence will largely be at the operational level, though the two higher levels will probably maintain an interest in event delivery. To evaluate the strategy any organisation uses for an event requires an understanding of how different levels of the organisation interact with, and influence, the event delivery.

A famous model used to explain strategy is Mintzberg's 5Ps of Strategy (see Table 4.1), where each of the Ps is its own definition of strategy. Thus he suggests that there is not one definition, but several. This implies that a range of different influences helps create a strategy. For example, this includes past experience, future plans and expectations (intended and unintended). Overall, this suggests that strategy is a combination, often unique, of both

Table 4.1 Mintzberg's 5Ps of strategy

Type of strategy	Explanation
Plan	A pre-determined, deliberate course of action, implementation and evaluation
Position	The means by which an organisation is located
Perspective	An organisation's ingrained, and collective, view of the world
Ploy	A means to outmanoeuvre competitors
Pattern	A series of actions which display consistency in behaviour

(Adapted from Mintzberg 1994).

predicting what will happen with events and also being able to respond efficiently and effectively to those events.

Strategy and events

> **Definition box 4.1**
>
> ### Strategic events
>
> A strategic event is one designed to help achieve wider corporate objectives, such as economic well-being, political gains or competitive advantage. The benefit could be for the host organisation or a third party, such as the local community.

The term strategy has not often been applied to events, not as much as it has to many other industries, probably because of the 'pulsating' organisational nature noted earlier. For example, Crowther (2010) suggested that traditional event planning models do not appear to link events explicitly with strategy. Yet historically events have for over two millennia been used as strategic tools. For example, many caesar's in Ancient Rome, in particular Caligula, used circuses and gladiatorial games, accompanied with free bread and food, as a means of gaining support, or at least acquiescence, from the masses. Events were used as part of their strategy for political survival: getting the masses (the plebs) supportive of them acted as a counterweight to any opposition they might have from within the political elite, such as the Senate. Beyond these overt political machinations, Korstanje (2009) refers to a more subtle use of events, where leisure was used to reinforce core values through the mythology of Roman life. For example, the original Olympics, held in Ancient Greece, were a means of demonstrating military prowess. In Ancient Egypt the Sed Festival was a jubilee that proved a king's health to continue to rule. It often took place after thirty years of the king's rule. Events were a means of providing an alternative to political reform, while still maintaining support and credibility.

Machiavelli (1505, translated by Bull 1975: 127) suggested that events could play a key part in political strategy: 'A Prince . . . at suitable times of the year he should entertain the people with shows and festivals.' This suggests the strategic role of events is to keep the minds of the people off issues the political elite does not want them to consider. Indeed, Raj *et al.* (2009) suggest that in the seventeenth and eighteenth century, European Kings provided organised events as a means of maintaining their political power. For example, the existence of a large number of religious and local community festivals gave peasants something to look forward to, which helped them forget how tough their lives were. The strategic role of events, therefore, was about political survival.

More recently, events have been used to present a positive image of a nation or society. In other words, not necessarily overtly to oppress people, but to give them pride in a country and, by association, its political leaders. The obvious examples are hosting mega-events such as the Olympics. China sought to use the Beijing 2008 Olympics as a means of shifting international opinion. China did not suddenly decide it was a good idea to host the games: rather, it had clear strategic goals about why it wanted to host them, which it believed justified the £20 billion cost (*Guardian* 2008).

Academic commentators and practitioners are increasingly viewing events as strategic tools. For example, Russell (2007) quotes research by George P. Johnson as showing that events can play strategic roles in driving business value. In another example, Pugh and Wood (2004) found that local authorities were increasingly using events as a strategic tool. Similarly, Getz (2008) noted that events were being used to meet strategic objectives for public policy organisations, such as pressure groups and governmental organisations. Table 4.2 shows some of the reasons why events are used as strategic tools. Increasingly, organisations are turning to events as a means of addressing core economic, social and political problems that they face.

Table 4.2 The strategic role of events

Sphere of interest	Role
Political	National prowess/prestige
	Maintain power
	Display power
	Provide safety valve
	Deliver representation
Economic	Deliver prosperity
	Regeneration
	Target pockets of poverty
	Make money
Societal	Reflect cultural interests
	Mobilisation
	Fun/enjoyment
	Encourage societal change

A clear example supporting Pugh and Woods' view is our case study on Edinburgh, where the city council has made a deliberate strategic decision to use events, and this in turn has shaped their core corporate messages.

Edinburgh City Council – the strategic use of events

Edinburgh is the capital city of Scotland and is host each year to hundreds of events. It is particularly associated with the Edinburgh Festival, considered the world's number one culture and Arts festival. It is also well known for its New Year celebration, Hogmanay, and hosts many major sporting events.

The city is heavily dependent on tourism for many jobs. As a result Edinburgh City Council seeks to offer events which both provide a backdrop for visitors already in the city, and to attract others to visit the city primarily for the events. The city council often works with EventScotland to assess the value of events.

When a proposal for an event comes in, or the city is considering bidding for an event, the event is assessed against clear criteria:

- *Economic impact* – sometimes they conduct a study to assess this. For other event proposals they have a broad idea already.
- How will it raise the profile of Edinburgh? For example, Edinburgh is bidding to host the Grand Depart of the *Tour de France* in 2017, which would attract a good deal of worldwide television coverage.
- *Legacy* – for sports events the city council also looks for evidence of a legacy from the event: so, once the event is over, how does it help the sports development of the Edinburgh public? For example, in 2011 Edinburgh hosted the World Tag Rugby championships and competitors visited local schools. So far this has led to at least twelve schools now playing tag rugby for the first time, and more are expected to follow.

The council recognises that occasionally events can lead to some inconvenience for residents in the form of additional traffic or road closures, but, while recognising this, believes that in terms of the bigger picture events contribute significantly to the economic wellbeing of the city.

Being a capital city helps Edinburgh attract events, but it is also blessed with an attractive centre around Prince's Street Gardens and the castle, where event organisers want to host their events. The location provides a striking backdrop for the media.

Events can help the city promote an image as a rugged romantic city. For example, the Great Edinburgh Cross-Country Race, held every January, is a great fit with the city's projected image. Moreover, it is probably one of very few major cities in the world with the landscape to allow a cross-country race to be legitimately held in the centre of the city.

In addition, the city has used events to help develop the image of the city. Research conducted found that Edinburgh was viewed as a cultural centre, but by attracting a number of sporting events, the city is adding to what it is known for. Furthermore, sporting events are helping promote a health agenda, which is part of an attempt to make Edinburgh the most physically active city in Europe by 2020.

Edinburgh finds itself in an increasingly competitive environment, with other major cities investing heavily in events, and so the focus is on preserving and enhancing the reputation of the Edinburgh Festival as the world's number one.

Edinburgh's future strategic use of events is set against the context of the current severe financial climate. Despite cuts in some other services, there is a political recognition that events are for Edinburgh an investment. If council budgets get smaller, however, this may raise issues for the funding of events in Edinburgh. Irrespective of this Edinburgh City Council continues to have an appetite for attracting bigger and better events.

Marketing strategy

Marketing strategy is vital to event marketers because it encourages them to ask the key questions of what they are trying to achieve – their marketing objectives – and how they will accomplish these. In reality, such questions make us ask whether an event is actually worth doing in the first place. The process of developing a marketing strategy has intrinsic value in encouraging key issues and ideas to be discussed. A marketing strategy helps organisations and events focus their efforts.

The marketing strategy for an individual event is different from, but allied to, the corporate strategy. The corporate strategy concerns the allocation of resources within an organisation to achieve the overall business direction and scope identified within specific objectives. Marketing strategy defines target markets and direction within the overall corporate strategy. While our assumption is that the link has to be an event we have organised, in January 2011 Microsoft used an event it did not actually attend, to meet corporate objectives. During the live television coverage of the Golden Globe Awards (Oscars), Microsoft ran television advertisements which launched its new corporate tagline 'Be What's Next' to a national audience.

Any event has only finite resources. The intention behind developing a marketing strategy is to work out how best to use those resources. Therefore, a marketing strategy is about matching an event's abilities and competencies to the environment (Crowther 2010), and doing so over a period of time. For example, technological developments, especially in IT, create new problems and opportunities. From a strategic marketing perspective, key decisions concern the overall direction of the programme and target audiences, the fit with other organisation/event activities and overall corporate strategy. Marketing should help reinforce core messages, reflect the mission statement and provide a means of using resources efficiently. Brennan *et al.* (2003:

17) note that: '*Strategic marketing decisions are concerned primarily with ensuring the effectiveness of the marketing organisation in the competitive struggle.*' We can, therefore, identify a number of key components which help construct an event marketing strategy: goals and objectives; positioning; target audience; marketing approach; and marketing activities.

Goals and objectives

Marketing goals may address general operational factors, such as delivering a memorable experience, but they can also seek to improve relationships with stakeholders. Objectives are based on awareness, acceptance or action. They should be simple, brief and measurable. Sponsors of an event might have as their marketing objectives to motivate staff, or gain sales leads from potential customers. Event organisers'/hosts' marketing objectives might include launching a product, building a brand or increasing sales.

Positioning

Positioning an event in the mindset of the market is an important strategic decision. Brassington and Pettitt (2005: 393) suggest

> The marketing strategy defines target markets, what direction needs to be taken and what needs to be done in broad terms to create a defensible competitive position compatible with overall corporate and competitive strategy within those markets.

Positioning describes how target market segments perceive the events offer in relation to competing brands. While positioning can be determined by what consumers think of an event, it should not be passive: rather, an event's marketer should identify where they think they are and where they wish to be. The concept of positioning is often associated with Ries and Trout (1982), who suggested that what mattered is not so much the product, but what consumers thought about the product. They suggest that marketers need to get a product into the minds of consumers, which can often be achieved by creating a unique position.

There are a number of different ways of assessing your event's positioning. One is to construct a perceptual map, measuring Quality along the y-axis and Price along the x-axis. As shown in Figure 4.2, your event or event portfolio might be considered in the middle in terms of price and quality, and so be at position **a**. But you note that your main competition in position **c** is close to you in terms of price and quality, and you want either your existing event(s) or a new event to take advantage of a gap in the market at position **b**. As a result, your marketing strategy will be designed to help create this impression amongst consumers.

Positioning need not just be about price or quality: for example, the website of the Saucony English Cross Country Relays (www. http://www.englishcrosscountry.co.uk) states that:

> The positioning of the event in early November makes it an ideal competition for athletes aiming to qualify for the Great Britain team to take part in the European Cross Country Championships a month later. . .

Other factors such as timing or venue can shape the positioning of an event.

Core to understanding the positioning of an event is to consider where it is *vis-à-vis* competitors. The appropriate strategy for the market leader is different from those with a smaller market share. Another means of assessing event positioning is to use the Ansoff matrix. This is formally a tool for identifying growth strategies, but in essence this requires an understanding

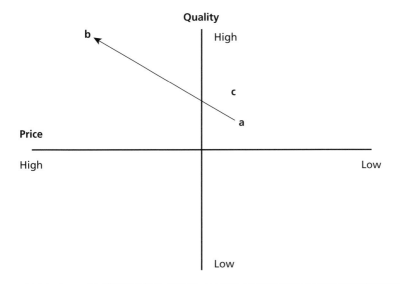

Figure 4.2 Positioning your event

of positioning. The key question that the Ansoff matrix tries to address is whether future growth should be based on new products or new markets. Figure 4.3 shows that the event marketer has potentially four strategies. If an organisation wishes to focus on current markets then they can either seek to increase market share within existing markets (market penetration), or through market development consider putting their existing products into new markets. Alternatively, they may believe that growth will be from new markets, and this could be through product development of new products to existing markets. Or, most riskily, it could be diversification, which is new products to new markets. As a general rule growth strategies on new products are less secure, but may be the appropriate choice if an existing product is in decline.

The BBC's Saturday evening flagship light entertainment programme, *Strictly Come Dancing*, has branched out to an event reflecting a range of positioning strategies. *Strictly Come Dancing. The Live Tour* in 2012 visited eleven different UK venues over forty nights. The live show represented a combination of strategies, and helped market penetration in that it is another way of reaching existing audiences, but by being a physical touring event and not just a television show it also allows the brand to reach new markets in major population areas. The audience is a mixture of the old and the new, and this is achieved through product development.

Markets	Products	
	Current	*New*
Current	Market penetration	Product development
New	Market development	Diversification

Figure 4.3 Using the Ansoff matrix for event positioning
(Adapted from Ansoff 1965)

Target audience

The positioning that an event marketer chooses is heavily reliant on identifying who the target audience is. As Fill (2009) notes the traditional approach to reaching an audience was to use the promotional mix. This involved a combination of the mix that was used, and the resources allocated to each. For example, an event manager of a charity fundraiser might decide to rely on media relations because it is financially cheap. However, Fill dismisses this approach for essentially putting the cart before the horse, by deciding the channel before assessing the needs and preferences of the audience. An alternative strategy to the promotional mix approach, therefore, is one based on the consumer.

We will assess the detail of segmentation in Chapter 6, but here we will just note that strategically it is unwise to rely on one single consumer group: rather, an event is best advised to target a number of segments. The event marketer needs to identify the possible segments. For example, at a major outdoor music festival these might be students, professionals aged 25–34 and couples with young children. They will then need to assess these segments, perhaps for factors such as ease of reaching them, spending power and likelihood of attending. Having selected the appropriate segments, the nature of the event may need to reflect this: a music festival that attracts young children is likely to be different in feel and facilities to one aimed at an adult-only audience. Once you have selected your segment(s), the event communicator should then check that it fits with the event positioning outline above.

For some events, such as Student Shopping UK in our case study, the audience determines everything that the event manager organises. This event is specifically aimed at only a student market, and the owner of the company, Alex Ludlum, realises that the student market can be further broken down.

CASE STUDY 4.3

Targeting niche markets

Some businesses specialise in providing events for discrete niche markets. Student Shopping UK (www.studentshoppinguk.com), as you might imagine, provides events aimed at students. They are best known for running student discount nights in many UK shopping centres: for example, they set up and managed the first Freshers Shopping Fest – the UK's largest student focused retail and social experience in October 2011.

Student Shopping UK's target audience is clearly students as a whole market, and they essentially help shopping centres and other retail businesses reach this market. Therefore, although experts in putting on events, they use their knowledge of this niche market to help their clients reach this audience. Student Shopping UK's discount shopping nights are the means by which they introduce the market (students) to their clients (retailers and shopping centres). Because they are market driven, Student Shopping UK can offer bespoke activities designed solely to enable clients to reach the student market.

Although a niche the student market is not homogeneous: rather, like all markets it is heterogeneous, with a range of different segments. Students are of different ages, gender, religions, live in different types of accommodation, and differ in the type of university attended. This necessitates some differences in how each is reached, though the message of exclusivity, saving money and having a good time, is universal to the market as a whole.

The needs of targeting, drive the actual event product. The venues chosen are only those shopping centres with a significant number of students nearby, otherwise the footfall is not large enough for the event to be a success. The nature of the target audience also shapes the communication channels used. As mostly younger people, students are reliant on certain communication channels such as texting and the Internet, so these are the prime means by which Student Shopping UK reaches potential attendees. In addition to online communication, student campuses are a discrete 'world', and there exist a number of direct channels within a university to reach students.

Managing Director Alex Ludlum said: 'Our whole business offer is shaped by the nature of our target market: students. Moreover, every one of our events is unique, reflecting the fact that the exact needs of students differs slightly from university to university.'

Marketing approach

The appropriate marketing strategy is usually shaped by the nature of the organisation *vis-à-vis* its competitors. In the BBC television show *Dragons' Den*, where business people present their ideas in order to secure funding, the questions asked often appear consistent with Porter's Four Forces Model (Figure 4.4). Porter's (1980) model suggests that the ability of an organisation to achieve its goals is influenced by its relationship with: the bargaining power of suppliers; the bargaining power of buyers; obstacles to new entrants; and threats of substitutes. The first two factors refer to an organisation's dependency: Are there very few buyers or lots of buyers? Are there few suppliers or plenty of suppliers? Where there are few buyers and suppliers the organisation's options are limited; where many, they have more choice. The third and fourth factors refer to whether the event is unique or fairly common. With the former you have much more independence of strategic movement. It is for these reasons that the 'dragons' often ask whether there are barriers to entry, such as patents, cost and expertise.

When two aspiring event managers, Ian Forshew and Celia Norowzian, presented their idea for Beach Break Live (http://www.beachbreaklive.com) the UK's first student festival to the 'dragons' in 2007, very unusually all four 'dragons' offered to fund them for a percentage of the business. The strength of the pitch was that it was the first to see the market opportunities, and had a clear ethos of being ethical. Implicitly or explicitly, the dragon's questions, and Ian and Celia's answers, reflected the very sort of issues Porter's Four Forces Model suggests it is strategically important to discuss. The 'dragons' were not assessing the idea of a single event: rather, they were assessing the concept's idea as a strategic approach for reaching the student market. They concluded that it would.

The importance of a marketing strategy

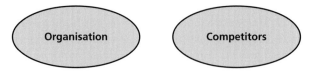

An organisation's, and its competitors' position is influenced by:

Organisation   Competitors

1   The strength of buyers
2   The strength of suppliers
3   Barriers to new entrants
4   Threat of substitute products/events

Figure 4.4 Porter's four forces model
(Adapted from Porter 1980)

Porter's Four Forces Model helps shape an event's likely marketing strategy. As Figure 4.5 shows, Porter identified four strategic approaches depending on the circumstances in which an organisation found itself. Each of these is designed to help an organisation gain competitive advantage, so that the organisation can either follow a cost-based approach or a differentiation-based approach. He identified two variants of each. Those who decide a cost-based strategy can seek to have the lowest costs, and so beat their rivals on price (dominant cost leadership). Or they can seek to lower costs and maximise market share (focused cost leadership). In both cases strategic decisions address how costs can be reduced. Those who seek to differentiate themselves can do so by either offering a product that is different from their rivals in some way (differentiation), or the differentiation is in the market, as with Student Shopping UK, and so they specialise in niche markets (focused differentiation). Decisions on these strategies are based on whether the aim of the event is to hold a leadership position in a region/city, or to have a narrower yet well defined market scope.

An event's marketing strategy can be influenced by:

● What the event is trying to achieve.
● The event's resources.
● Attitudes to risk and innovation.
● What competitors are doing.
● The nature of the market.

The marketing strategies outlined above are essentially customer focused, but a different approach exists: namely, basing marketing strategy and positioning on what competitors are

Approach	Appropriate strategies
Cost based	Dominant cost leadership or focused cost leadership
Differentiate event	Differentiation or focused differentiation

Figure 4.5 Porter's generic strategy model
(Adapted from Porter 1980)

doing, and what the event could do to the competition. This approach, marketing warfare, was first outlined in an article by Kotler and Singh (1981) and then popularised by Al Ries and Jack Trout's book, *Marketing Warfare*, in 1986. They were influenced by military writing such as Sun Tzu's *The Art of War*. They suggested that the orthodox approach was that size mattered – that the event with the largest sales team, most financial backing or market size would automatically win. However, looking at military battles when smaller armies had beaten larger ones, Ries and Trout suggested that planning, manoeuvring and overpowering the opposing side were key. The role of marketing warfare strategy is to overpower the competitor somewhere with superior force.

Depending on the size and market share of a company they suggest that there are four possible marketing strategies: defence; attack; flanking; guerrilla. Defence is the preserve normally of the market leader, who seeks to entrench their position to make it difficult for competitors to take away their market domination. They might achieve this by tactics such as launching new products, improving quality or significantly increasing promotional activity. The attack strategy is typically the recourse of the second or third largest company in a market, and directed at the market leader. This might be achieved by tactics such as reducing costs, price reductions and creating a perceived market differentiation, often of reputation/position. Flanking attacks are designed to address those areas which are not core to the defender's interests, and so likely to be less well defended. Typical flanking attacks seek to gain a bridgehead, such as in a particular geographical market or segmented audience. Guerrilla attacks are usually the preserve of those companies with a small market share or new entrants. The attacker seeks to gain entrance to a niche market. Thus in the dance field there are a number now, such as Zumba, Samba and Salsa, where a new entrant can set up classes. If it meets resistance from the large established dance classes then the guerrilla withdraws.

A similar approach to marketing warfare is game theory, which came to prominence in 1944 when von Neumann and Morgenstern published *Theory of Games and Economic Behavior*, where mathematical theory was applied to economics. Game theory suggests that events can be viewed as akin to strategies used in games. Within events there could be a number of different 'players' each of whom has different preferences and dislikes. Each player has to select preferences or 'plays' for reaching a preferred outcome. This requires them to gauge how best to juggle preferences to achieve the best outcome in relation to other players. There are two main categories of game theory:

● *Zero-sum games (competitive)* – the better one player does, the worse the other fares.
● *Non-zero sum games (conciliation)* – player's compromise so each gets something.

During a crisis, game theory might provide a framework for deciding at what point you inform the media and other stakeholders that there is a major problem. If you go for zero-sum you might wait till the last minute, hoping that there is a resolution so you do not need to tell people about the issue. But if there is no resolution and you have delayed communication, then this may add to the criticism you might receive. Similarly, if two promoters are planning to organise rival music festivals in the same geographical area at a similar time, their choice of game theory strategy would influence whether they decide to 'fight it out' and see who wins, or seek to find an accommodation whereby they jointly promote an event. They might each share the money with the latter, but with the former at very best one will win, and quite possibly they will both lose. Game theory can help explain the strategic approach event managers take to competitive situations.

Marketing plans

A well structured marketing plan can increase the chance for business success. The marketing plan takes the broad strategy and works through the detail required to deliver it, and so seeks to convert the strategy from general ideas to operational detail. The plan seeks to adapt the organisation or event to take into account the external situation, so a marketing plan is about finding a strategic fit between what the organisation wants to achieve and what the environment will allow. The marketing plan provides a clear and unambiguous statement about the strategies and actions that will be implemented, by whom, when and with what outcomes.

Plans are at the heart of managing events. However, a marketing plan does not necessarily follow exactly the format of an event plan. While there is a range of different styles of marketing plan, the core to any marketing plan is:

- An understanding of the environment (internal and external).
- Clear objectives.
- Marketing activities.
- Marketing programmes (action plan).
- Marketing budgets.
- Control.
- Contingencies (What if?).

Environment

The starting point for most marketing plans is a marketing audit, which requires an assessment of both the internal and external environment, with typically the former being conducted first. A common tool for internal audits is a SWOT analysis, where you go through an honest assessment of your Strengths, Weaknesses, Opportunities and Threats. This is designed to help identify internal factors that could shape the future of an event, both positively and negatively. Carlsen and Andersson (2011) found that festivals took a different strategic approach to their use of SWOT, depending on their ownership structures. Publicly owned festivals, being more dependent on primarily one funding source, took a narrower approach to funding and stake-holder opportunities than private and not-for-profit sector festivals.

A typical tool for assessing the external environment is PEST, which Kotler (2005) suggests is a strategic tool for understanding an organisation's market. The core components are:

- P – *Political* factors, such as the introduction in the UK of the 2010 Bribery Act, which may have a direct impact on the corporate hospitality sector.
- E – *Economic* factors which influence the wider environment, such as recession. For example, in October 2011 Luminar, the UK's largest nightclub owner, went into admin-istration (Sibun 2011), leaving some events potentially without a venue.
- S – *Society* develops: for example, taste and fashion. Certain activities are popular for a while and then replaced by something new.
- T – *Technological* changes: for example, the widespread use of social networking sites is having an impact on both the promotion and content of some events.

An event which understands the external environment is more likely to seize on new marketers and avoid introducing an event just as the economic, social or political tide is moving against it.

Objectives

Core to all marketing plans is a need to identify exactly what you wish to achieve. We have noted earlier the widespread application of the mnemonic SMART.

Marketing activities

This comprises two related parts. First choosing which channels, tools and activities will be used within the promotional mix: for example, direct mail, public relations and a sales team. Second, the scheduled plan of actions, often tactical, using promotional mix variables to gain advantage within target markets. This is normally detailed in the marketing plan, so that it might include when particular press releases are going to be sent, the dates and messages of any direct mail campaign and updates to the website. All the previous sections of the plan are working towards this detailed action plan.

Whether an event is following, deliberately or not, a transactional, relationship or experiential marketing approach will shape significantly not just the whole plan, but specifically the action plan. A transactional marketing approach is much more likely to make use of short-term sales methods such as sales promotion. An event using a relationship marketing approach may well be more likely to use direct mail and e-newsletters over a long period of time. An event using, or being used as, part of experiential marketing is more likely to have an action plan based on physically meeting consumers. The action plan is the end of a long tail, but without it the strategy and plan is merely meaningless paper.

Control

We may have a clear and strong strategy, and a detailed well thought through plan, but an event also needs to know what is happening once the plan is implemented. The control system covers what is ensuing with the budget, and monitoring what is happening with the event's communication. This is then used to help the event communicator make the necessary changes. Core means of maintaining control are:

- Talk to consumers, suppliers and participants – How do they view the event?
- Be very clear what you do and do not control, including people, processes and activities. What is beyond your control, and how might you respond?
- Keep written documentation on all decisions and who has been tasked to do what and by when.

Practical checklist

- Justify your event by creating a strategy – always.
- Consider strategy as a circular process not a linear process – evaluation at all stages.
- Create clear lines of strategic responsibility.
- Identify the strategic purpose of an event: if there isn't one, do not have the event.

- Dovetail the marketing strategy to overall corporate goals.
- Ask simple questions: Where are we? Where do we want to go? How can we get there?
- Never view your event in a vacuum. It is affected by, and affects, a wider environment.
- Create a visual action plan of what you are going to do, by when and who will do it – put it up on a wall so your team can see it.
- Check what is happening to attendee numbers, such as which tickets are selling, which are not. Do we need to consider, for example, a sales promotion to get interest in some tickets?
- If something goes wrong keep asking: Why? You will eventually get to the heart of the problem and be able to address it.
- Write up the lessons.

This chapter suggests that Scotland, as a relatively small country reliant on limited natural resources, is acutely aware of the importance of events to its future. Our second case study looked at how an individual city, Edinburgh, developed its strategy. Our last case study looks at how a government body, EventScotland, considers the use of events across a nation. It is no accident that Edinburgh City Council and EventScotland work closely together.

CASE STUDY 4.4

EventScotland

EventScotland (http://www.eventscotland.org), the national events agency, was established in 2003 with the aim of strengthening and promoting Scotland's events industry. EventScotland does this by attracting, generating and sustaining a portfolio of world-class events in Scotland.

In 2009 EventScotland launched the national events strategy, Scotland The Perfect Stage, which will lead Scotland's events industry into and beyond 2020 and outlines a clear mission and vision to further establish Scotland as a world-leading event destination. Scotland's cultural identity and heritage are strong differentiating factors and the friendliness of its people is renowned throughout the world. Scotland boasts a rich natural landscape as well as impressive architecture and cityscapes, and a range of sports facilities and arenas. Scotland has a range of iconic sporting and cultural events, which form the backbone of its events portfolio, and reinforce a reputation as a world-leading events destination.

The strategy also defines the seven key impacts by which EventScotland will measure the successes of Scotland's events industry: tourism; business; image and identity as a nation; media; participation and development; environment; and social and cultural benefits.

EventScotland has invested in hundreds of events, through the international programme and the national programme. These have included sports, festivals, food and drink and music.

Launched in 2009, BusinessClub Scotland is an initiative to help Scotland's business community benefit from the country's ambitious events programme in the run up to the 2014 Commonwealth Games and beyond. Supported by the Scottish Government, EventScotland and the country's leading business organisations, BusinessClub Scotland will ensure that Scottish companies are supported, engaged and given the chance to maximise the commercial opportunities generated by Scotland's current and planned investment in major events.

The exchange rate with the Euro is currently favourable, which creates a great position for bringing European events over to Scotland.

Your task

- Why was EventScotland created?
- What alternative solutions to the problems it seeks to address might have been adopted? (Think about by whom, how and why?)
- How does EventScotland help achieve the overall strategic goals?
- Who are likely to be EventScotland's stakeholders? What do you think the relationship is likely to be? What does EventScotland need to do to address any problems?
- How would you assess how successful EventScotland is?

Discussion questions

Not all events, especially one-offs, recognise the importance of strategy, yet it enables them to assess the purpose of the event in a clear and measurable way. This chapter highlights that event marketers are faced with key issues:

1 What are the possible consequences of not having an event marketing strategy?
2 How would you go about constructing an event marketing strategy?
3 What are the key questions you need to ask in developing your marketing strategy?
4 In what ways could an organisation use events as a strategic tool?
5 How does constructing a marketing plan differ from the other planning activity an event organiser undertakes?

Further information

Other sources which might help you consider the issues outlined in this chapter include:

Books

Brennan, R., Baines, P. and Garneau, P. (2003) *Contemporary Strategic Marketing*, Basingstoke: Palgrave Macmillan – the section of case studies is particularly useful.

Hooley, G., Piercy, N. and Nicouland, B (2008) *Marketing Strategy and Competitive Positioning*, Harlow: Pearson Education – oft-quoted book on strategy.

O'Toole, W. (2011) *Events Feasibility and Development: From Strategy to Operations*, Oxford: Butterworth-Heinemann – the only events management book that looks at strategy in any depth.

Slack, N. and Lewis, M. (2008) *Operations Strategy*, Harlow: Pearson Education – well known strategy textbook.

Websites

Visit EventsNSW at http://www.eventsnsw.com.au/home.aspx – makes clear the strategic value of events within destination awareness.

http://www.mplans.com/event_planning_marketing_plan/marketing_strategy_fc.php – one of many websites that give basic details on how to construct a marketing plan.

Chapter 5

The event marketing mix

Introduction

This chapter will outline those components of the marketing mix which apply to events. We will first consider what it is the event consumer is purchasing, and then the price they will be willing to pay for this. We will then assess what impact the fact that most events have a venue has on the concept of place and distribution. Finally, we will highlight the detailed techniques available to promote your event. By the end of this chapter students will be able to:

- Understand what the event marketer is marketing to consumers.
- Assess the applicability of the 4Ps versus the7Ps.
- Identify unique aspects to events marketing which differentiate it from other industries.
- Evaluate the most appropriate marketing communication channels.

The marketing mix

The event marketing mix is the means by which the strategy and plan will be implemented. It is normally associated with US marketer Neil Borden, who is believed to have first used the term in 1953. The marketing mix is those components of an event which McCarthy and Perreault (1987) suggest relate to the factors the marketer can control. By changing the different components of the marketing mix, the event marketer will alter the nature of the final event delivered. The marketing mix is like a recipe: an event is the result of the blend of ingredients selected by the event marketer.

There are a number of different approaches to the appropriate marketing mix for events, but most event marketers normally adopt either the 4Ps or the 7Ps. The 4Ps developed by Jerome McCarthy in 1960 identified the importance of (in no particular order): Product; Price; Place; and Promotion. This was long considered the orthodox view, and as we saw in Chapter 3 is associated with transactional marketing. Hoyle (2002) refers to the 5Ps for events of: Product, Price, Place, Public Relations and Positioning. The use of public relations instead of promotion is too narrow, and positioning is part of a strategic approach. Moreover, these 5Ps do not necessarily address the specific requirements of a service based industry such as events. The 7Ps, sometimes referred to as the Extended Marketing Mix, reflects limitations of the 4Ps and is associated with Booms and Bitner (1981). The three additional Ps are: People; Processes; and Physical Evidence. This approach is considered to be more consistent with relationship marketing. There does not yet appear to be a model of Ps, or any other term, which fits with experiential marketing, though people and physical evidence make an obvious fit. The 7Ps has been considered a better fit with service based industries, because of the importance of the interface between the seller and buyer, and the intangibility of many services (for a wider discussion of why the 7Ps is more appropriate see Rafiq and Ahmed 1995).

The event product

Definition box 5.1

Defining the event product

The event product is what staff, participants, sponsors and attendees experience. It is therefore affected by all aspects of the event, both the obvious public ones and those less obvious, more 'hidden' ones. The event product is not one thing, but the composition of various different components. Moreover, the experience of every different attendee is personal to them, and can be different to the next person.

Technically a service is different from a product, so should we not be talking about the event service? A service implies an interaction between human beings or an entity, and essentially we are buying that interactivity, possibly in the form of advice, expertise or experience. The marketing literature is fairly clear on the exact meaning of a service as opposed to a product. For example, Kotler *et al.* (1999: 646) suggest that: '*A service is any activity or benefit that one party can offer to another which is essentially intangible and does not result in the ownership of anything.*' This suggests that the key difference between a product and a service is that the former is physical and tangible, and that the latter is not. However, this can be a rather simplistic division, especially concerning events. You may go to a concert and enjoy a non-physical service in the form of an artistic performance, but at the same time you may buy a physical memento such as a tour T-shirt.

The characteristics of services are (not in any logical order):

- *Intangible* – consumers cannot use all their senses to access it, the service is not physical and cannot be viewed or touched. It is difficult for consumers to tell in advance exactly what they will be experiencing.
- *Inseparable* – production and consumption are not separate processes, rather they happen at the same time. The consumer will normally have contact with the service provider, there is no intermediary.
- *Perishable* – services cannot be stored before purchase, so that each service is unique at the time of manufacture and consumption. There may be peaks and troughs in demand.
- *Heterogeneous* – each service varies, for instance depending on contact with the service provider and the exact nature of the service.

Each of these characteristics raises questions which the event marketer must address. Although the event itself might not be tangible and something the potential consumer can touch or smell, it is possible to provide tangible evidence of the event, such as videos, photographs and testimonials. For example, BlueSky Experiences, an events company based in Perth, Scotland, has a whole page given to some fourteen testimonials from happy clients (http://www. blueskyexperiences.com/testimonials.cfm). Inseparability usually means that the event will come into direct contact with the consumer, and because an event is perishable, an absence of consumers to one sitting is revenue lost. With the heterogeneous nature of events it is difficult to standardise the service provided. To minimise differences in event performance necessitates focusing on operating systems, staff training and quality standards/assurance.

Most commentators tend to use the term 'product', so although it is technically erroneous for events we shall use the term 'product' as well. There appears to be a consensus that the event product is based around the experience attendees (and indeed participants) gain from attending. For example, Getz (2008: 280) suggests that: *'The "product" is in fact the event experience.'* It is for this reason that Getz believes the event marketer should apply a relationship marketing approach. Event marketing needs to address all the factors which might shape the consumer's experience, not just that component of the event they are coming to see.

One strategic tool used by many event marketers is the product life-cycle. It assumes that all products from birth to death go through four stages:

- *Introduction* – the marketer needs to launch the product, as consumers do not know about it.
- *Growth* – as awareness grows and product sales increase, so competitors come into the market. The event marketer needs to defend their product/brand by differentiating the features and/or benefits.
- *Maturity* – sales, and hence revenue and profit, are at their highest, but so is competition. Typically, marketers seek to build on relationships with consumers to maintain loyalty.
- *Decline* – eventually all products decline, but marketers seek to put off this stage for as long as possible, often by using sales promotions, such as discounts, gifts and prizes.

However, it can be difficult to tell which stage you are at.

The World Nettle Eating Championships was held at the Bottle Inn, at Marshwood near Bridport in Dorset (http://thebottleinn.co.uk) in the UK. It began in the late 1980s, and attracted significant media coverage. Based in a public house, the organisers also offered a beer festival, live music and children's entertainers. It was a local community event which attracted tourists, and although apparently a success, the 2010 championships appears to have been the last. Presumably unable to resist the economic travails which the UK licensed premises industry is facing the pub closed, and so this event appears to have reached the last stage of the life-cycle.[1]

New products

The life-cycle implies that eventually every event will either decline, or at least become unprofitable. To maintain market share and income this strongly suggests that the event marketer needs to consider the development of new events. If the event marketer wants to gain market share and increase revenue then they will have to develop new events. New product development is, then, either a defensive or offensive process depending on the event marketer's strategic goals.

There may be an assumption that new means originality, in the form of a completely new technology or idea that has never been seen before in the whole world. In fact such new products are rare, especially in a non-technological field like events. However, there are a number of different levels to new products, which imply far less exacting forms of originality, so that you do not have to be the first person in the world to think of a new event.

Occasionally a new event may be the result of a eureka moment where the event marketer is stimulated to suddenly think of an original idea. However, unlike Archimedes we do not have to sit in a bath to get such inspiration; rather, there exist techniques for identifying possible new events. A common method used and adapted is the new product development process, which involves eight separate stages (Cravens and Piercy 2006). At any one of these stages it may be decided that the event simply does not justify being launched. The eight stages are:

- *Idea generation* – set up project teams to systematically identify new ideas. This might include conducting research amongst existing staff, suppliers and consumers.
- *Idea screening* – the creative idea needs to be looked at more closely. Is it compatible with our current objectives, resources and production abilities?
- *Concept development* – this is where the idea is tested to see if it might work, which is rare for intangible events. However, it would be possible for larger events, such as a conference, to use computer design programmes to construct virtual images to address how the event might look.
- *Business analysis* – here we look at likely profitability, both for financial and any non-pecuniary objectives we might have.
- *Product development* – this is usually where a prototype is produced, again possibly feasible with physical products but not so with services. For an event, this stage will often have to be missed out, which may lead to some uncertainty as to whether it will work on the day.
- *Test marketing* – the product might be introduced to a restricted market segment, such as one geographical area, to learn lessons in what consumers think. Again, with service based events this stage is difficult to achieve, though many West End plays are tested first in small provincial theatres.
- *Launch* – the event is produced, and here the marketing mix is key.
- *Monitoring and evaluation* – an event provides a host of data, such as how ticket sales are going, which allows us to tweak an event's marketing. Once over, how do we then learn the lessons?

We have on the one hand the suggestion that event marketers will from time to time think about new events, but this is not an easy process to get right. Moreover, it involves expending resources in the form of money, time and expertise, and so we cannot afford to develop too many ideas which do not actually get off the ground. Edgett and Cooper (undated) estimate that 46 per cent of the resources that companies devote to the conception, development and launch of new products go to projects that do not succeed – they fail in the market place or never make it to market. Thus it is imperative to consider new products, but huge health warnings exist about how difficult this is to actually achieve.

Edgett and Cooper (2005) identified a number of reasons for why new product ideas fail. Their core argument was that a range of factors was not in place. There needed to be a clear brief, the developing team needed to be cross-departmental and to include the appropriate resources, the product needed to be clearly differentiated and not just a 'me too' product, and there had to be clear 'kill or go' decision timeframes built in to the process. Therefore, they revised the eight stages above with a gate and stage model. The stages were broadly similar to above, but they introduced four gates, at each of which the development team decides whether to go the next stage.

This suggests that events do not fully fit with the orthodox norm of product development, and the next case studies demonstrate how different events can be to other products.

CASE STUDY 5.1

Developing new specialist conferences – a collaborative model

US based Forecast Technology Group, (www.conferencestrategists.com) specialises in scientific and engineering conferences, which includes new product development. Its core market is non-profit organisations, such as charities, and start-up professional associations. It starts by assessing an organisation's overall strategic goals, and then identifies how best to ensure that the organisation's vision becomes reality. New events are derived from this process.

The reason why Forecast Technology Group suggests new event products stems in part from its approach. It is an atypical conference planning group, in that it focuses more on defining the strategic goals for (and with) a non-profit organisation, then utilising conference and educational products to achieve those results.

One successful example of a new product development is the concept of Innovation Discovery Labs. Since many biotech groups are so small, they rarely have a staff/administration to do much beyond member requirements. Forecast Technology Group serves as an extended 'staff' (outsourced) by producing the meeting, and then Forecast Technology Group has enhanced the main meeting by developing a new product (Innovation Discovery Labs) to provide complementary education via a 'pre- or post-con' specialty workshop.

Forecast Technology Group finances the add-on workshops, absorbing the upfront production and staffing costs, then recoups its investment after the registration and sponsorship monies come in. If there's a loss, Forecast Technology Group absorbs it. If there's a profit, it is split with the client. This is a form of collaborative new product development.

The key to new event product development is innovation, then following your instinct and realising if it's something you believe in enough to finance. It's challenging and rewarding to be able to apply these product development skills to the biotech industry – especially with the extreme promise that some of this new emerging research provides, which can help lead to everything from finding cures for major diseases to building organs in the laboratory.

Price

Price provides all the money for the other Ps. Any profit is based upon getting the price correct. Constructing the pricing strategy is a complex process which involves balancing competing factors, such as when the event is to be held, the nature of the target audience, the costs of the event and the positioning of the event.

Any pricing strategy is based on what the event marketer will ask people to pay to attend. Therefore, price is simply the amount of money charged to attend the event and the consumer has to decide whether the price asked for attending the event offers value for money. However, price can be more than just what the consumer is asked to pay: it can also include how payment will be made. For example: Does it have to be up front, or paid in instalments by direct debit? Are credit terms available? A season ticket to a professional sports team may cover up to twenty or so games, but the money is usually paid up front. Many entertainment venues include a small booking fee which is additional to the ticket price.

Pricing involves important management questions for the marketer. Price is rarely plucked from the air: it is based on data of what consumers might pay, and involves collaboration between the finance and marketing sides of the event management team. Moreover, as Hoyle (2002) suggests, the event marketer must fully understand the financial aspects and not leave these up to others. The event marketer must also understand, and respond to, the financial objectives of any third party involved with the event, such as a sponsor. For example, increases in price might bring in more total money through the turnstiles, but sponsors may be alarmed if the number of attendees is significantly lower as a result.

The event marketer can choose from a range of pricing strategies, but first they need to identify what their costs are. Event organisers usually take into account two types of cost:

- *Fixed* – fixed costs do not change but remain the same irrespective of how many attend your event. For example: venue, insurance, equipment and signage.
- *Variable* – variable costs vary with the number of attendees. For example: staff, artistes and refreshments.

Having identified their costs, the event manager can then decide the appropriate pricing strategy:

- *Cost-oriented pricing* – a common strategy where the event marketer works out all the costs, adds on a portion for profit and then decides what the price will be. This is typical for larger events that may be less influenced by competitors, such as sporting events.
- *Competition-oriented pricing* – where smaller events, especially new entrants, look at the pricing strategy of the market leader. This is fine if your objectives, approach and costs are similar, but a problem if not.
- *Prestige pricing* – appropriate for a small number of high-end or very popular events. The price is set high and so implies a quality event which attracts high-income consumers, such as the Glyndebourne Festival Opera held next to an English country home, where many of the attendees have picnics in the grounds. It attracts those interested in culture, with a high income, where seating varies from £40 through to £230 per person (http://glyndebourne. com/seating-plan-and-ticket-prices-festival-2012). However, Getz (1997) warns of the danger of a 'customer backlash' if the price is too high.
- *Yield-management* – very common to many events, especially those with more than one 'sitting', or several different segmented markets attending. For some events there are quiet periods of demand, and attractive prices can help increase demand. For example, professional cricket that typically lasts from 11 a.m. to 6 p.m. has long had a tradition of letting people in for a low fee late in the day. Those events with different markets can provide a different service quality which reflects different prices: for example, the English Premier League team Chelsea Football Club offers restricted viewing tickets in one stand at £23.50, but for the rest of the tickets in that stand they are up to £61 (http://www.chelseafc.com/

Figure 5.1 Gabor–Granger demand response curve
(Adapted from Gabor and Granger 1961)

page/ExtraInformation/0,10268~2363834,00.html). Yield management can also reflect different tickets such as group passes, season tickets and age groups.

One useful tool that the event marketer can use is the Gabor–Granger (1961) Demand Response Curve (see Figure 5.1), which tries to research and identify what might be the effect on consumer demand of different event prices. Questionnaire respondents select whether they would or would not buy a ticket depending on different price points. This allows the event marketer to construct the response curve. Applying primary research data to consumers, this tool can help the event marketer predict what the market will take, and therefore what is the best price to gain maximum attendance/and or profit.

Place

Place focuses on distribution: namely, how will the seller get the right amount of product to the consumer at the right time in the right location? For most industries, therefore, it requires a detailed understanding of distribution and supply chain management. For events, however, place is generally a much more simplified concept that, with the exception of cyber-events, equates to the venue.

However, there is some disagreement as to what place means in an event marketing context. Rogers (2006: 102) defines it as: '*Place focuses on the activities used by a destination or venue to make its product available and accessible to prospective clients.*' For Rogers, place is a channel for how people market themselves, in terms of what and how. This seems to suggest that how people get tickets to the event is the main purpose of place. This appears to be a fairly narrow description, and a broader possibly better definition is offered by Allen *et al.* (2005: 210): '*Location(s) where the event is held and its tickets are distributed, its physical setting and on-site processes.*' This definition adds two features: that the event venue is central to place as a marketing concept; and it develops the ticketing idea to including online processes, which may well add value to ticketing.

Because of the centrality of venue to event place, this actually has an effect on the product in the way that place, for many consumerable goods, does not. For example, Hoyle (2002) points out that in choosing the correct venue the event marketer must be aware of its potential impact on consumers. Place may actually shape the nature of the event itself. Koh and Jackson (2006) conducted a questionnaire of attendees to The Mesa County Fair in Colorado, to ask what they thought of the venue. The fair was in an open field – two buildings, an arena, with two parking areas. They made use of flags, streamers and potted plants to create the ambience. Country music was played throughout the fair. The average daily temperature was in the 90 degrees Fahrenheit. Respondents felt the venue was too spread out, with poor parking and that not enough was made to make it a pleasant experience given the high temperatures. The results suggested that place would have a significant detrimental effect on attendance in future years.

For the vast majority of events, place is geographical: a physical venue such as a conference centre, stadia or a farmer's field. However, there is a small niche market of virtual events, which can be accessed virtually. For example, UnisFair (http://www.unisfair.com) presents itself as a virtual means of engaging with customers by creating a virtual event. Virtual Event World (http://www.virtualeventworld.co.uk/) offers itself as a virtual trade exhibition. Other forms of virtual event are webinars and video conferencing, so that on its website *Infosecurity Magazine* offers a range of webinars (http://www.infosecurity-magazine.com/webinars). The advantage of such events is that they can take place at almost any venue, and a worldwide audience can access it. They are more likely to be attractive to a business audience, where they can access the information without having to necessarily pay for travel, accommodation and other costs. However, despite some evangelising by their supporters, they still largely remain a very small part of the worldwide event industry, probably because we want primarily physical not virtual experiences.

Hybrid events are physical events that offer added value through some aspect of a virtual event, so the virtual and physical coexist. Attendees and delegates to the physical event can download or access online activities such as discussion forums, videos and social media such as Twitter and Facebook. For example, Event Camp Europe (http://eventcamp.eu/), held in September 2011 at Down Hall near London for event professionals, explained how hybrid events worked, and offered the virtual add-ons for event organisers to try them. The George P. Johnson (2010b) *Virtual Market Outlook Report* found that of 889 participants in the virtual events market, 37 per cent produced hybrid events with both physical and virtual components. This might suggest that if virtual events remain a niche product, then hybrid events might become much more mainstream, simply because they are an added service to an existing physical event.

One of the key developments has been the common use of e-ticketing, which relates to both place and process. E-ticketing is e-commerce: the ability for consumers to buy tickets direct online. As well as avoiding having to physically visit a box office, or hanging on the telephone waiting for it to be answered, e-ticketing allows the consumer not just to buy the ticket, but to see where tickets remain and look at a range of options. For the event marketer, e-ticketing reduces many of the costs and allows them to sell outside office hours, because processing is reliant on computer software not people hardware. Event marketers can host their own e-ticketing system, but, as this can be expensive, more typical is outsourcing to specialist e-ticketing agents such as Ticketmaster and Ticketweb. Others hire a software package from companies such as Eventbrite, so that they can run their own operation. So the key management decision for the event marketer concerning e-ticketing is to decide whether they run it in-house or outsource.

E-ticketing systems for the B2C (Business to Consumer) market are very popular in certain types of event. For example, Guo *et al.* (2002) found that sports, music and Arts events in Macau were particularly likely to apply e-ticketing. The use of e-ticketing is especially prevalent in sport, so Mignerat and Audebrand (2010) assessed its use in the UEFA European Football Championships of 2000, 2004 and 2008. They found that there have been no real problems, and there is no turning back for such mega-sporting events. However, it is too narrow for the event marketer to view e-ticketing as merely a selling tool that enhances their processes. Research by Beaven and Laws (2007) of a popular music tour suggests that e-ticketing can have an effect on customer service and on how consumers interact with the artistes. They found that on the down side some fans were unclear about the process by which tour tickets would be available, and the commission was resented by some. Yet conversely they found that e-ticketing, if used as part of a relationship building approach, can help to enhance consumer loyalty. Therefore, e-commerce could be an important part of an event's place, processes and promotion.

A current trend worth noting is the use of RFID (Radio-Frequency Identification) technology. This is typically used at events to help with access, such as with VIPs, and can be controlled line of sight. The tag that a person is wearing is 'read' by an electronic scanner. This is quicker and less intrusive than a barcode, and can contain key information about the person – for example, runners at some marathons have a RFID chip on their shoes to accurately record their time (Swedberg 2011).

Promotion

All organisations have to communicate to a range of stakeholders. By promotion we are talking about marketing communication, and the application of the communication mix. Marketing communication seeks to address issues such as customer attraction and retention, corporate branding/image/identity – so a main audience is customers. At the same time marketing managers are under pressure to find new ways of communicating, and to do so cost-effectively. Underpinning the promotional process should be that communications are integrated (this is the key management aspect), and that they should seek to build relationships (with customers and others).

As Table 5.1 shows, there are several promotional tools available to the event marketer. These can categorised as to whether they are 'above or below the line'. This mythical line, which is commonly used within the marketing industry, has no agreed definition, but what we can say is whether commission is paid or not is crucial for determining which position is being referred to. With above the line, a commission is paid; and below the line there is no commission

Table 5.1 Promotional tools available to the event marketer

Promotional tool	Event use
Direct sales	1: 1 dialogue
Advertising	Rent a channel to deliver a message
Public relations	Gain wide attention
Sponsorship	Tap in to other networks/gain funding
Sales promotion	Address sales shortfalls
Direct marketing	Present complex messages
Trade shows and exhibitions	Encourage face-to-face communication
Cause related marketing (CRM)	Gain credibility

due. The first two tools in Table 5.1, direct sales and advertising, are considered above the line because a commission is paid. The other six tools are considered below the line, and although they obviously incur costs, they do not require the payment of a commission to a third party. We will not address the last CRM (Cause Related Marketing), which is a specialised area where a part of the purchase price will be donated to a named good cause. It is used more by retailers but rarely at events.

Direct sales

The gold standard for communicating with consumers is face to face (Mutz 2001), as it is considered the most effective, and hence is why direct sales teams are often considered central to marketing. However, employing them is also the most expensive in terms of staffing resources. It is probably most appropriate where there are few customers, or some customers buy big purchases, such as corporate hospitality and training. Therefore, while there may be some sales teams for B2C (Business to Consumer) markets, it is more likely to be the case for the B2B (Business to Business) sector, such as team building, training and corporate hospitality. It is important to note that we are not talking about passive sales involving cashiers who distribute tickets: rather, we are talking about active sales people who go out and find consumers. Cravens et al. (1993) suggest that selling effectiveness is the result of the sales manager and the sales force. The sales manager should control the sales inputs and ensure rewards for meeting clearly defined targets. The salesperson is the link between the supplier and the customer. The primary and traditional sales channel is the field sales force, whose job is to find prospects, demonstrate products and persuade prospects to buy.

One event that is heavily reliant on its sales team, but has developed its own unique model, is Beach Break Live (ww.beachbreaklive.com), which is targeted at an exclusively student audience. In each of its target universities Beach Break Live recruits a sales force of students with a promotions manager, who in turn manages a team of reps who sell tickets, earning commission dependent on how many they sell. This sales force is the main tool for ensuring 20,000 tickets are sold.

Advertising

With advertising, the event marketer is renting a channel – be it television, newspaper, radio, billboard or whatever – to deliver their message. This provides a high level of control in terms of content, timing, location and frequency, but it comes at a cost: paid-for advertising can be very expensive, especially for small community based events. Advertisements inform, remind or persuade existing or potential consumers of the existence of an event. Irrespective of the channel, an advertisement can really only get across one simple message; where more complex messages are required, other channels such as direct mail are more suitable. There is an assumption that advertising is solely about getting people to purchase something, but its role can be much more than this and could be to:

● Inform
● Remind
● Persuade
● Differentiate
● Build awareness
● Encourage dialogue (if only on an internal basis)
● Position brands

There are generally accepted to be two main models that explain how advertising works: strong and weak (see Figure 5.2). The strong model assumes that advertising is capable of effecting a degree of change in the knowledge, attitudes or beliefs of target audiences. Jones (1997) suggests that the strong model is based on using advertising for conversion by applying psychological techniques. This implies that an advertisement is persuasive, and can make people buy products they have never previously bought. The strong model assumes that consumers are passive/apathetic/non-rational. The weak model (Ehrenberg 1988; Brannan 1995) assumes that consumers buy brands out of habit, not from exposure to promotional messages. Consumers are active problem solvers, and therefore advertising provides them with information. Advertising is therefore a process of Awareness, Trial and Reinforcement (ATR). Awareness is required before any purchase can be made, the trial purchase followed by reinforcement, which provides reassurance (usually in the form of cognitive dissonance – see Festinger 1957) to repeat the purchasing pattern. These two models can apply in different circumstances, so the strong theory may be appropriate for increasing sales in the short term, whereas the weak is better for long-term sales building. As a result, as noted by Hill and O'Sullivan (1999), the successful advertiser needs to apply both models.

Sponsorship

Sponsorship has been defined by Meenaghan (1983: 9) as the: '*Provision of assistance either financial or in kind to as activity by a commercial organisation for the purpose of achieving commercial objectives.*' Sponsorship potentially presents the event organiser with three key benefits: access to a new revenue stream; contact with new promotional opportunities; and an enhancement of the event experience. It can, then, affect price, promotion and product. From the perspective of a company considering sponsoring an event, there are two main purposes for why it might consider sponsorship. First, sponsorship is a means of promoting or selling

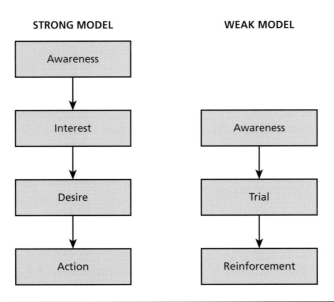

Figure 5.2 Models of the advertising process

specific products, which could be in the form of give-aways, competitions or tying it into the merchandising of the event venue. Second, more strategic in nature as a means to enhance the corporate reputation of the sponsor. For example, Schwaiger *et al.* (2010) found that sponsorship of cultural and arts events had a positive impact on the likeability aspect of corporate reputation. A sponsor could view sponsorship of an event as helping to meet either or both of these overall goals.

At the top end, sponsorship can be for considerable amounts of money. In 2011 the London 2012 Organising Committee (LOCOG) confirmed that it had secured £700 million in sponsorship from UK companies for the 2012 London Olympics (www.London2012.com). The 2014 FIFA World Cup in Brazil has FIFA 'partners' and event sponsors, including Coca-Cola, Emirates and Sony. However, although we may tend to consider large events and large companies as sponsors, smaller companies increasingly look at sponsoring local events, such as fairs and sports competitions, as a means of increasing their visibility within the local community.

Sponsorship can be at a range of levels. Thus in UK football the Premier League is sponsored by Barclays, one of the biggest clubs, Arsenal, plays in the Emirates Stadium, England's star player Wayne Rooney has a range of personal sponsorships including Nike, and for 2011–12 the best-known football competition is the *FA Cup with Budweiser*. Therefore, just in one sport in one country, sponsorship can be of league, clubs, venues, competitions and individual players. Different sports, be they professional or amateur, also attract sponsors: Adidas was the kit sponsor of the 2011 Rugby World Cup champions, New Zealand, and in December 2011 British athletics sprinter James Ellington auctioned his sponsorship for at least £30,000 on eBay to get funding to train for the 2012 London Olympics. The fact that sponsorship is an almost everyday fact of sports, arts and cultural events suggest that both sponsor and sponsoree automatically assume it is a key part of putting on an event.

Sales promotion

Sales promotion is normally used when sales appear to be dipping, or are simply not bringing in enough revenue. Hence, sales promotion is a means of attracting a sale by offering a value enhancement, but one which is only available for a temporary period. Sales promotions tend to be used when the product life-cycle is in decline, and is a means by which event organisers can try to stave off an event no longer being financially tenable. There are two types of sales promotion: value increasing, and value added. Examples of value increasing which are price based, include discounts, coupons, payment terms, refunds, guarantees, multi-buys, quantity increases, buybacks and BOGOFs (Buy One Get One Free). Value adding are not price related, and include samples, special features (limited edition), valued packaging, gifts, clubs or loyalty programmes competition/prize draws and visuals. Where value increasing is directly related to price, value added can relate to events. So a marketer may attend an event, perhaps with a stall for give-aways or contests to help raise their profile.

Sales promotion has to operate according to legal guidelines, and in the UK the Institute of Sales Promotion provides guidelines, and the Advertising Standards Agency polices them. Particular areas where you need to be careful are scratch cards, alcohol, tobacco, promotions involving children and anything which creates databases. Note that legislation is different in other countries, and can be tighter in some European countries, so consult an expert when conducting international sales promotion.

Public relations

Although we shall deal with public relations in depth in Chapters 7–10, here we shall just signpost the core features, as it impacts upon events management. It is a much used, and sometimes abused, term, but it is increasingly viewed as a growing part of event promotion. In part this is because it is cheaper than advertising, but also because sometimes it is viewed as more effective as well. Public relations is designed to reach a range of stakeholders, such as funders, consumers, the media, and other interested parties. Such audiences can be reached directly or indirectly, using a wide range of media.

Hoyle (2012) suggests that public relations is the means by which an event organiser shapes what their audience thinks or feels about the event. This implies both an emotional and a rational attachment, designed to change attitudes and behaviour towards your event. This could be to launch an event to the world, maintain interest in it, counter negative activity or enhance its overall reputation. Adding to this, Masterman and Wood (2006) suggest that public relations is particularly of relevance to the events industry because for many medium and smaller sized events the costs of mass communication advertising are too high. This, combined with the credibility that public relations campaigns can add to a message, has led them to suggest that public relations is a critical part of event communication.

Direct marketing

The introduction of personal computers (PCs) and desktop publishing (DTP) programmes in the 1980s made direct marketing an affordable and effective method, whereas up to this point it had been a marginal marketing channel. It has increasingly become a major growth area as a means of bypassing third parties and reaching your audience direct, which the Internet in the form of email and e-newsletters has further encouraged. Thus, Palmer and Koenig-Lewis (2009) note that as the cost of communication has steadily come down, direct marketing becomes a more attractive proposition.

According to the Direct Marketing Association (www.dma.org.uk), the trade body in the UK representing direct marketers, direct marketing is

> Communications where direct contact is made, or invited, between a company and its existing and prospective customers, and results are measured to assess return on investment.

Direct marketing has an impact on place because it allows the event marketer to bypass intermediaries and communicate directly with potential consumers. It is, therefore, designed to manage consumer behaviour and build long-term relationships.

There are two key factors the event marketer needs to address to make best use of direct marketing: the database; and the message. Egan (2008) notes the importance of getting the database right. The event marketer needs either to buy or to build up a database. A range of companies sell databases. Some are comprised of businesses for the B2B events market whilst others offer lists of individual consumers, which you buy by the thousand. It is possible to approach companies such as Database Manager, Electric Marketing and Markets. who can, amongst many others, provide general lists. This might be useful when going into a new market, but you would always be better advised to build your own database of contacts once the event has been running.

The second issue is content, and being a rich media channel it allows for the presentation of sometimes complex arguments in the way many other channels cannot. Consumers will look to direct mail as a means of providing some form of tangible or intangible benefit, such as shopping convenience, time utility and offering different products. Direct marketing presents the events communicator with the opportunity of conducting one-to-one relationship building with key consumers.

Trade shows and exhibitions

An exhibition is where a range of items is presented, whilst a trade show is where those within a specific named industry or interest can come together to present what they have to offer. Both therefore are showcases designed to encourage relationships between exhibitors and visitors. As Varey (2002) suggests, exhibitors can use attendance at trade shows to directly sell products or to promote themselves, so sales are not necessarily the immediate concern. Exhibitors will be concerned with things such as parking, how to set up, space available to them (and their competitors) and the ease by which footfall can visit them. Visitors are interested in the range of exhibitors and whether big names are present, and the facilities available to them such as food and drink, toilets and rest areas. Research by Skerlos and Blythe (2000) suggests that there may exist a gap between what exhibitors want (to meet potential and actual clients) and visitors want (to gather information on products).

Trade shows and exhibitions can be for both B2B and B2C markets. Those organisations which exhibit at consumer based shows, such as Home 2012 at London's Earls Court, and the BBC's Good Food Guide at Birmingham NEC, are able to reach in one day many thousands of consumers who are interested in their product specialism. Trade shows are especially important for targeting B2B markets. Trophex at the Birmingham NEC is solely for those in the trophy, awards and engraving industry, whilst the London Asia Expo at London Earls Court is for European buyers interested in products from Asia. Typically a stand holder at a trade show is not seeking to sell one or two items, but to get orders from retailers. Trade shows and exhibitions give the exhibitor access to a captive audience, and the success or failure of an event depends on getting the right audience to visit.

The insurance company RIAS (www.rias.co.uk) launched a new policy, its 'insurance hub', a one-stop shop for the over-50s, at a series of exhibitions where they might find potential consumers. So in 2011 RIAS travelled more than 4,500 miles taking their stand to events such as the Edible Garden Show in Warwickshire, BBC *Gardeners' World* Live in Birmingham and the Retirement Show in Glasgow. RIAS viewed these exhibitions as a way of engaging with their target consumers.

Selecting the correct channel

The communications mix is essentially about how an event marketer reaches consumers. This is in part a judgement call, so how does the inexperienced event marketer decide the appropriate channel to use? Table 5.2 provides a simple means of assessing the marketing problem in the form of purpose, and this suggests certain routes are more applicable.

Our next case study suggests that promotion of major sporting events differs according to the audience, and at what point in the event cycle the promotion is taking place.

Table 5.2 Selecting routes to market

Purpose	Appropriate channel(s)
Consumer attraction	Direct sales
	Advertising
	Public relations
	Sales promotion
	Direct marketing
	Trade shows
Consumer retention	Advertising
	Public relations
	Direct marketing
Image shaping	Advertising
	Public relations
	Direct marketing
Relationship building	Public relations
	Direct marketing
	Trade shows

CASE STUDY 5.2

Promoting a major sporting event

Lord's Cricket Ground in north London (www.lords.org) is considered the Home of Cricket. The ground is owned by the Marylebone Cricket Club (MCC), and usually hosts Test Matches between England and two touring countries each summer. A Test Match is scheduled to last five days, and the ground has a capacity of 28,000 spectators. MCC aims to have a full house for every day of each match.

The target audience, and hence the appropriate marketing communication, varies depending on the day and the opposition. The first two days of each Test, Thursday and Friday, being working days are weighted more towards corporate days, where the focus is on hospitality packages. Saturday and Sunday are when more families attend. The driver to encouraging families is that tickets for children are only £5 each.

MCC conducts a ballot, first of Members and then the public, to generate interest in each Test. MCC has a substantial database which it uses to encourage interest in the ballot. In some years, such as the Ashes series when Australia visits, demand exceeds supply. Overall, MCC looks to generate interest once the ballot is open.

The first Test, in early summer, tends to be against the smaller sides that are less of an attraction. These Tests can need more targeted communication. For example, when in 2010 Bangladesh toured, the MCC targeted heavily the Bangladeshi community in east London and elsewhere.

In terms of routes to market, MCC is doing more and more web-based marketing, such as through Facebook and Google pay-per click. MCC also uses a lot of email communication based on its databases, which is designed to engage past attendees. Public relations is becoming more important, especially in the London based media such as the *Evening Standard* and *Metro*. Strategically, MCC links the online advertising campaigns with media relations activity, so they are at the forefront of people's minds.

Sales promotions have been used especially for the less popular Tests. Thus, for example, it used Travelzoo during the Bangladesh Test. However, it is always low key, so that its use does not upset full-price ticket purchasers.

The combination of communication channels to be used is decided by when in the year the Test is, which day, the opposition, ticket prices and the type of people who have bought tickets for this match in the past. Having worked out its budget the MCC will bring in a media buying agency to work out what is the best way to reach the key audiences. There is no single formula: rather, it is decided on a case by case basis depending on the opposition.

In the near future, MCC expects that more of its communication will be digital, via mobile phones and websites. Cricket has not been at the forefront of this, but MCC aims to be much better at being relevant to the individual customer, rather than relying on large batches of communication.

Practical checklist

- Remember the importance of the event experience.
- Carefully consider whether you need new events.
- If you want new events make them distinctive not 'me too'.
- Don't base price on guesswork – get the right data on costs and consumer expectations.
- Use the Internet to add value by creating a hybrid event.
- Mix and match your promotional tools, do not rely on just one.

Our last case study presents the lessons of not one event, but of a specialist agency organising many events internationally. The importance of collecting the appropriate data is stressed.

CASE STUDY 5.3

Choosing the right communications mix

MCI (www.mci-group.com) is a communications and events management company with offices in forty-five cities worldwide. It specialises in the field of association management (AMC), Congress and Exhibition (PCO), live communication, meetings, events and incentives and performance improvement programmes.

The purpose of communications for its clients depends on the nature of the event. For internal events MCI seeks normally to motivate staff, and create a buzz for why they should attend and then keep the momentum generated post event. For external audiences who have to pay, communications is about information – what people are getting from attending – so the emphasis is on benefits. With free events to external audiences the main issue is minimising the dropout rate, so it is important to make every person feel that they are the only person being communicated with.

For events with external audiences, MCI uses a range of ways of identifying key targets to reach. There will normally be lists of who attended the previous event, and there will be marketing data captured since, such as a website or social media, which may generate further client interest. Clients may also buy in postal address databases. However, targeting is not just about numbers: reaching the right level of attendee is important, as having a lot of people attend without the right level of influence is a waste of energy.

MCI's clients tend to use a range of communication channels. Direct marketing in the form of buying postal mailing lists and sending information through direct mail is still valid depending on the client type. A lot of communication is now by email, and so is direct marketing by email. Social media platforms (Facebook, Twitter, LinkedIn) are now very popular, and for it to work activities such as competitions and downloads of free material help to 'entice' the user into your brand/product or culture.

Martin Richardson, Director of Meetings and Events, has noted that one of the key trends in communicating for events is that there has been more communication in the online world. The world has become a smaller place thanks to the Internet, but with every person effectively having a voice to the outside world good and bad feedback can travel equally as fast – how you use the online world has to be planned carefully.

A lot of clients are interested in using social media, more so when they hear of good event examples that have intrigued them. However, they do not always know what they want to achieve or why they want to use social media. It is important that any communications campaign, no matter what platform is used, has a strategy behind it; something should not just be used because 'everyone else uses it'. MCI consults with clients to evaluate the best means for a client's specific project.

Discussion questions

At its very heart the event marketer is offering an experience to their consumers. This chapter highlights that event marketers are faced with key issues:

1 What is the product you are offering participants and attendees?
2 Which is the most applicable approach to event marketing: the 4Ps, the 5Ps or the 7Ps? And why?
3 What might be the peculiar effects events have on how you market them, compared with other industries?
4 How might you determine what is the appropriate communications mix for your event?

Further information

Articles

Close, A., Finney, Z., Lacey, R. and Sneath, J. (2006) 'Engaging the Consumer through Event Marketing: Linking Attendees with the Sponsor, Community and Brand', *Journal of Advertising Research*, 46 (4): 420–33 – detailed understanding of sponsorship.

Keller, K. (2001) 'Mastering the Marketing Communications Mix: Micro and Macro Perspectives on Integrated Marketing Communication Programs', *Journal of Marketing Management*, 17 (7/8): 819–47 – detailed assessment of the communications mix.

Nadav, S., Smith, W. and Canberg, A. (2010) 'Examining Corporate Sponsorship of Charitable Events in the Greater Charlston Area', *Event Management*, 14 (3): 239–50 – provides a clear sponsorship case study.

Pitt, L., Parent, M., Berthon, P. and Steyn, P. (2010) 'Event Sponsorship and Ambush Marketing: Lessons from the Beijing Olympics', *Business Horizons*, 53 (3): 281–90 – addresses a growing area of sponsorship importance.

Websites

http://www.jempp.com.au/corporate-events-marketing – comment on the event marketing mix.

Chapter 6

Understanding the consumers of your event

Introduction

This chapter will seek to address the concept of the consumer, but specifically consumer behaviour for events, as you will be faced with unique ideas, problems and solutions. The consumer is not a single concept, and we will start by identifying the various different types of consumer that exist. We will then assess the practical means by which you can codify your consumers, and then assess the factors which influence buying behaviour. This discussion leads us to a consideration of how an event marketer can use segmentation to reach the right people for their event. The last section will consider the specific nature of the event consumer, especially the importance of customer service. By the end of this chapter students will be able to:

- Identify the importance of understanding buying behaviour.
- Explain how buyers can be profiled.
- Explain how buyers can be influenced.
- Identify buying behaviour models.
- Assess the importance of customer service to events.

The importance of consumers

Without knowing who the general market(s) is, and ideally the specific consumers within broad markets, the event marketer will not know how best to use their finite resources. The event marketer needs to know the answer to the question: 'Who is the consumer of our event?' For most products and services the concept of the consumer is usually fairly simple to define. This is not necessarily so with an event. Events raise an issue of consideration concerning the consumer which is unique to the industry. With most products and services the consumer is the person(s) or organisation that buys/uses the product, hence the act of consuming. However, events can be viewed as having other 'consumers' who do not necessarily consume the event: namely, participants. While some of these, such as artists, might separately be considered suppliers, many display consumer characteristics. For example, an elite sporting event such as a professional football match has players, referees and officials from the opposing team. The essence of consumer orientation is to understand their needs, and if referees and players feel that they are being mistreated or not listened to, they could theoretically withdraw their active participation. Events, therefore, have both internal and external consumers.

One dominant theme is the centrality of the consumer, and hence the desire to place the consumer as central to the marketing process. This desire manifests itself as a belief that any marketing should be consumer oriented. Hartline *et al.* (2000) suggest that customer orientation is the belief that consumers' interests should be considered as primary among all considerations, which implies the marketing manager must build these into their planning and implementation processes. Walsh (1994) has suggested that this requires the provision of more choice, improved communication with consumers and the existence of vigorous systems of redress. Therefore, customer service should be a core part of event marketing. This implies a consideration of the importance and nature of customer service at the event itself.

Who is the consumer?

Definition box 6.1

The event consumer

The consumer of an event is anyone – individual, team or organisation – that gains some form of gratification from the existence of, or attending, the event. Consumption can be passive – just attending – or active as part of the production of the event.

There is a potential issue of confusion we need to address at the outset. This chapter's title stresses 'the consumer', but many commentators also refer to 'customer service'. As we shall see below there is technically a clear difference between the two terms. However, in vernacular language the two terms are often used interchangeably.

For events, we may hear a range of terms that approximate with consumer, such as audience, spectators and crowd. The specific terminology concerning buyers is:

- *Customer* – individual or organisation that buys on behalf of others or for themselves.
- *Consumer* – end-user.
- *Client* – a service customer.
- *DMU* – decision making unit.

We can further identify two different types of customer: individual or organisational. The first is often referred to as B2C (Business to Consumer), where individuals buy products and services. So when you and your friends buy a ticket to a music festival, a sports competition or Arts show, you are an individual consumer. The second type of consumer market is B2B (Business to Business), where the consumer is an organisation (commercial or not-for-profit). The events being sold could be the same as for B2C, though for a different type of ticket – for example, corporate hospitality seats. In addition, B2B businesses may also be based on completely different events that are aimed primarily at an organisational market, such as trade conferences, exhibitions, training courses and award ceremonies. The audience for such events is those who own or work for commercial and non-commercial organisations. B2B and B2C consumers are often interested in different types of events and demonstrate different characteristics, and the marketer may have to reach and persuade them in very different ways.

As indicated above, two of the core concepts that the event marketer needs to understand are the consumer and the customer. We can identify three particular areas where the event marketer is more likely to have to differentiate between consumers and customers. First, as noted above, with events aimed at, or which have a component of, B2B consumers, very often the attendee is not the person who formally buys/pays out of their budget. For example, typically the Human Resources (HR) department will select and buy training for staff. Similarly, sales and marketing might buy corporate hospitality for clients. Second, the buyer for events aimed at primarily or even secondarily children, are usually their guardians, family, schools or activity clubs. Third, event tickets bought as gifts by family or friends. Some events are specifically tied around key dates and so may be gifts relating to this, such as pantomimes at Christmas. Primarily the event marketer will aim to reach the consumer, but for specific events or markets they also have to target those who may not actually attend the event.

There is a tendency for the event marketer to focus on external consumers only, by whom we mean those who pay to attend the event. However, we must not forget internal consumers, not only because they matter in their own right, but also because they engage with and may influence the view of external consumers. Internal consumers can include staff, volunteers, suppliers, participants and funders such as sponsors. They should be informed of what is happening, why and what is expected of them.

Events open up a fairly unique aspect of the consumer concept: namely, that there are sometimes attendees who are not required to pay at all. Often, non-profit making events invite consumers to attend, and may even have a ticketing system, but do not actually charge for attendance. For example, a political meeting on behalf of a pressure group is usually open to all with no formal charge. For open-door events, such as the Virgin London Marathon, spectators watching on the sidelines throughout the 26-mile route are an integral part of the event. Apart from the probable impracticality of charging them, their presence adds to the atmosphere, encourages the runners and helps sponsors reach wide audiences.

As suggested in Chapter 3, how the marketer views an individual consumer reflects their overall approach. The transactional marketer essentially views the consumer as a one-off, and so the consumer is seen as pretty much a number, whereas, the relationship marketer wants to build long-term loyalty, and so engages with the consumer as a person. They are more likely to consider the rational aspects of buying behaviour. The experiential marketer seeks to engage with the consumer through a shared memorable experience, and so tends to focus on the emotional aspects of buyer behaviour. There is not necessarily one simple single view of the event consumer.

Identifying consumers

The key to understanding consumers, and providing what they want, is information and data management. This can take place in two ways. The first is to find out information about a market through market research, and is usually appropriate if you are considering changing your products, your positioning or going into new markets. It can provide the sort of information which allows the event marketer to decide whether an event should go ahead, and what audience it should be targeted at. The second form of information is that held by the event about their customers. Such data could include how they heard about the event, buying behaviour across and within events, and contact between events. Collating such data is a deliberate, unsexy and time consuming process, necessitating some form of marketing intelligence system, but one which could give your event a competitive advantage.

Market research

Market research is particularly useful if an event organiser is thinking of entering a new market. By new market we could mean an emerging market, such as environmental events, or a market which is new to an existing event, such as a different geographical area. The Market Research Society (2010: 8) refers to research as

> The collection and analysis of data from a sample or census of individuals or organizations relating to their characteristics, behaviour, attitudes, opinions or possessions. It includes all forms of market, opinion and social research such as consumer and industrial surveys, psychological investigations, qualitative interviews and group discussions, observational, ethnographic and panel studies.

This definition implies that event marketers need to know who attends events, why and what influences them. Overall, the focus is on markets, and not necessarily individual consumers.

The first decision the event marketer must make is to be clear what they want to find out: unless the research problem is clearly defined any subsequent market research will not provide useful answers. This assumes that the event marketer knows what the underlying problem is, which is not always the case. However, a typical generic research question could be whether there is a profitable market for an event. This would consider the broad parameters of whether enough people exist who might be interested in a proposed event, and what they might be prepared to pay to attend. Having decided on the research question, the event marketer needs to decide whether they should use secondary or primary research, or both. Table 6.1 identifies the different types of research an event marketer can use. Secondary research utilises existing sources of information, and therefore tend to address a broad area, and is unlikely to directly address the research question. Say we were trying to see if there was a market for a Scottish Highland Games in other countries: secondary research might be an effective way of identifying which countries had the highest number of Scottish expats or descendants. Secondary sources can be free, such as the *General Lifestyle Survey* carried out by the UK government agency, the Office of National Statistics (ONS), or they may incur a cost, such as MDD's Commercial Due Diligence Ltd *UK Corporate Hospitality Market Research Report 2010*, which costs £600.

If secondary research is insufficient, or only the starting point, then the event marketer may conduct primary research, which can enable them to identify very specific new data. The main advantage of investing the time, skill and money into primary research is that it can be directly tailored to the research question, the main downside is cost. Quantitative data, such as the use of questionnaires, focus on gaining large numbers of information. Qualitative data such as interviews, seek to gain more depth of information about what people think. This is not an either or situation; many researchers use both approaches.

Event organisers are always looking to better understand their markets. Our next case study is an example of an event which conducts research, and offers this as an add-on product for existing attendees.

Table 6.1 Classification of market research

Type of research	Nature	Methods
Secondary	Uses a range of hard and electronic sources produced by an external body	Trade magazines/journals General magazines/newspapers Sector reports (e.g. Euromonitor, Mintel) Government publications
Primary – Quantitative	Statistically reliable, based on large samples	Internal data Questionnaires/surveys Polls Panels
Primary – Qualitative	Rich in meaning, narrow in scope	Interviews Focus groups Observation Respondent record

CASE STUDY 6.1

Market research of the UK musical festival industry

Festival Awards.com (www.festivalawards.com) which organises the annual UK Festival Awards, also conducts research on the UK musical festival industry as part of its Festival Conference. The research report produced for conference delegates, and available at a cost to non-delegates, is based on two data sources: the Festival Census; and market trends. The Festival Census runs concurrently with online voting for the Festival Awards, with some 4,000+ respondents who are engaged and regular festival attendees. The market trends are derived from analysis of developments within the industry over the previous year.

The UK festival industry is quite disparate, a collection of what might be termed cottage industries. The industry can be opaque, based heavily on the experiences of those involved, with limited access to independent and industry wide scientific data. There exist good economic impact studies, but limited research that provides clear and quantifiable information of how the industry is performing. The Festival Census, and accompanying report, was designed to help inform those in the industry, irrespective of their specific role, of broad festival trends. The data are designed to help individual events, and the music festival industry as a whole, become stronger by sharing information.

Respondents answer 50 questions, which cover information about their demographics, their opinion of the festival business, what they like at the festivals they attended, what they did not like at those festivals, how much they spent at each, and their views of branding at festivals. Such consumer opinion provides a broad health check of how the UK music festival industry is performing. It also provides detailed information of use to promoters, event organisers, venues, sponsors and the media. Decisions and improvements can therefore be driven by hard data, rather than guesswork. This can help enhance not just individual festivals, but also collectively the industry as a whole.

The data presented are used in two main ways depending on who receives it. Some, such as promoters, may use the data as a means of identifying market trends: for example, where are the opportunities for them to get involved with in future years? Others, such as event organisers, tend to use the data as a means of making improvements to their festival.

Green events reflect the growing political, economic, social and policy importance of environmental issues. One of the key questions any organisation seeking to provide such events has to assess is whether a market exists for it. For example, Holy Trinity Environment, a church based environmental group in Clapham, London, organised in December 2011 its first ever Green and Ethical Christmas Fair (http://holytrinityclapham.blogspot.com), a slight twist on a more common seasonal event. The research which suggested that the event had a market was twofold: first the congregation, and second the Green Community Champions Officer at the local council, suggested that there was a wider interest. Aimed more at a B2B market, Talk Action (www.talkaction.org), which specialises in training for environmental issues, was asked to run Environmental Sustainability in the Workplace courses. Based on running similar courses for businesses, charities and local authorities, it realised that there was a huge market for this type of event – many organisations would want to save money through sustainability, and enhance their image by doing so.

Marketing intelligence

A marketing intelligence system will combine external data from market research and internal records. Where the former are often generic, the latter allow for a bespoke system to be designed to meet the needs of each event. By collecting data on consumer behaviour, as well as aspects of an event that will influence this, such as the venue, artists and ticketing, the event marketer is able to identify problems and opportunities and to address them. A marketing intelligence system is a means of collecting everyday information about the interface between an event and its consumers. In particular, marketing intelligence requires the event marketer to speak to consumers and to record their behaviour. Such systems could include direct consumer feedback which is deliberately sought – for example, this could be evaluation sheets for training attendees and conference delegates; or it could be a questionnaire to event attendees, possibly with some

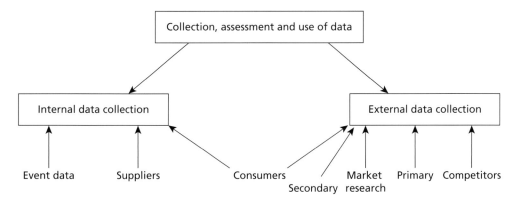

Figure 6.1 Marketing intelligence system

form of incentive such as a prize to encourage responses. However, feedback can also be received that is not deliberately sought. This can include general letters and emails from attendees, and should be collected and analysed. It is also possible to have more structured qualitative feedback in the form of advisory panels. Figure 6.1 suggests that a marketing intelligence system is comprised of two core components: collecting the data; and using it. One without the other is of no use.

Our next case study demonstrates the importance of creating a marketing intelligence system to decide first whether to run an event, and then to drive marketing decisions. It is clear that the data will heavily shape the nature of the second year of this event.

CASE STUDY 6.2

Marketing intelligence systems – London International Technology Show

The first ever London International Technology Show (www.litshow.co.uk) was held at the ExCel Centre, London in October 2011. The exhibition was designed to showcase leading technology brands, and in addition to the stands there was a series of seminars and free clinics. It was organised by the events team at Dennis Publishing, which owns a number of technology based magazines and websites.

The idea for putting on the show came from a range of sources. The magazines within the Dennis group regularly conduct questionnaires of their readers, one question of which was whether they would be interested in events related to the publication. This gave a range of data that suggested what potential consumers would be interested in. The idea came from the sales team listening to the desires of Dennis's advertisers who wanted to be able to interact more closely with their end-users, so that their consumers could experience their products. This led to the idea of the live show.

To determine the appropriate charge for ticket prices the organisers used their experience of running a number of events, and used this to assess the correct price to charge for year 1 of an event. Over 50 per cent of the tickets had a code, and so could be tracked as they were bought through an outsourced specialist ticket agency, Ticketmaster. This enabled the organisers to keep track of how well the event was selling, and from which publications they were purchased from.

At the beginning they assumed that the target audience would be primarily high-end technology buyers, but they found from data collected that the audience was more of those who are very serious about technology and gaming. The information collected suggested that the profile was more specialist than generalist in terms of their interest in IT.

At the show the organisers conducted a survey and it was available online as well. This was designed to identify who attendees were in terms of profile, and what they thought of and did at the show.

Evaluation of the event included an assessment of the questionnaire, what was said on social media sites, but the main measurement was on the revenue – did the event make a profit?

The organisers conducted a series of meetings afterwards to determine how well the event went, and to assess the learning curve for making it better next year. One of the key stakeholders in the evaluation process were the advertisers of the magazines: for example, SCAN Computers, who got on board with the event early on. Therefore, data were collected from consumers, the organisers, the exhibitors and the advertisers.

The marketing communications of the event led to data being collected not just about the show itself, but also of non-show spin-offs such as advertising of the magazines.

The second year of the London Technology Show presents the organisers with new challenges in terms of maintaining their information systems. Where the use of vouchers helped them track data, new systems will have to be created for future shows.

Influencing buying behaviour

It is not enough to know who your consumers are: the event marketer needs also to know what influences how and why they buy. While there are generic factors such as social, cultural and personal influences, the experiential nature of most events shapes the buying process. When we are faced with fairly simple decisions, such as which washing powder to buy, we tend to use heuristic factors such as habit or special offers. With more complex decisions, such as buying a car, consumers will be influenced by a range of factors, often of an emotional and/or rational nature. Such complex buying decisions usually take longer and require an assessment of more factors and information gathering, and may involve more than one person in the process. For most individual consumers, choosing to go to an event is not a very complex decision unless we are dealing with luxury events. For many consumer based events, marketing can apply heuristic messages. For business consumers this process is likely to be more complex in terms of who chooses, but also how the value of event attendance will be measured and evaluated. So B2B event marketing needs to be more rational, using the central route of persuasion process.

Buying is an intensely personal process, but there are three key questions about why and how your consumers buy, which help construct your marketing messages:

Q1. Who are your buyers?

Utilising a marketing intelligence system, the event marketer needs to understand who actually attends their event, what their needs and wants are, and how to reach them. The event marketer needs to identify different consumer types, and consider whether each type needs a tailored targeted offer. Once we know who the potential buyers of our event are, then we can address what types of events are appropriate for them, our pricing strategy and how best to reach them.

Q2. Why do they buy?

We will address segmentation in more depth, but at this stage we note that there are four types of influence which shape why a consumer might attend an event:

● Personal characteristics of consumers.
● Psychological characteristics of consumers.
● Social variables of consumers.
● Marketing activity from the event marketer.

Buyers seek to acquire 'bundles of benefits' to satisfy a range of functional and emotional requirements by attending an event. At the same time the consumer is aware of what such benefits cost them, be it in terms of time, effort or money. Consumers, therefore, look for value from attending an event.

As noted in Chapter 5, attendees are buying an experience. For example, Agrusa *et al.* (2008) suggest that participants of the 2006 Honolulu Marathon attended because they viewed it as an experiential service. Getz (2008) adds that such event experiences provide the consumer with a 'utility', such as survival, pleasure, happiness and satisfaction.

Q3. The decision making process

One way of understanding the decision making process is that buyers consciously or unconsciously decide whether to attend an event through a sequential 'problem solving' approach. One way of presenting this decision making process is the Problem Solving Continuum:

● *Routinised Response Behaviour* – rapid decision making, applicable for low-value products such as sweets, food and newspapers.
● *Limited Problem Solving* – some consideration of alternatives and shopping around. Tends to apply to consumer durables, fashion clothing and entertainment.
● *Extensive Problem Solving* – deliberate/protracted movement through all stages of the decision making process. Tends to apply to expensive or important occasional purchases such as cars, mortgages and university.

Most events would probably fit into Limited Problem Solving given that there are likely to be some alternatives, and they usually involve travel, refreshments and sometimes accommodation issues. A very small number, namely luxury and one-off special events, which are very expensive and might necessitate foreign travel, could also be Extensive Problem Solving. It is unlikely that events would be considered a Routine Response Behaviour.

Segmentation

Segmentation is the attempted solution to two related problems. First, no event marketer can reach all their possible markets. We need a means of using finite resources, and most marketers rely on segmentation: breaking down the overall market into manageable parts. This does not mean, however, that all segments are equal in size or importance, and so the event marketer also has to prioritise segments. Second, markets are not homogeneous. All consumers are not the same: rather, they are heterogeneous, with a range of different characteristics. By identifying such key target markets, marketers can tailor their marketing communications. Event marketers try to find something, or several somethings, which a group of people share in common as a means of reaching them with a shared message.

For segmentation to be of value each segment needs to be:

● Measurable.
● Substantial in size.
● Accessible.
● Affordable.

Brassington and Pettitt (2005) suggest that B2B and B2C markets are segmented differently. Table 6.2 suggests that the key difference between segmenting B2B and B2C markets is who makes the decision, and what influences their decision making on what to buy.

There is a wide range of approaches to segmentation that the event marketer can take. For some events one type of segmentation alone may be enough, but for other events the marketer may need to apply a range.

Geographic segmentation

One of the easiest and most common forms of segmentation is geographic, which could be by country, region, county, city, district or village. This is fairly simple to do. For example, it is often applied to entertainment events, so that Bournemouth Pavilion Theatre (http://www.bhlive.co.uk/) generally targets those who live within a 20-mile radius of Bournemouth. For certain events, particularly shows that are running for one week or more, this is expanded to approximately a 45-mile radius. However, geographical segmentation has limitations because it does not indicate interest in a particular topic, theme or activity.

Demographic segmentation

One of the most common forms of segmentation is to identify demographic differences. Indeed, several event observers (Formica and Uysal 1995; Lee *et al.* 2004; Reid 2011) have identified the possible impact of demographic change on the future development of events. Typical measurements of demographics are:

Table 6.2 Differences between B2B and B2C segmentation

Factor	B2B	B2C
Decision making unit	Can involve several different people	Usually one person
Nature of product	Buying criteria can be complex	Buying criteria are fairly simple
Decision making	More likely to be rationally based	Can be both emotional and rationally based
Importance of personal link	Very high	For many products, especially lower value such as most events, of no real importance
Numbers	Usually smaller markets, so corporate hospitality is usually a niche event market	Typically larger mass markets

(Adapted from Brassington and Pettitt 2005).

- Age.
- Gender.
- Level of education.
- Income.
- Socio-economic class.
- Ethnicity.
- Religion.

These might shape who you communicate with, and how, but they can also influence the nature of the event: if your target audience has less disposable income, for example, this will determine what you offer them. There is criticism of just how much such criteria will help identify different behaviour. Moreover, the class based classifications can lead to generalisations that are not accurate predictors of buying behaviour of events in a rapidly changing society. It is worth noting that Michael Eavis, the organiser of the Glastonbury Music Festival, suggested in 2007 that the audience was becoming too middle aged, and so potentially deterring younger music fans (Addley 2007).

Geo-demographic segmentation

A more sophisticated, and therefore more expensive, approach is geo-demographic segmentation, often associated with what is called postcode profiling. Recognising the limitations of geographic and demographic segmentation, this is based on micro-cultures and the belief that individuals of similar economic, social and lifestyle backgrounds tend to cluster together in certain areas. The assumption is that if people demonstrating certain characteristics in one postcode are interested in an event, then those in other postcodes with similar profiles will also be potentially interested. Commercial packages include ACORN, MOSAIC and PINPOINT, which are all based on census data and postcodes. Political events, especially election campaigns, are often associated with this form of segmentation.

Psychographic segmentation

Most commonly associated with William Lazer (1964), this looks at the relationship between consumption and lifestyle of a social group. Marketers do not just rely on data on which products we buy, but also focus on three key features based on individual consumer's characteristics:

- *Lifestyle* – such as personality, motivation and family stage.
- *Social stereotypes* –such as over-55s have more disposable income.
- *Segmentation* based on *attitude, motivation, values and lifestyle.*

This approach seeks to assess:

- *Activities* – where they are observable and measurable; often concerned with issues such as shopping habits, sources of entertainment and holiday preferences.
- *Interests* – such as family, work and the local community.
- *Opinions* – product related issues/associations.

This form of segmentation may be more relevant for some events than others. For example, people who consider themselves hedonists would be very interested in entertainments which are essentially about having fun. However, it can be difficult to identify such people, and to identify enough to make it worthwhile contacting them.

Behavioural segmentation

This approach focuses on how consumers know of, use or respond to an event. Therefore, Kotler *et al.* (2008) suggest it is based on a marketer's knowledge of a consumer's use and attitude towards a product. They suggest that the behavioural variables which help the marketer determine a consumer's behaviour include:

- *Occasions* – when and where a consumer buys. For example, if a consumer is celebrating an anniversary, birthday or some other special day, they are more likely to want higher quality or buy related activities such as food.
- *Benefit* – what benefits of attending your event are consumers looking for? For example, is it a romantic date, a group celebration or just something to do on a wet Wednesday afternoon?
- *Usage rate* – how much of an event do you consume? This could be in terms of the type of ticket available: do you buy the cheapest, a middle option or the most expensive package?
- *User status* – are event attendees occasional, regular, or those devoted who always attend?
- *Attitude* – what do consumers think of an event? This could be not a lot, neutral through to very enthusiastic.

Figure 6.2 offers a snapshot of the profile of festival-goers. It was a based on a survey of 4,300 festival attendees, and gives an insight into the type of person that visits music festivals, and what they do there. It includes mostly demographic data, but also includes behavioural as well.

28 Years
Average Age

Average Salary =
£17,000

19%
have children

'Single & Unattached'
Marital Status of 46%

20% have tried
'Cannabis'

2.3 p.a.
Average festivals attended

11 p.a.
Average gigs attended

17%
Download music for free

25%
have left their tent at a festival

10%
use Twitter

Spend most on
'Socialising'

'Rock'
Most popular music genre

Public Transport
Used by 39% to travel to festivals

31–50 units
Average alcohol consumption at a festival

Figure 6.2 Profile of festival-goers
(Adapted from *The UK Festival Report* 2009, www.virtualfestivals.com)

Event consumers

Can we simply apply to events the general lessons above concerning identifying the consumer, assessing their buying behaviour and who they are? In reality the answer is no. There are peculiarities about who the event consumer is, their role within an event and what makes them buy. One of the first issues is that the name given to the consumer can be different from type of event to type of event. Bowdin *et al.* (2010) suggest that at concerts and festivals they are referred to as the audience, for sport they are spectators, at an exhibition they are visitors, for a conference we use the term delegates and at corporate events usually client. This nomenclature does not take into account another peculiarity of events: namely, that the participants in the form of artistes, players and trainers are also consumers, with their own needs and wants.

We can also see differences in the type of events consumers attend depending on social, economic and educational factors. While Table 6.3 can only be based on generalisations, and there will always be exceptions to the rule, it strongly suggests that likeminded people 'herd' together in terms of the events they like.

One very important question the event marketer needs to be able to answer is whether all consumers are equal. Fashion United.com (2009) noted that during the recession fashion houses used special in-store events to tempt customers. Where once they might have used traditional sales promotions such as discounts, they now offered standard trunk shows (the designer turns up with a trunk of clothes to show off to a select audience), art exhibitions and meet-and-greet a brand's designer. The idea behind these is to help break through a psychological barrier to discretionary spending. For example, Fashion United suggested that in early 2009 Prada invited the world's most reputable stylists to revamp its stores in key cities such as London, New York, Milan and Paris. The intention behind this was to create consumer interest in the brand among new and existing high-end consumers. This suggests that luxury brands may consider experiential marketing accompanying segmentation.

This chapter, and most marketing orthodoxy, largely focuses on meeting the needs of consumers. The corollary to this is that the consumer is always right. In fact, we need to occasionally

Table 6.3 Types of event consumer

Type of consumer	Events attended
High end – social class A and B, high income, senior managerial and professional jobs, usually attended higher education	Arts and cultural events, corporate hospitality, career related events such as conferences
Middle – social class C1, C2 and D, middle income, supervisory, skilled or semi-skilled, usually tertiary or further education	Sporting events, entertainment, popular music
Low end – social class E, typically unskilled and often unwaged, school level education	Tend not to attend events

challenge such axioms. What if there is demand to attend a violent or environmentally destructive event? Should we consider putting it on simply because there is demand? Conversely, what if there is not a commercial market. Should we avoid putting it on? There may be limited demand – say for an eating healthy road show – but there may well be strong non-commercial reasons why it should be organised. Moreover, some events such as an Arts festival may have an intrinsic value in its own right, and not necessarily require a demand for it. Market demand does not always have to drive the supply of events.

Event consumer trends

We have noted earlier that the role, nature and impact of events have evolved over time, and we can identify some trends in event consumer behaviour. For example, Masterman and Wood (2006) suggest that there are four trends in consumer behaviour which have an impact upon events:

- An ageing population.
- The nature of Generation Y (born in the 1970s to the 1990s).
- Changes in family structures.
- More information is available through technologies such as the Internet.

Common to these four trends is the changing nature of where and how consumers gain information, and what they are looking for. With an overload of information sources, many people, especially those who are older and those from generation Y, relied on personal sources of information such as family and friends through word of mouth. This implies that for the event marketer existing consumers, rather their own promotional activities, may be the most appropriate means of influencing new consumers.

   The focus on event trends has often been on identifying demographic changes, technological developments and the impact of legislative frameworks (Goldblatt 2000; Getz 2009; Bowdin *et al.* 2010). While it is important for an event marketer to be aware of broad societal and economic changes, this will not automatically help fit events to target markets. There are social, cultural and political issues which are helping to develop new events. The event marketer's research could include an assessment of possible events that address a developing problem. Current event trends include:

- *The rise of personal milestones* – many have become important statements about an individual, or a means to maintain social networks. These could include challenges such as running a marathon, which are a means of saying something about the dedication and achievement of someone. In a world where families and friends are often not in close geographic proximity, events are increasingly the glue which brings people together. Christenings, naming ceremonies and funerals have always played this role, but they are becoming more theatrical and complicated in nature. Another event reflecting societal change, but also making a personal statement, has been the growth of divorce parties. We can also identify some global trends: so the High School Prom, so long a rite of passage for American teenagers, is now increasingly common amongst schoolleavers in other countries.
- *Issue influenced events* – the news, political debate and often private discussion reflect the importance of certain key issues facing humans, and this has led to new event markets. Currently, there are in most Western nations several interrelated issues which dominate the public agenda to varying degrees. Most readers will have heard of the ozone layer, the greenhouse effect and renewable energy. They represent an interest in environmental issues, which is reflected in a potential market for green events. These could be events which are about green issues, and there are many conferences and exhibitions that meet this market. For example, in November 2011 the University of Damman in Saudi Arabia hosted Sustainability Through Biomimicry: Discovering a World of Solutions Inspired by Nature. Or it could be that increasingly events seek to present 'green' credentials as part of their USP (unique selling proposition). For example, Event Live Expo 2011, held in Los Angeles, sought to tackle sustainability in the live music industry by hosting a seminar on how the industry could present its green credentials. The Shambala Festival (http://shambalafestival. org/), a music festival, prides itself on being 99 per cent powered by wind, sun and sustainably sourced vegetable oil, and encourages low-carbon transport to reach it. For many the food chain is a key issue, so that there is an interest in food miles, organic products and exploitation. In the UK there has been a significant increase in local food festivals. The impact of wider issues on events is not restricted to individual consumers: greater interest in corporate business behaviour has led to the growing importance for businesses of acting socially responsibly. For example, in America the Committee Encouraging Corporate Philanthropy (http://www.corporatephilanthropy.org/) hosts networking events for corporate giving professionals, and its Corporate Philanthropy Summit has in the past had former US President Bill Clinton address it. The effective event marketer is aware of what are the key issues in society, and considers how their events might reflect them.

The next case study shows how even a global sporting event cannot ignore its social responsibilities, and the impact of green issues on its reputation.

- *Luxury events* – a growing niche market based on the idea that attendance at an event can be a means of celebration. There is a long tradition of the perceived value of luxury. In 1899 Veblen identified that there are goods people want to buy because the high price gives them a greater status. Luxury events have the same qualities as luxury items – experiences that are exclusive, rare, unique, and/or expensive, or provide a networking opportunity. This could be paying for special and expensive VIP tickets to an event – perhaps for a special family occasion such as a major anniversary or birthday – or it could be going to an event

The greening of the Super Bowl

America's largest professional sporting event is the annual Super Bowl, the American football championship game run by the National Football League (NFL). The NFL (www.nfl.com) has incorporated environmental principles and projects into the management of Super Bowl since 1994. Initially, the NFL focused on reducing solid waste through recycling. Over the years, environmental activities expanded to include donation of extra prepared food, donation of reusable materials (including office supplies, building materials and decor), collecting used books and sports equipment for distribution to local schools and youth programmes, and a Climate Change Initiative that brings together a series of projects aimed at reducing the carbon footprint of this huge event.

As part of the Climate Change Initiative, thousands of trees are planted each year in the host community, and major event venues including the stadium are either powered directly by renewable energy or offset through use of Renewable Energy Certificates (RECs). The NFL also incorporates biofuels into its transportation fleet each year whenever the local infrastructure exists to support biofuelled vehicles.

Since the 2010 Super Bowl the NFL provides event managers, contractors and staff with a guide on how to make their operations more environmentally friendly. Each host committee is now required as part of the bid process, to work with the NFL to address the overall environmental impact of Super Bowl and the many activities connected to it.

For 2012 the Indianapolis Super Bowl XLVI Host Committee and the NFL extended the use of 'green' power to all six major Super Bowl facilities. Everything was powered by green energy, provided by Green Mountain Energy Company, which bought 15,000 megawatt hours of renewable energy certificates generated at wind farms in North Dakota to offset the power associated with the event. This will avoid more than 14,000 tons of greenhouse gas emissions associated with Super Bowl electricity consumption, over the course of the month-long period leading up to and immediately following Super Bowl XLVI.

Green Mountain and the NFL provided a solar power installation for one of the homes being renovated as part of the Host Committee's urban legacy project, and together they will support urban forestry projects. They planted additional trees post-Super Bowl in Indianapolis neighbourhoods in partnership with Keep Indianapolis Beautiful. The final tree planting event included the annual passing of a 'golden shovel' to next year's New Orleans Super Bowl XLVII Host Committee – a tradition that began in 2008.

which in itself costs a lot of money. For example, the Barmy Army is a group of largely middle-aged, middle-class England cricket supporters who can pay many thousands of pounds sterling to follow their team for several months in long-haul places such as Australia, the Caribbean and Sir Lanka. Those living in America with $125,000 to spend can have a Tequila Avion Private Party at their home for up to 75 guests hosted by A-list event planner Colin Cowie (http://www.neimanmarcus.com/store/sitelets/christmasbook/fantasy.jhtml? cid=CBF10_O4839&r = cat33500731). Essentially, a luxury event is perceived to be so because of its price, exclusivity and the fact that as an attendee you are treated like royalty.

The importance of customer service

As noted above, the consumer of an event does not differentiate between the event and customer service: they are part of a whole experience be it good, indifferent or bad. Therefore, customer service is part of the product. The band you went to see at a gig may have been brilliant, but the fact that someone was in your seats and the stewards would not help you, or the toilets were disgusting, or a pickpocket stole your money, could undermine the whole experience for you. As an event consumer you were not just 'buying' the main part of the event – be it music, sport, education or whatever – but your interaction with the organisers and other consumers will influence your view of an event. The event experience comprises a number of parts, to which we may give different weighting, but collectively they make up the whole that shapes our evaluation of it.

One of the key areas of customer service which affects our enjoyment of an event is the behaviour and demeanour of all the event 'staff' we as consumers come into contact with. A surly or non-helpful approach from any member of staff to a query for help or information, may cloud your view of the event. If you ask the first member of staff you see what time the main event is on and they reply 'Dunno', this is not very helpful. Your expectations are clearly not being met. And such customer service begins before the event itself. For example, if you ring the event organisers a few days before to gain some specific information – say on car parking – and no one answers the phone, or if you leave a message and no one replies, then even before the event occurs you are feeling potentially negative towards it.

Similarly, bad behaviour by other consumers can negatively affect your experience. One of the major society events of the English summer season is Royal Ascot, ostensibly a horse race meeting, but because it is patronised by Her Majesty The Queen, it is where the great and good meet to see and be seen. One of the main days is Ladies' Day. which matches fashion with sport, where a range of extravagant millinery is on show. As a consequence this social event secures significant mainstream broadcast and print coverage. Yet in 2011 the headlines were less innocent than what some wealthy lady might be wearing on her head, as several drunken 'gentlemen' wearing expensive top hat and tails were photographed fighting wielding champagne bottles as weapons (Gabbatt 2011). Being present at such violent behaviour would probably make you think about attending again.

The event marketer has to recognise that event service and event consumption are part of the same package, and needs to introduce management structures and policies to address consumer service issues in advance of the event. Excellent service accompanies and is part of a high-quality experience. The meaning of quality service has been defined in a range of ways. One of the most basic approaches is to suggest that it requires conforming to existing standards and expectations (Crosby 1984), so that Edosomwan (1993) identified requirements. Another approach is to suggest that it is what consumers say it is (Feigenbaum 1990), but this is really rather vague. A third approach is made by Juran (1982): quality service is associated with fitness for purpose, so that the event is appropriate for intended purpose. For example, an event designed to improve staff morale, probably needs to include entertainment, fun and some element of reward. The wise event manager seeks to exceed consumers' expectations.

One of the most common systems applied to ensuring service quality is SERVQUAL. This model is based on Parasuraman *et al.*'s (1988) interpretation of service quality, which they suggest is centred on the consumer perception, comprised of five dimensions:

- *Reliability* – everything happens in the way the marketing communication has promised.
- *Assurance* – presents an appearance of being knowledgeable.
- *Empathy* – understands the consumer needs and delivers caring attention.
- *Responsiveness* – to the needs of the consumer.
- *Tangibles* – the physical appearance of the equipment, venue and catering.

SERVQUAL is a method of measuring service quality by producing a gap analysis of an organisation's service quality performance against consumers' service quality needs. It uses a questionnaire in the form of consumer surveys that assesses these five key service dimensions. It does this by measuring the difference between visitor expectations and perceptions, so that when the consumers' perceptions of the event match or exceed their expectations, a quality experience has been delivered.

Practical checklist

- Consider the needs of both internal and external consumers.
- Participants should be considered like consumers.
- If you have B2C and B2B consumers at your event, tailor the product, delivery and message.
- Remember attendees at free events and watching on television or listening on radio are also consumers.
- Rarely rely on one segmented audience: mix and match your segments.
- Introduce mechanisms for measuring consumer satisfaction.

Our case study exercise highlights the fact that the consumer can be a multi-layered concept.

CASE STUDY 6.4

The John Smith's Grand National

The John Smith's Grand National (www.aintree.co.uk) is the climax of three days' jump racing at Aintree Racecourse, and one of the highlights in the racing calendar. But the Grand National is more than just a horse race: it's one of the UK's most iconic events, a race that stops the nation and is a sporting institution.

The festival is three full days of the highest-quality jump racing in the UK. Starting with Liverpool Day on the 12 April, followed by Ladies' Day on the 13 April and culminating with the world's greatest steeplechase, the 2012 Grand National on Saturday the 14 April.

Grand National tickets and badges go on sale from the previous August. They are available online via the website and by telephone.

Season tickets holders for Aintree, get priority access to the Grandstand of their choice, and are able to experience every race day at Aintree in 2012 for an additional £60. For Grand National day there are seventeen different types of ticket, based on which stands or areas the ticket gives access to. These vary in price from £20 per person for the Steeplechase Enclosure through to £220 per person for a seat in the Winner's Bar. Child tickets apply to some enclosures. Where no child price is stated, children are charged at full price. Group discounts are available in some enclosures, where groups of 50+ can get 15 per cent off the ticket price.

Hospitality packages with restaurants or private boxes are also available. For the Grand National, restaurant packages vary from £246 to £499 per person, and boxes from £437 to £507 per person.

The John Smith's Grand National has been televised live since 1960, and is a major part of the BBCs live sporting calendar. Footage is distributed to 140 countries and it is estimated the worldwide audience is 600 million people.

Your task:

- Given the wide range of tickets available, how would you segment your audiences?
- Do you treat the key participants (Jockey Club officials, owners, trainers and jockeys) as consumers? If so, how would you meet their needs?
- What of the non-paying customers, watching on television or listening or radio? How important are they? And how would you try to meet their needs?
- With a wide range of tickets, enclosures, and refreshment options, how would you maintain excellent customer service? How important to the race day experience is customer service?
- The John Smith's Grand National is clearly Aintree's 'Crown Jewels', so how would you use the opportunity to cross-sell other racing and non-racing events at Aintree to attendees?

Discussion questions

The idea of an event buyer is not a single concept: rather, we need to understand the different ways in which an individual or business buyers purchase events. This chapter highlights that event marketers are faced with key issues:

1 What would happen to your marketing activities if you could not identify your target markets?
2 How would you determine which are your event's most important groups of consumers?
3 In what practical ways could you incorporate and apply the buying behaviour models outlined in this chapter?
4 Why should the event marketer be especially concerned about the quality of customer service delivered at the event?

Further information

Other sources which might help you consider the issues outlined in this chapter include:

Books

Doole, I., Lancaster, P. and Lowe, R. (2005) *Understanding and Managing Customers*, Harlow: Prentice Hall – a comprehensive assessment of the importance of consumers within marketing.

Williams, C. (1989) *Behavioural Aspects of Marketing*, Oxford: Heinemann – addresses the social aspects of consumer behaviour.

Articles

Fox, D. and Edwards, J. (2009) 'A Preliminary Analysis of the Market for Small, Medium and Large Horticultural Shows in England', *Event Management*, 12 (3/4): 199–208 – analyses the characteristics of horticultural show consumers.

Oakes, S. (2003) 'Demographic and Sponsorship Considerations for Jazz and Classical Music Festivals', *The Service Industries Journal*, 23 (3): 165–78 – identifies the similarities between festival-goers at two different music festivals.

Taylor, R. and Shanka, T. (2002) 'Attributes for Staging Successful Wine Festivals', *Event Management*, 7 (3): 165–75 identifies the importance of location for consumers.

Thompson, K. and Schofield, P. (2009) 'Segmenting and Profiling Visitors to the Ulaanbaatar Nadaam Festival by Motivation', *Event Management*, 13 (1): 1–15 – motivation of Mongolian event attendees.

Wohfeil, M. and Whelan, S. (2006) 'Consumer Motivations to Participate in Event-marketing Strategies', *Journal of Marketing Management*, 22 (5): 643–69 – identifies the importance of having fun in consumer motivation.

Chapter 7

Building your reputation – the use of public relations

Introduction

Events both are a tool of public relations and use public relations techniques to promote themselves. Indeed, in recent years events have increasingly recognised public relations' added value. This chapter will first introduce and assess the practical implications of the meaning of public relations. We will then introduce one of the key differentiations with marketing: how audiences are codified and reached. Last, we will introduce the main theoretical framework through which we can understand the use of public relations within an event context.

By the end of this chapter students will be able to:

- Define public relations.
- Assess the importance of publics.
- Understand the impact of the meaning of public relations on events.
- Assess the relevance of a range of public relations models.

The meaning of public relations

As noted in Chapter 1, I suggest that public relations should not be considered a single concept. Rather, as noted by Moloney (2006), public relations can be divided in two related, but nonetheless separate, components: marketing public relations (MPR); and corporate public relations (CPR). MPR is the view typical of many event managers, namely to secure visibility by using, for example, media relations and stunts to gain attention for events. This is a legitimate use of public relations, but one that is narrow, tactical and short-term. CPR supplements event marketers' use of MPR, because it is much more strategic, is longer term and seeks to influence corporate reputation (Fombrun 1995) through tools such as issues management, crisis management and internal communication. As noted in Figure 7.1, what CPR adds for the event communicator is a different world outlook. Where marketing relies essentially on a north/south way of viewing communication issues (straight ahead to consumers and directly behind to suppliers), CPR supplements this by adding an East/West visibility (other audiences on the side).

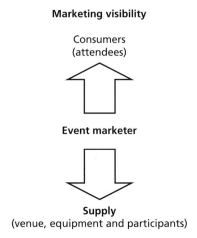

Marketing visibility

Consumers
(attendees)

Event marketer

Supply
(venue, equipment and participants)

Public relations visibility

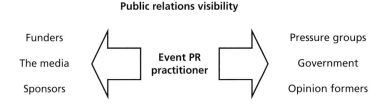

Funders		Pressure groups
The media	Event PR practitioner	Government
Sponsors		Opinion formers

Figure 7.1 How the event communicator views the world

If public relations is so different from, and adds value to, marketing, then what actually is it? This is not a simple question to answer, for as with our definition of marketing the exact meaning we ascribe to public relations implies a much wider understanding and use of the term. Public relations is at one level a widely understood term. We all conjure up images of what it means – often it is linked to spin – but in truth do we really mean the same thing? In 1976 Harlow identified 472 different definitions of public relations, and we must assume especially with enhanced use of new technologies and the development of issues and crisis management, that this number has significantly increased since that time. However, the wide range of definitions does imply that while there may be some common themes across definitions, in all likelihood there can never be one single agreed definition; rather, they cover a wide range of different details.

Ashley Wirthlin of the GTC Institute (http://publicrelationsblogger.com) suggests that the person responsible for event public relations needs to create awareness and interest within the event as well as outside. To do this Ashley outlines the importance of you knowing what the whole story of an event it, so that you can share it with outside audiences.

Typically, textbooks (Cutlip *et al.* 2006; Theaker 2008; Gordon 2011) offer a few definitions that provide the headline components of public relations, its role, what it might cover and the nature of how it might work in practice. However, as suggested above this approach has severe limitations, and indeed a single definition is probably not attainable. More relevant to understanding public relations is to identify common threads amongst definitions, in the form of approaches or schools of thought (Hutton 1999; Mackay 2003; Ruler and Vercic 2005; L'Etang

2008; Jackson 2010). Each of these authors rather than offering a single definition has identified typologies of public relations. Just as we introduced three marketing philosophies in Chapter 3, then so shall we assess three different public relations approaches as a means for assessing how, why and with what impact public relations may be used: the Grunigian paradigm; Persuasion; and Relational. It is worth noting that in addition to clear differences between these approaches there is also both common ground and grey areas, and so they are not rigidly divorced or mutually exclusive from each other.

Definition box 7.1

Defining public relations

Public relations is the art and science of how an event communicator can defend, manage and change the reputation of their event. It can be both a 'loud' tactical tool, designed to draw attention to an event, especially among potential attendees. At the same time it can also be a 'quiet' strategic tool, designed to shift opinion of an event, typically that of both attendees and influential non-attendees.

The Grunigian paradigm

This approach[1] is named after the American academic James Grunig. It is believed to be the dominant view in the Western world (L'Etang 2008), and suggests that the role of public relations should be to establish mutual understanding between an organisation and its publics (Newsom et al. 2000; Baines et al. 2003; Cutlip et al. 2006; Guth and Marsh 2006; Fawkes 2008). This implies the development of a mutual benefit (Grunig and Hunt 1984), for both the organisation and its publics. By entering into symmetrical communication with each other, both the organisation and its audiences learn what each wants, to mutual benefit. An event, therefore, would seek to engage its key audiences through dialogue to find out what they want, and then deliver this.

A typical example of a Grunigian definition of public relations is offered by the Chartered Institute of Public Relations (CIPR)

> Public relations is about reputation – the result of what you do, what you say and what others say about you. It is the discipline which looks after reputation, with the aim of earning understanding and support and influencing opinion and behaviour. It is the planned and sustained effort to establish and maintain goodwill and mutual understanding between an organization and its publics. (www.cipr.co.uk)

The CIPR, which is effectively the trade body for public relations in the UK, is therefore suggesting that public relations is a strategic tool designed to address an organisation's reputation by generating enhanced goodwill through understanding.

The Grunigian paradigm does not necessarily rely on any particular public relations tools: rather, it will use what is appropriate for each situation. However, it seeks to be strategic in nature by addressing the big communication issues facing an organisation (Grunig and Grunig

1992). The core to this approach is the need for developing dialogue. Originally this viewpoint suggested that normatively any feedback should be two-way symmetrical (Grunig and Hunt 1984; Springston *et al.* 1992), though this was later amended to recognise that this might not be appropriate for all organisations in all situations (Grunig and Grunig 1992). The approach recognises public relations involves power relationships, and that these may be weighted to the benefit of one interest (Dozier *et al.* 1995). However, the sub-text of this approach is nearly always that for communication to be effective, long-term and strategic, there needs to exist a win-win situation for both an organisation and its publics. When one side feels it is being used, or is getting a poor deal, there is unlikely to be a long-term relationship.

This approach may be easier to achieve where the event communicator controls what is delivered, as is often the case with B2B markets such as training, award ceremonies and conventions. However, it is much more problematic where the event communicator does not control all facets of the event, such as the line-up of a music festival which may be subject to frequent or last-minute changes. The principle of being open in communication is sound, but in practice the Grunigian paradigm may be difficult to achieve with some events.

Persuasion

Suggesting that public relations is a persuasive activity implies a pluralist approach, and so the public relations role is to give voice to competing groups (Bimber 1998; Moloney 2006). This approach is a critique of the idea of mutual understanding within the Grunigian paradigm. The purpose of persuasion, therefore, is to reach, inform and then change the attitudes/behaviour of key audiences, not to develop goodwill. Among critics of public relations it is this purpose which has drawn a comparison with propaganda (Ewen 1996; Miller 2003), although Moloney (2006) draws a distinction by suggesting that public relations is 'weak propaganda', in that in representing interests it does so within a competitive, if not always equal, public arena. Public relations, therefore, acts as a cheerleader for a particular interest, be it commercial, public sector or the not-for-profit sector. This could be the use of media relations to attract people to an event, community relations to enhance the reputation of the event among the local community, or to lobby local politicians to change a policy which affects the event.

This approach has its roots in the ancient Greek rhetorical school of Aristotle (Heath 2001; Mackay 2003; L'Etang 2008). This implies that the message, in the form of symbols, is just as important as the process, if not more so (Miller 1989). However, persuasive techniques and messages need to be ethical to be distinguished from propaganda (Messina 2007). An ethical approach may be achieved if communication is based on discourse, and hence is inherently dialogic (Heath 2008). Because it represents interests, the persuasive approach encourages competing interests to enhance the information flow to the wider public. Communication for one individual event can also be viewed as part of a bigger picture, cumulatively improving knowledge on events in your field/area.

Given that persuasion is based on exerting symbolic control (Miller 1989), it can use a very wide range of direct and indirect public relations tools. Moreover, it can be both tactical – for example, persuading a consumer to purchase an item – and strategic in shaping the view of key stakeholders to an organisation. Essentially there are two, not mutually exclusive, ways in which public relations can persuade. First, informational through logical argument, but this assumes that recipients make decisions rationally, and so the head rules. For example, Ewles and Simnett (1985) and Williams and Wells (2004) note how public information campaigns based on rational argument and statistics, have sought to inform key audiences to help them change their behaviour. Second, if the heart rules, then a more emotive approach to the message may be suitable. Considering the power of linguistics, Holtgraves and Lasky (1999) found that the style of the speaker and not just the message had an impact on their persuasive power. The persuasive approach stresses that the message can be a combination of rational and emotive argument and symbols.

The next case study shows how the events industry as a whole is applying the persuasion approach through a lobbying campaign.

CASE STUDY 7.1

The voice of events

Event managers have traditionally focused on their own event, but there is increasing recognition that the industry itself has to have its voice heard. One of the tools chosen to achieve this is political lobbying and media relations. In 2010 the Business Visits and Events Partnership (www.businesstourismpartnership. com) launched its Britain for Events Campaign. This campaign highlights the value to the UK of the events industry, and aims to highlight some key issues facing it. In particular, its core message is that events bring £36 billion to the business tourism industry, and need government support.

The emphasis by campaigners has been to use public relations to gain support amongst political influencers and decision makers. For example, the Business Visits and Events Partnership kicked off its campaign in October 2010 with a reception in Parliament where 43 MPs and 150 people from the events industry attended. A tangible result from this was the setting up of an All-Party Parliamentary Group for Events, chaired by Nick De Bois MP. This committee and the Britain For Events campaign in turn received a supportive letter from the Prime Minister David Cameron in November 2011. This was followed up in January 2012 when the trade association responded to a government consultation document on 'UK Subvention Policy and Bid Support Practices for International Conferences'. The cumulative effect of this lobbying activity, and accompanying media coverage, has been to raise significantly the profile of events generally, and the Business Visits and Events Partnership specifically, within the British policy making community.

Relational

A paper by Ferguson (1984) can be viewed as the beginning of the relationship management approach to public relations. Ferguson did not deny that public relations might seek to build mutual understanding, indeed there has been an attempt to link the Grunigian and relational approaches (Grunig and Huang 2000). Rather, what was central to public relations was building relationships with key stakeholders. The relational approach focuses on a small number of influential stakeholders, and as a consequence takes a long-term strategic view of public relations. This approach utilises a wide range of tools but, as it seeks to build networks, it is likely to stress personal interaction such as meetings, lobbying, sponsorship and corporate hospitality. There are clear links to the Grunigian paradigm because a dialogic approach is assumed, and as a result interactive Internet technologies are considered to support the relational approach (Taylor *et al.* 2001; Seltzer and Mitrook 2007). The event communicator identifies and engages with key decision makers and influencers, such as the media, commentators, politicians, sponsors and pressure groups. The relational approach is far less interested in the attendees of an event: rather, the focus is on other audiences who can influence the event.

The ultimate aim of the relational approach is to build the reputation of an organisation based upon trust (Ledingham and Bruning 1998). This usually requires focusing on a small number of key stakeholders, such as funders, the media and political decision makers, and so issues management is one of the main applications of relationship building (Bridges and Nelson 2000; Bruning *et al.* 2008). It is also suggested that building relationships can create loyalty, so that during a crisis those organisations with higher levels of loyalty amongst key stakeholders are more likely to survive (Coombs and Holladay 2001). Building relationships is akin to a favours bank, which can be called in when circumstances are either very unfavourable or your event is facing a crisis or threat. There is evidence that the relational approach applies to some cultures which have had only recent exposure to public relations. The *quanxhi* tradition in China (Chen and Culbertson 2003), has influenced the use of public relations so that it is very relational based. Similarly, Taylor (2004) has noted that in Eastern Europe in general, and Croatia specifically, there is a heavy reliance on a range of relational methods, such as personal invitations to events. Whilst the relational approach may encourage organisations to respond to concerns of society, as articulated by pressure groups, it does suggest a strategy that may place customers into the second level of communication priorities. It also suggests that the use of relationship building can differ depending on the country your event is in.

Table 7.1 compares the three approaches, and in particular suggests that the implications are not just in how you communicate, but also the type of events that each approach fits best with. The Grunigian perspective does not really support most commercial events, with the possible exception of B2B events. The persuasion approach is more flexible, and could apply to nearly all events. The relational approach could apply to all events, but this is an approach which most events do not currently adopt.

What are publics?

Where marketers use the term 'markets' or 'consumers', public relations practitioners tend to rely on the term 'publics' or sometimes 'stakeholders'. This difference in terminology is not simply one of professional lexicon, but can reflect a significantly different approach. Publics is a much broader concept than markets, implying that the public relations practitioner takes note of a wider range of internal and external audiences. Public relations can simply be viewed as relations with publics – this is the key concept that frames how public relations practitioners approach problems, situations and opportunities.

Whereas a marketer can decide which market they wish to reach, this is not the case with publics. Put simply a public is all the individuals and groups of people an event wishes to be in communication with or is in communication with. The essential difference with markets is the term 'is in communication with'. This implies that some of the people an event is in contact with may not be people they actually wish to deal with, but they have no option. An event cannot choose all of its publics – some decide themselves that they will be a public, that then cannot be ignored. A local residents' association or pressure group may be unhappy with the effect of, say, traffic, and will lobby to get changes, or sometimes even try to stop the event

Table 7.1 The application of public relations approaches

Approach	Purpose	Tools	Type of event
Grunigian perspective	Mutual understanding Mutual benefit	Symmetrical two-way communication based upon feedback	Political events Non-profit events
Persuasion	To inform and then change attitudes &/or behaviour	Media relations Promotional campaigns Lobbying Community affairs/CSR Issues management Uses both rational logic and emotional messages	MPR based, such as product launches CPR, such as building reputation amongst key audiences
Relational	Develop influential relationships Mutual benefit	Target key influencers Build networks Personal interaction Sponsorship CSR Online PR Media relations Lobbying Corporate communications *Quanxhi*	CPR Consumer based relationship building

(Adapted from Jackson 2010)

happening. For example, when the Glade Festival proposed to move to Matterley Bowl near Winchester local residents were concerned about noise and traffic problems (Payne 2009). In 2010 the event was cancelled four weeks before it was due, on police advice. There is some argument as to the reason, but Hampshire Police in a press release did make reference to 'a formal review became necessary to meet concerns raised by members of the local community, which we always take very seriously' (Hampshire Constabulary 2010). Such groups may not be potential consumers, and so ideally the event organiser would not want to have to spend time dealing with them, but the event communicator ignores such groups at their own peril.

While we note above that local residents may be a lobbying thorn for some events, they can also be a very positive force for encouraging or actually setting up events. For example, the Muswell Hill and Fortis Green Association in London set up the Muswell Hill Festival in 1976, and have maintained a role in its organisation since (http://www.mhfga.1to1.org/). In Gloucestershire the Barton Residents Association claims the credit for lobbying the local council to revive the ancient Barton Fayre in the City of Gloucester (http://www.visit-gloucestershire.co.uk/gloucester/barton.htm). The event, by closing a high street, became in their words 'a genuine community effort'. Indeed, it appears that where local pressure groups get involved they act as a support for traditional community and cultural events.

An event's publics are those individuals and groups who share some interest, perception or beliefs about that event, which can be positive or negative. Each event will have a range of publics, often with slightly different views of the event and sometimes they may even be in conflict. Table 7.2 identifies type of publics for an event. It is worth noting that a person can be part of more than one public. So you can be an employee of an event, a local resident and a consumer, all of which the event might impact in slightly different ways.

Not all publics have the same value or importance: some are more crucial to an event's success than others. As noted above any individual event could have many publics, but at any

Table 7.2 Event publics

Stakeholder	Who	Their event interest
Consumers	Prospective attendees Event attendees	What is happening? Why should I go? What does attending this event say about me?
Participants	Artistes Performers Sports players Supporting officials Speakers	Will I get paid/expenses? Will my needs be looked after? What does participation at this event say about me? Will participation help further my goals?
General public	Anyone who might hear about, and so construct an opinion of, an event	What is it? Will it have any effect on me? Overall impression/image
Suppliers/contractors	Equipment Support skills Refreshments Merchandising Sales/ticketing	What will I get paid? What do I have to do? Who else is involved? Is it worth my while being part of it? Will there be spin-offs for me?
Staff/Volunteers	Full-time Part-time Temporary Volunteers	Do I feel ownership of the event? Am I a mushroom in the dark? Where in the order of priority are we?
Funders	Banks Shareholders Owners Sponsors	Will I get a return? What does supporting this event say about me? Will anything go wrong?

Stakeholder	Who	Their event interest
Regulatory authorities	Governments Individual politicians Emergency services Judiciary	Should we be supporting this event? Have they done the right things? Will this be a well run worthwhile event? What are the tangible benefits?
Media	Local National International Online Trade Special interest	What is the story? How important is this event for my readers/viewers/listeners?
Pressure groups	Local/residents National Cause	Will this help/hinder our interests/cause?

(Adapted from Jefkins 1982)

one time there will be a few core publics. An event will have finite resources in reaching all its publics, and to make best use of them the concept of core publics helps the event manager focus on the most important first. At different stages in the event process these core publics might change, or external factors to the event may necessitate change. So at the start of a new event the funders may be core, but as we get closer to the event the participants may grow in importance. Equally, a crisis could affect an event. When, for example, when some farms in the UK were inflicted with foot and mouth disease in 2007 many rural areas had to cancel or radically change their events because of quarantining affecting a farmer's field that was being used, or because a nearby village or town was affected by travel restrictions. When developing their communications plan an event manager needs to recognise that not all publics are equal in importance to their event. The trick is working out which are core and which are secondary.

Typically, an event will have three core publics at which the bulk of its communication effort is directed. The type of core publics may be different depending on the nature of the event. Most events expect paying consumers in the form of spectators or delegates, and being a major source of revenue these would normally be a core public. However, many other events are not funded by spectators, such as the Saab Solomon South Downs marathon (http://www.209events.com/event.php?event=33), where typically for such events participants and sponsors are key. Another event with different publics is the 2012 Heart Truth (http://www.nhlbi.nih.gov/educational/hearttruth), a series of health road shows to raise awareness and targeted at American women. Here the funders would primarily be sponsors, government or charity sources or the host organisation. Funding is not the only factor which shapes whether a public is core or not: another probable core public for most events are the participants, such as artistes and speakers. For example, the speakers at TED Ideas Worth Spreading (www.ted.com) are central to such events. Core publics may also include those such as the local authority or public services such as police and fire service who may not actually be directly involved but have statutory powers or political influence to shape the nature or even actual existence of the event.

Non-core publics are not ignored, but the concept of core publics means that all publics are prioritised in order, and depending on factors this may change. Core publics are central to an event actually happening probably in terms of how it is funded, organised or what is delivered.

Technology has had an effect upon the concept of publics, and many events now need to consider online publics, as well as offline. In Chapter 11 we shall discuss the Internet in more depth, but virtual publics can be very different from offline publics. The first obvious difference is that online publics need not actually attend your event, but any musings on forums, weblogs and in social media can affect the reputation of your event. For example, Birdevent is a global community on Facebook interested in the sport of Badminton; and at http://apps.facebook.com/whitehouselive people can comment about events screened on the White House channel. The second difference is that their nature can be very different. For example, a pressure group offline assumes a level of support and resources that are not necessarily required online. A single disgruntled person with the appropriate skills could run an effective web campaign against your event in a way they could not do offline. Online publics can reach a wide range of global audiences, cheaply and whenever they want, requiring a different approach to dealing with them.

There is no single way of identifying the publics of each events but two different approaches are discussed below:

Jefkins' basic publics

Frank Jefkins' (1982) how-to book for the non-specialist on conducting public relations constructed a simple framework for an event communicator to identify their audiences. He suggested eight simple publics, which acted as headings. These are:

- *The Community* – this could be physical, virtual or an interest group.
- *Potential employees* – this might be of more relevance to larger regular events.
- *Employees* – for events this means full-time paid, part-time/occasional staff and volunteers. Potential and actual employees are important to an event because they are an important part of the experience attendees receive.
- *Suppliers and services of materials* – such as AV equipment and marquees.
- *The Money Market* – whoever funds an event, and this could include third parties such as sponsors.
- *Distributors* – probably of limited use to events, but could include box office and online ticket agencies.
- *Consumers and users* – clearly this means both spectators, delegates and participants.
- *Opinion leaders* – this could mean influential individuals such as bloggers, but also the media and pressure groups.

Jefkins' basic publics model does not address the detail – every event defines and determines what each public means. It implies that the organiser of a music festival, conference and community event could have the same overall framework though the detail for each would be different. This model is fairly unsophisticated, but is ideal for smaller or new events. Our next case study shows how a small event might apply this model.

CASE STUDY 7.2

Applying Jefkins' basic publics

The World Conker Championships (www.worldconkerchampionships.com) is organised each year by the Ashton Conker Club, and is held near Oundle in Northamptonshire, UK. There are separate Men's, Ladies and Junior competitions, held in the autumn, typically October/November.

The community

- Residents and businesses in and around Oundle
- Conker players worldwide, but primarily UK

Employees

- Volunteers

Suppliers

- Conker collectors
- Open-air venue
- Fairground
- Entertainers
- Providers of associated activities such as classic cars

The Money Market

- Individual and team entrants
- Stalls and refreshment providers

Distributors

- Website
- Schools

Consumers and users

- Anyone individual or team interested
- Charities benefit if contestants get sponsored

Opinion leaders

- The media

Situational theory

A more complex approach, situational theory, has been developed by James Grunig since the late 1960s (Grunig 1966; Grunig 2005). This model seeks to assess scientifically where an event organiser should spend their finite communication resources. Grunig (1989) believes that the theory addresses:

- What are publics and how do they arise?
- With which publics is it possible to communicate?
- How can one communicate most effectively with each kind of public?

It is referred to as situational as the appropriate target audience varies from situation (event) to situation (event).

Figure 7.2 shows that situational theory is divided into dependent and independent variables. The event communicator should identify active communicators, as these deliberately go out to find some information about a specified topic. For example, some people are interested in rock music and will look for information on this, and are therefore more likely to be interested in rock music events such as the Fuji Rock Festival held up a mountain in Japan. Others may simply to want to know what is on locally for them to do, perhaps by accessing a 'what's on' website such as *WhatsOnWhen*, a global events guide (www.whatsonwhen.com). In both instances they are active communicators. Passive communicators discover and process the information, perhaps by reading an article or listening to a radio programme, but as they did not actively seek out the information they will not actually do anything with it: they are unlikely to attend your event. Those who are active communicators for one event may be passive for another. This means that unlike Jefkins' basic publics, situational theory implies that the approach a music festival, conference and local community event will take to identifying its audiences will be very different.

The dependent variables assess how interested a person is in a topic. Those that are considered passive for an event should not be contacted at all, except indirectly or by accident, as they are unlikely to be interested in attending. The independent variables then address whether those who are active might actually be likely to attend the event. There are three independent variables, each of which acts as a filter narrowing down potential to likely or actual attendees. Grunig conceptualised the first independent variable in terms of problem recognition: Do people detect that something should be done about a situation? Assuming the answer is yes, and for many it won't be, the second variable is constraint recognition: Do people perceive that there are obstacles in a situation that limit their ability to do anything about it? If their answer is no they will proceed to the third variable that assesses their level of involvement. This is the extent to which a person connects themselves with a situation. For example, a person or group of people may decide that they want to go out on Saturday night, and look for possible options:

Dependent variables	*Independent variables*
1 Active information seeking	1 Problem recognition
2 Passive information processing	2 Constraint recognition
	3 Level of involvement

Figure 7.2 Situational theory
(Adapted from Grunig and Repper 1992)

this is the first variable. Having recognised the problem (the desire to go out), they then need to decide what they can/want to do (are there any constraints). This might include issues such as cost, venue, timing and transportation. Assuming that these do not deter them, they then move to the final variable: Are they going out all night or only for a portion of it?

The theory assumes a simple yes/no answer, but in reality with events a person may decide not to attend one event, but using situational theory may decide to attend another. This process, and situational theory is a process, could equally apply to a B2B consumer looking at a conference: for example, do they need to go, if so which ones, and how long will they be there for? The event communicator is looking for those people who recognise that there is a problem, that they can do something about it and that they will do something about it.

Our next case study looks at how different it is to focus on luxury markets, where the potential number of consumers can be very small, exclusive and wealthy.

CASE STUDY 7.3

Targeting your audience in a niche market

Itspr (www.itspr.co.uk) is an events and PR specialist run by Waj Hussain which focuses mostly on the luxury high-end market. Itspr's clients use events as a means of reaching a very select group of potential buyers of their high-end products. Although Itspr does run events to a wider audience, the requirements of luxury goods is that reaching the key audience is very important and probably different from many other public relations campaigns.

Given the nature of the events that Itspr organises, aimed at the high-end luxury market and so primarily very wealthy people, attendees at events are normally referred to as guests.

Itspr suggests that identifying the correct audience is one of the most important components of any successful event. It identifies them by starting with the client's objectives, and works out from there who they should seek to reach. For example, does the client want to raise awareness of a brand, or increase sales from the event? It is from this starting point that an event can be used to build trust in a brand.

For example, Itspr has as a client a five-star resort in the Mediterranean, which wants to attract those interested in a luxury holiday and/or investing in luxury real estate. So it has identified 20–30 potential buyers, and the resort has a high-class golf course, so one of the events organised is a golf day, because this is the sort of activity this audience likes.

As well as identifying the client's objectives, it is also important to understand the product, and what the expectation of it is. For example, at a recent convention in Barcelona Itspr organised the Embee Diamond Reception (www.embee-diamond-reception.com), where 96 per cent of attendees turned up because they were intrigued by the concept of Diamonds in Champagne Glasses.

For small private parties, the client's focus is on customers, but for public parties there is a much wider range of audiences. For example, there is a need to look after performers and staff at events, so that they have food, sometimes address transportation and make sure they meet the right people, too.

In the luxury market Itspr often has partnerships with others, such as concierge companies, to provide access to the best venues, celebrity clubs, hotels and bars. With luxury products the main target audience is very wealthy people, but by also reaching the media and celebrities there is a trickle-down effect, whereby others also want to attend.

In the luxury products market, online publics play a limited role: the key is to meet people face-to-face at events.

One of the latest trends in this market relates to the similarity of target demographics, so there is an increase of co-branding within events, so that for example a luxury car and a luxury drink manufacturer may come together to put on an event. The key is to meet like-minded people face to face.

Public relations tools

For many event communicators public relations equates almost exclusively with media relations; indeed, Raj *et al.* (2009) note that the terms public relations and publicity are often interchangeable. In large part this widely held belief that media relations is the prime, if not only, public relations technique was driven by the fact that mass communication channels such as television, radio and newspapers dominated how individuals received information. Hence, organisations tended to rely on these channels to reach their core audiences, be that through paid advertising or with media management creating news stories. This principled use of mass communication channels applied equally whether an event was national or local. What differed was the exact channels used.

In Western countries such as the USA, Australia and Britain, the rise of the mass media began in the 1950s and 1960s, often associated with national cultural or political events such as the coronation of Queen Elizabeth II in 1953, the assassination of President Kennedy in 1963 and the landing on the moon by Apollo 11 in 1969. By the 1970s and 1980s in most Western countries the main route to reaching large event audiences was via the mass media. However, from an event communicators perspective relying on mass communication alone can be expensive, it is difficult to stand out from the crowd and may not always reach the right audience. For example, while a village summer fair might well send a press release to the local newspaper it is more likely to rely on banners, leaflets and posters to remind local people directly when and where it is happening. By the mid-1990s the dominance of mediated communications had been increasingly challenged by direct communications such as exhibitions, direct mail, the Internet and sponsorship. Event managers are, therefore, more likely to use a wider range of communication tools.

Despite the initial reliance on media management, public relations makes use of a wide range of tools. Indeed Newsom *et al.* (2000) note that the Public Relations Society of America (PRSA) identified fourteen different activities, while White and Mazur (1995) suggested thirteen. Whoever is correct, the lesson is that public relations can provide the events communicator with a wide range of tools, each of use in different circumstances. While the initial focus may be on how events can utilise media relations, Table 7.3 suggests that there are at least eleven tools that the event manager needs to consider.

Table 7.3 Selecting the correct event public relations tools

Tool	Why use	How use
Media relations	To gain attention for an event	Generate news stories for press releases and stunts Generate visuals to support an event story Run up to the event, during and post-event stories
Copywriting	Writing features, newsletters, brochures and websites	Construct well crafted and persuasive messages to support an event
Online PR	To raise awareness of an event To build relationships with an event	As a means of delivering news stories Reinforcing messages by using all channels Generating viral campaigns
Press conferences	To get across a message to a wide number of journalists at the same time	You have a major story Your event is in crisis
Crisis management	To minimise the adverse effect of a crisis	Reactive to when something has gone wrong Managing key audiences who determine how well you have performed
Issues management	Construct the means to avoid crisis, or to identify opportunities	To identify and build relationships with those other than consumers who might affect, or be affected by, your event
Meetings/briefings	To mobilise people To communicate complex information Face-to-face is expected	To encourage a sense of belonging To encourage dialogue

> **Table 7.3** continued

Tool	Why use	How use
Internal communications	Our people matter – they affect the event experience	Regular internal meetings and briefings Encourage dialogue
Sponsorship	To generate money To access the sponsors' publics	To give credibility to an event Reach the sponsors' audiences Use the sponsors' resources to reach key audiences
Public/community affairs	To raise profile locally To reach key decision makers	Work with or for local community groups Build mechanisms for talking with decision makers Invite the right people to your event
Events	Raise awareness of your event	Attend someone else's event to publicise yours (and reciprocate) Construct your event

Public relations models

Until fairly recently public relations theory has relied on adapting existing theory from other disciplines such as sociology, marketing and psychology. It is only really since the 1970s that specific public relations models have been created. Probably the best known is Grunig and Hunt's (1984) Four Models of Public Relations. Based on research conducted, they identified four public relations practices: press agentry; public information; two-way asymmetric; and two-way symmetric. They therefore suggested (see Table 7.4) that the four different types reflected two key variables: Direction (one-way and two-way); and Purpose (asymmetrical or symmetrical). Grunig and Hunt thus identified the characteristics of their four models, and suggested that each had its own set of values and patterns of behaviour that determine how it is used in practice.

Press agentry is one-way and primarily seeks to gain attention, usually through manipulating the media by creating stories. It is a field of public relations largely criticised, but we tend to find it where either people need high visibility to generate income, as with celebrities, or to 'get bums on seats' as with some entertainment related events. For example, the boxing promoter Don King often uses hyperbole, stunts and colourful language to suggest that his latest fight is the best, meanest, toughest or whatever adjective he believes will sell tickets, both to attend directly and to buy pay-for-view television. When celebrities who marry enter into an exclusive deal with a publisher, there is an inevitable requirement for publicity to help sell the story. For example, when Victoria and David Beckham married in 1999, *OK* magazine wanted publicity from the wedding to justify their expenditure. This is not to say that all events are susceptible to this approach, but it is clearly a factor with some events.

Public information is also one-way in direction, but the key differences are that it uses a wider range of tools, and truth is central to the credibility and impact of the message. It seeks to persuade the receiver through the power of its message based on rationality and facts. While some commercial events may apply this model, it is especially linked to not-for-profit organisations. For example, governments and pressure groups may try to persuade us to change our diet, fitness or be more environmentally aware, and if such messages are not seen to be true they will have limited effect.

Grunig and Hunt divided two-way communication into asymmetrical and symmetrical. Asymmetrical is where the communicator seeks to change the behaviour of publics without changing the behaviour of the organisation. It is therefore unbalanced. For example, an event organiser may want to establish through research how a potential audience wants to find out about the event, so that they can be more persuasive by using the preferred channel for that person/audience. Grunig and Hunt believed that such an approach, although using dialogue, is really about manipulation, and not likely to be socially responsible. They believed that symmetrical communication was balanced, based on mutual understanding, and more likely to be socially responsible. For example, an event manager upon receiving feedback from consumers may change the nature of the actual event. Of their four models Grunig and Hunt normatively preferred this last model over the other three.

However, there is limited evidence that their preferred model is the dominant approach. Shirley Harrison (2000) estimated that public information was the most popular with 50 per cent of all public relations being within this model. She suggested that two-way asymmetrical accounted for 20 per cent of public relations activity, and the other two models 15 per cent each. Such figures are fairly hard to support and represent a lot of guesswork, but conceptually Grunig and Hunt's models were criticised for a number of reasons. They were based on data from Anglo-Saxon countries such as the USA, Canada and the UK, and so might not apply to other countries and cultures. Some of the models were considered more relevant to certain situations, such as fighting a general election, than others. Normatively Grunig and Hunt preferred the two-way symmetrical model, but if you are in the entertainment or celebrity event field, press agentry is perfectly normal. If your event is trying to change attitudes and personal behaviour then public information is an applicable approach. Moreover, it was felt that an organisation might use more than one model at the same time. As a result subsequent versions of their models recognised and addressed these criticisms (Grunig and Grunig 1992; Dozier *et al*. 1995; Grunig *et al*. 2002).

Table 7.4 Grunig and Hunt's (1984) models of public relations

Model	Characteristics	Event example
Press agentry	Propaganda, one-way communication, truth not essential. Heavy use of publicity tools such as media relations to create hype	Events that need to get 'bums on seats', typically commercial and public launch based. Can be applicable to some event industries, such as music and entertainment

Table 7.4 continued

Model	Characteristics	Event example
Public information	Dissemination of information, one-way communication but truth is important for the credibility of the message. Will often rely on providing facts through written documents and educate people through events such as road shows.	Events that promote a message, such as meetings and road shows. Designed to help a government or pressure group in their awareness raising campaigns.
Two-way asymmetric	Scientific dissemination, two-way communication but imbalanced towards the needs of the message sender. Research based, but designed to ascertain how audiences' attitudes are created. The prime beneficiary is the message sender, who finds out how to be more persuasive.	Commercial organisations seeking to gain competitive advantage through feedback.
Two-way symmetric	Mutual understanding, two-way communication and with balanced effects benefiting both the sender and the receiver of the message. Heavily based on research to find out what audience wants from a product, but then uses a range of communication tools to reach them. Sender is likely to change the product as a result of feedback received.	Organisations seeking longer-term relationships with key audiences.

(Adapted from Grunig and Hunt 1984)

As Table 7.5 notes, we can see a link between the four models outlined by Grunig and Hunt, and the three approaches that are a theme of this book: that the three approaches do not apply to all the models. We note that press agentry has the least application, and two-way symmetrical the most.

Table 7.5 Applying public relations approaches to Grunig and Hunt's four models

Press agentry	Public information	Asymmetrical communications	Symmetrical communications
Persuasion	Grunigian persuasion	Relationship persuasion	Grunigian persuasion relationship

Practical checklist

- Even for one-off events take into account the importance of reputation.
- Introduce an east–west approach to viewing your audiences to identify those which affect the reputation of the event.
- Identify your approach or philosophy to public relations at the outset.
- Construct a framework which identifies your key audiences.
- Prioritise your audiences; spend most of your efforts on three or four key publics.
- Reassess who your publics are at different stages of event planning.
- Do not ignore participants and suppliers as publics.
- Do not rely on one public relations tool, mix and match several.
- Use whichever of Grunig and Hunt's models fits your needs, so if you need to 'get bums on seats' press agentry is appropriate.
- Use more than one of Grunig and Hunt's models.

Our last case study shows how an events agency breaks down all the aspects of their public relations strategy. Given the commercial nature of their events, return on investment drives much of their communication decisions.

CASE STUDY 7.4

How an agency helps its clients communicate

Big Cat Group (www.bigcatgroup.co.uk) is a full service agency and consultancy with offices in Birmingham, London, Paris and Barcelona. The agency offers a range of services including events management, marketing, PR, design and social media. It is particularly known for specialising in three key areas; B2B, third sector and leisure and entertainment. Big Cat uses a broad range of communication styles to create and develop strategies to achieve both long- and short-term objectives.

Due to the diversity of clients and events Big Cat works with, the objectives of each will vary considerably. Whilst some events will be directly related to community engagement others will be linked to financial outcome and of course making a profit.

For example, an event in Birmingham run in conjunction with music development agency Punch Records, celebrated Jamaican culture and targeted both the local Jamaican community but also wider West Midlands residents of all creeds. The aim of this event was to showcase Jamaican heritage and the importance and being proud of where you have come from.

An alternative to this was the Gala Dinner, run in conjunction with professional networking body, Birmingham Forward. This event was a ticketed event and provided both members and non-members with an opportunity to shout about the success of the organisation and engage with forthcoming developments.

Both of these events utilised a multitude of methods in order to raise awareness and drive ticket sales. These methods include e-marketing, direct mail and press release. Often, clients will seek a quick fix in order to drive ticket sales for a regional or city event. In this instance, media relations are often the most effective method of brand awareness. By utilising press releases and features, Big Cat is able to maximise the coverage it achieves and reach a market that may not necessarily be reached by direct marketing.

After any event or campaign, clients will obviously wish to analyse how successful it was and whether it is worth hosting the event again. Dependent upon the event, clients will have set initial objectives they wish to have achieved. These may include increase in turnover/profit, attendance numbers, or even just positive feedback, all of which are valid measurements of ROI. Each department within the organisation has its own unique way of evaluating a campaign.

Discussion questions

Applying the full suite of both MPR and CPR may be new to many events. This chapter highlights that event communicators are faced with key issues:

1   How and why should you determine whether your approach is based on mutual understanding, persuasion or building relationships?
2   Given the differing nature, size and purpose of events, how will you identify your publics, and how will you prioritise them?
3   When and why would you choose to use each public relations tool?
4   Which public relations model, or combination of models, would you choose for your event?

Further information

Other sources which might help you consider the issues outlined in this chapter include:

Websites

www.cipr.co.uk – UK's main public relations trade body.
www.prweek.com – weekly publication for practitioners good for case studies.
www.iabc.com – US based global network of business communicators.
http://spinsucks.com – critiques the use of public relations.
http://prstudies.typepad.com/weblog – long-established blog by PR educator.
www.mediawatch.com – educational body that challenges some use of the media.
http://www.prca.org.uk – another UK trade body representing practitioners, especially known
    for representing lobbyists.
www.spinwatch.org – monitors the use of public relations and spin.

Chapter 8

Gaining visibility – marketing public relations (MPR)

Introduction

Many people, perhaps erroneously, associate MPR solely with media relations, yet this chapter will only address this in broad terms, as the next chapter will go into the practical details of using media relations. This chapter will start by assessing the relationship between marketing and public relations. We will then consider the meaning of MPR, and its possible application by event communicators. Lastly, we will consider which MPR tools individually and collectively an event communicator can use.

By the end of this chapter students will be able to:

● Understand the relationship between marketing and public relations.
● Assess the role and application of MPR to events.
● Evaluate the tools of MPR.

The relationship between marketing and public relations

As suggested earlier, marketers and marketing texts largely equate public relations with publicity, and with one whose role is essentially to support marketing. This is indeed a valuable part of the public relations function, but as we shall see in Chapter 10 it is much more than this. However, this chapter and the next will address this perfectly legitimate attention-gaining function which public relations can offer events. Very few events can assume that their profile is such that target audiences will automatically know that they are happening, and be persuaded to attend/watch. And even those which might normally be able to gain attention, such as the Olympics, will still want to make sure that spectators buy tickets, companies sponsor the event and that television and radio stations want to buy coverage. Rather, it is the case that nearly all events have to reach and persuade some or all of their target audience. Marketing public relations (MPR) is a major weapon in the event marketer's armoury.

For the event marketer MPR is a tactical way of raising awareness about their event. In effect it acts like a metaphorical megaphone. The role of MPR is to gain attention and so it is not normally subtle. Given that your message has to stand out from many others, MPR is usually 'loud'. Reinforcing this propensity for 'loudness' is the fact that most MPR techniques are indirect, generally employing mass communication channels.

More importantly, the growing role of events within the marketing and public relations practice is changing the nature of MPR. Reflecting the orthodox view, Moloney (2006) suggests that the main expression of MPR is in the form of writing. In particular he focuses on two forms of the written word: press releases and promotional copy. This suggests that MPR relies on the ability to draft news releases that catch the attention of the reader/listener/viewer, or that the public relations professional is able to draft interesting copy for advertisements, brochures and posters. However, this reduces the MPR practitioner to primarily a wordsmith. Rather, I suggest that the growth of events as a promotional tool is changing the nature of MPR, widening it beyond the written word. The input of events means that MPR now also includes the widespread use of experiences to communicate directly with potential audiences. It is this development which has created a close link between experiential marketing and MPR. These event based experiences can indeed be 'loud' like other forms of MPR, but they can also be 'quiet', because they can allow longer contact with the target audience, and so get messages across more subtly. In the previous chapter we introduced different approaches which help us understand public relations. Orthodox MPR is within the persuasive school, but event based MPR can also be within the relational approach.

Figure 8.1 shows that this combination of loud and quiet suggests that at least four different MPR strategies are open to the event communicator. The main determinant of which is the correct approach depends on the message to be conveyed. If the information is quite simple, such as trying to make potential attendees aware of an event, then they would seek to gain attention (through press releases and posters) or create a visual stunt. When the message is more complex, however, such as telling volunteers what to do, then Inform (written briefings/ brochures) or Build Relationships (a meeting or road show) is the more appropriate approach.

Where do marketing and public relations come from?

The relationship between marketing and public relations engenders much comment. For academics the issue is usually focused on the meaning of each discipline and how they interact, in particular whether one is dominant or not. For example, Hutton (1999) argues that marketing is taking over many public relations functions. For practitioners this is not an idle discussion: the exact nature of the relationship in their organisation will have an impact on

	Simple message	
	Written MPR	**Events MPR**
	Gain attention	Stunts
	Inform	Build relationships
	Complex message	

Figure 8.1 MPR strategy

salaries, who reports to whom, the purpose of their work and the size of budgets they control. While academics have constructed different generic models to understand the relationship, in the workplace the relationship between the two functions will be unique. The exact problems, opportunities, resources and experience of one event will always be slightly different from others. As a consequence we can offer an overall theoretical framework that might guide the event practitioner, but it can be no more than a general guide.

Before we address the specific meanings of both marketing and public relations, and the impact this might have on the event communicator, it is important to realise that current debate is shaped by the historical development of both disciplines. Although there is a clear relationship between the two, they have been developed and shaped in different ways, both as a practice but also how they are taught and studied in universities and professionally through training. In turn the historical development has affected the meaning, perception and status of each discipline, especially how they are considered by those outside the maelstrom of each discipline.

While marketing has been traced back to the ancient Greeks, Dixon (1979) and Hollander *et al.* (2005) identify periods of marketing back to the tenth century, the orthodox view is that what we know as modern marketing only started in the early twentieth century (Jones and Shaw 2002). The interest in marketing is probably driven by the growth in the nineteenth century of the discipline of economics, and the growing size of international economies and markets. Sheth and Parvatiyar (2000) suggest that marketing grew out of selling and advertising, and developed an understanding of market behaviour to establish its credentials. Bartels (1976) identifies eight stages to the history of marketing, starting in 1900, with each stage roughly equating to a decade. Indeed, it was during the first decade, 1900–10, that the first marketing course opened at the University of Pennsylvania and the Harvard Business School was founded. By the 1930s and 1940s marketing was a well-established discipline, both in practice and increasingly in universities. As we shall see, this gave it a head start on public relations.

Public relations has a very different historical development to marketing, and one which suggests that it has often been considered more of a niche that is not necessarily central to organisational development. Unlike marketing, public relations often had to struggle to gain acceptance as a strategic, as opposed to tactical, tool within organisations. In this way some public relations practitioners consider marketers as competitive rivals, out to encroach on their communications domain. However, I would suggest that a more useful approach is to recognise the different backgrounds of each discipline, and use their complementary strengths to promote your event.

It has been suggested that public relations has a very long history. For example, when the Viking Eric the Red in the tenth century 'discovered' a cold and probably inhospitable place and called it Greenland, this could be viewed as a public relations trick to encourage more settlers by conjuring up a positive image of a verdant and pleasant place to live. The Boston Tea Party, although clearly part of a revolutionary struggle, can also be viewed as a simple 'stunt' to gain attention. We might assume that the skills required in Ancient Rome to promote a gladiatorial contest would be little different from promoting a pop-star today. The first example above deals with CPR; the latter two are of MPR.

Like many facets of management, public relations took time to develop. Despite the examples above, and many more, most commentators agree that as a discrete, systematic and strategic tool public relations actually stems from the nineteenth century (Moloney 2006; L'Etang 2008). Moreover, the initial use of public relations was strongly associated with events, and how they sought to get people to attend. The American circus impresario P.T. Barnum (1810–91) provides a classic example of how public relations can be used to 'get bums on seats'. Barnum created amazing stories about the attractions at his circuses. One well known example was in 1835 when Barnum exhibited Joice Heth, a slave whom he claimed was 161 and had been nursemaid to George Washington. He presented a yellowing 'birth certificate' as proof. When ticket sales tapered off, Barnum wrote an anonymous letter to a Boston newspaper claiming that Heth was a fake – she was actually a machine, made up of whalebone and old leather. As a result, crowds flocked again to see her (Joice Heth Archive). Such showmanship raised ethical issues over the use and reputation of public relations.

During the twentieth century, public relations moved away from being event and publicity based, and tarnished with a slightly disreputable status, to a profession that played a more central role in a much wider range of organisations. The first public relations agency was created in 1900 when George Michaelis founded the Publicity Bureau in Boston, USA. The first known book about public relations was written by Edward Bernays (1891–1995) in 1923, *Crystallizing Public Relations*. Bernays, who became known as the father of public relations, as the nephew of Sigmund Freud was aware of the possibilities of psychology for developed persuasive messages. Over a long career his clients included governments, pressure groups and commercial organisations. Bernays created the first ever public relations course, at New York University in 1923. This suggests that in both practical and academic terms public relations has a history as long as, if not longer, than marketing.

However, in reality marketing is often considered the senior of the two, with a longer practical and academic background. For example, in the UK the first degree course in public relations did not start until 1989 at the University of Bournemouth, and the UK trade body representing public relations practitioners started in 1949 and was not granted a Royal Charter until 2005, when it became the Chartered Institute of Public Relations (CIPR). The forerunner of the body representing UK marketers (the Sales Managers' Association), however, was founded in 1911, and received its Royal Charter as the Chartered Institute of Marketing in 1989 (see www.cim.co.uk). As well as being perceived by many to be the senior discipline of the two, marketing is also commonly viewed to be broader in scope. This highlights that there has sometimes been professional envy or conflict between the two, though we should not overstate this.

Marketing and public relations

As noted above there is some biased interpretation of the relationship between the two disciplines, yet the two subjects are very close. They should be complementary, especially within MPR when the two disciplines are likely to work symbiotically. Moreover, for most small to medium-sized events the reality is that both functions are usually provided by the same person, consultant or by a very small team responsible for a very wide range of communication functions.

From Chapters 3 and 7 we will have a sense of some differences between the two: notably that marketing focuses on markets, consumers and getting the right product to them profitably, whereas public relations is more associated with reputation building aimed at wider publics. Alison Theaker (2008: 305) sums this up by stating: '*All organizations have a need for PR, but not all are involved in marketing.*' By this she means that many non-commercial organisations such as governments or public bodies including the emergency services do not necessarily sell a pecuniary based product, but will use publicity and reputation building tools to help them achieve their goals. Very often we cannot construct a divide between short-term publicity and longer term reputation building. If used well, the former can lead to the latter.

Probably the two best known academic commentators on this debate are Philip Kotler (marketing) and James Grunig (public relations). Kotler and Mindak (1978) predicted that the separate marketing and public relations functions would eventually converge, with marketing likely to be dominant. Grunig (1992) takes a very different view and suggests that public relations should be separate. He maintains that where marketing spends money, public relations saves money. What he means by this is that the strategic use of public relations in the form of corporate communications and issues management, means that an organisation can respond before a crisis incurring costs in terms of money, effort and market share occurs. There is an alternative to these two diametrically opposed viewpoints: marketing public relations.

Although some commentators stress the differences between the two disciplines, for the event organiser it is probably more helpful to consider the similarities and how they can complement one another. Marketing and public relations share the following:

● Functions of management.
● Communication focused.
● Means of building relationships with human beings.
● Creative.
● Derive their objectives from overall corporate objectives.

Moreover, the success or failure of marketing and public relations can often threaten the success or existence of an event.

What is MPR?

> ### Definition box 8.1
>
> ## Defining marketing public relations
>
> Marketing public relations is the application of public relations to support marketing objectives. It is led by the relatively narrow and precise needs of marketers to reach suppliers, distributors and consumers. It applies to those public relation tools which help achieve this by drawing attention to the existence of an event. Event marketing public relations addresses both supply and demand. It can persuade participants that the event is credible and has a market, and at the same time attract that demand to want to see the participants.

Put simply MPR is where the public relations function supports marketing by creating visibility and attention primarily through publicity (Shimp 1993; Haywood 1997; Harris and Whalen 2006). Shimp (2010) goes further and suggests that MPR's strength is as a credible source, so it is particularly useful at educating a new market, building up interest and launching a product (Kotler and Keller 2006). This approach is generally limited to certain industries such as entertainment (King 2005), books and music (Grunig and Hunt 1984) and sports (Cutlip *et al.* 2006). MPR, therefore, is applicable to some, but not all, event fields. Hype may help marketers promote their products through 'puffery', and so imply they have more value than they may have (Moloney 2006). Harris and Whalen (2006) suggest that we need to distinguish between hype and buzz. They suggest that an audience may not view a hyped product as authentic, but that product communication which creates buzz is seen as 'cool' by the audience (Lewis and

Bridger 2001). Many events, especially those in sports and entertainment, are ideally suited to creating a buzz.

Indeed, Rebel Bingo (www.rebelbingo.com), by presenting itself as an underground Rebel Bingo club, seeks to establish an exclusivity which makes it appear a cool event to attend. For example, club rules include:

- No old people.
- No boring people.
- No customer service.

The event takes a normal entertainment, Bingo, and re-packages it in a way that suggests that attendance at Rebel Bingo says much about the 'coolness' of the attendees.

In Chapter 1 we briefly introduced the concepts of Integrated Marketing Communication (IMC), which is the orthodoxy amongst event marketing commentators, and Integrated Communication (IC), which challenges this. Ultimately, the debate between IMC and IC is over which discipline dominates: marketing or public relations? Such a power struggle is unhealthy for anyone promoting their event, as it uses up energy on internal squabbles rather than reaching external audiences. Kotler and Mindak (1978), updated by Pickton and Broderick (2001), identified five models for the relationship between the two disciplines, which may be of use to us. These are:

- Marketing and public relations as separate and autonomous functions.
- Marketing as the dominant function.
- Public relations as the dominant function.
- Marketing and public relations as discrete but overlapping functions.
- Marketing and public relations within a wider communications function.

Marketing by focusing on markets is good at identifying what events may help meet the needs and wants of customers, and dealing with suppliers and funders. Public relations provides a much wider perspective by considering the views and actions of other stakeholders, such as pressure groups, government and local communities. Each discipline has much to offer the other within an overall events promotion approach, but in the last chapter of this book we will outline a different approach.

One of the debates concerning MPR is whether it is a discrete discipline in its own right separate from marketing and public relations. Kotler (1991, quoted in Kitchen 1997: 258) suggests that it is:

> A healthy offspring of two parents: marketing & PR. MPR represents an opportunity for companies to regain a share of voice in a message-satiated society. MPR not only delivers a strong voice to win share of mind and heart, it also delivers a better, more effective voice in many cases.

As a result Harris (1993) predicted that MPR would split from corporate public relations and would focus on marketing support, and so would become a new discipline. In fact, the orthodoxy, and practical experience, suggests that MPR is a core component of marketing and public relations, rather than a separate discipline in its own right. The event communicator needs to view MPR as a tool, and not waste energy on worrying about structural issues of who provides it and how.

In the models of the relationship between the two disciplines (Kotler and Mindak 1978; Pickton and Broderick 2001), MPR is the point in the second model where the separate functions overlap, and in the final mode where marketing and PR are within one integrated approach where they also overlap. It has been suggested that about 70 per cent of organisational communication spend is allocated to MPR activities (Kitchen and Papasolomou 1997). Thus an events use of MPR represents a primarily tactical and short-term use of public relations, and indeed it is quite likely that the bulk of their activity in 'getting bums on seats' is within this sphere.

For example, the Watkin Glen Grand Prix (www.grandprixfestival.com) celebrates the US heritage of motor sports by returning to the original grand prix with road courses. In 2011 some 20,000 attended, and the promotional activity through its website and media relations was clearly designed to use 'nostalgia' as an emotive marketing tool. Moreover, the website makes frequent use of participant and attendee testimonials, and visual images to support the message.

A different approach to marketing and public relations is presented by Moloney (2006). He suggests that there are five forms of the relationship between the two disciplines: domination; subordination; separation; equality; and identity. He is not necessarily suggesting that one of the disciplines is automatically in the ascendant and the other submissive, but that in some circumstances one might dominate, whilst in a different set of circumstances the other one does. This slightly less partisan model looks at the actual relationship, not automatically suggesting that one or the other will have the upper hand. It provides a means for assessing which approach is appropriate for each different event.

When considering the relationship between marketing and public relations it is important not to get carried away with a sense of marketing versus public relations. In fact the two disciplines should work close together. For example, public relations practitioner Roger Haywood (1997) notes how important it is for public relations and advertising to get together. He strongly suggests that public relations and advertising activity be strongly coordinated during product launches. In terms of an event, you might consider sending out a press release prior to a planned advertising campaign, and either educating the target audience or gaining attention. The different tactics should dovetail and support each other. This adds to the value of each, so by reinforcing messages, the whole is greater than the sum of the parts.

The benefits of MPR

It is suggested by commentators such as Kotler (1997; Baines *et al.*, 2004; Harris and Whalen 2006; Theaker 2008) that public relations is able to help marketing by:

- Launching new products.
- Product promotion.
- Defending a maturing product.
- Product education.
- Defending products that have encountered public problems.
- Building a strong corporate image.
- Advertising support.
- Sales support.
- Providing credibility.
- Building up trust.

MPR is considered particularly relevant for educating a market to the efficacy of a new product. For example, one trend that originally developed in North America and is now moving to other countries is the idea of the divorce party. Event agencies which organise divorce parties use media articles, interviews and specialist websites to raise general interest. For example, Christine Gallagher, who in 2003 wrote 'How to Throw a Break-Up party' on her website (http://divorcepartyplanner.com), gives prominence to broadcast media appearances she has given. These raise awareness of the event idea, but also promote herself as a leader in this field. We are likely to witness a similar educational use first through MPR in other new markets such as green, luxury and milestone events.

There are two different approaches to the role of MPR. Kotler and Keller (2006) suggest public relations helps marketing by 'gaining share of mind'. What they mean is that public relations is more likely to provide a persuasive narrative which gains the attention of consumers in the first place. Marketing can then help to deepen that contact after the initial interest is achieved. Other commentators, however, such as Guth and Marsh (2006), suggest that MPR does more than gain initial interest, that it can help to build long-term relationships. An explanation for this difference of view could be that Kotler focuses on merely the media relations aspect of MPR, but others such as Guth and Marsh also recognise the event aspects of MPR.

One of the main reasons for the rise of interest in MPR is that one component part of marketing – advertising – is in a slow decline, with media relations becoming more important instead. This implies that events are more likely to be spending less money on advertising and more on media relations. The well known New York advertising executive Al Ries (Ries and Ries 2002) suggested that advertising is in decline, and public relations is taking over its brand building functions. The reason for this shift is a belief that public relations may offer more 'bang for the buck'. It has long been held that advertising is an inexact science, indeed the late nineteenth/early twentieth century US retailer John Wanamaker is often quoted as the source of the phrase: '*Half the money I spend on advertising is wasted; the trouble is I don't know which half.*' What has made many event marketers question their use of advertising is that it is increasingly more difficult to reach target audiences. Harris and Whalen (2006) suggest that there is increasing evidence of reduced returns in advertising. The fragmentation of audiences makes it more difficult to reach the same number. In the 1960s and 1970s there was in the UK only one national station with advertisements – ITV – and audiences were frequently of the order of 10–15 million people. Advertising was a way of reaching huge numbers of people. UK television viewers can now access hundreds of television stations, and the popular flagship television programmes have viewing figures half those of thirty years ago.

Many marketers are turning to public relations to help generate editorial coverage because it is considered not only cheaper than many marketing activities, but also third-party endorsement is believed to be more powerful and effective. This is particularly important during economic recession, when marketing departments need to look at their budgets, and media relations in particular can look very cost-effective compared to expensive advertising. Not all sources believe that public relations is automatically growing at advertising's expense. Doyle (2000) notes that although cheap, MPR is less controllable and certain than advertising. In the current difficulties that the world's economy has found itself in for several years, and which appears to be a legacy for several more to come, public relations offers a realistic option to traditional marketing tools. This issue of the cheapness of media relations is particularly relevant to events with a very small budget, such as community events, many arts festivals and charity fundraisers.

MPR is better suited to certain products and circumstances and Tom Harris developed the Harris Grid (Harris and Whalen 2006) to identify where public relations works best. By assessing high and low media and consumer interest he suggested that some products are more likely to attract media interest, and so are more suited to MPR. Figure 8.2 applies the Harris Grid to events to identify those most likely to benefit from an MPR approach.

Variables	Likely events
High media and consumer interest	Sports Music festivals
High media interest and low consumer interest	Arts festivals Political events
High consumer interest and low media interest	Conferences Trade shows
Low consumer interest and low media interest	Specialist interest

Figure 8.2 Harris grid applied to events
(Adapted from Harris and Whalen 2006)

MPR tools

Although most literature focuses on only media relations, there are in reality many MPR tools. Moreover, as the next chapter deals with media relations in depth, in this section we will only briefly introduce the importance of media management. Although MPR is associated with 'loudness' several of these tools are in effect a soft sell.

Guerrilla tactics

Sometimes referred to as guerrilla marketing or guerrilla PR, this is a clear MPR tactic. The concept was first associated with Jay Conrad Levinson who wrote *Guerrilla Marketing Excellence* in 1984. It can be linked with experiential marketing and stunts, because the idea is to use unconventional methods such as flash mobs, viral campaigns and street art. As we noted earlier guerrilla tactics is part of the marketing warfare approach, and is designed to be used by small businesses and organisations that do not have large advertising budgets. Therefore, rather than spending money, guerrilla tactics is based on creativity to design ideas which gain attention by creating buzz. It can be a pure stunt or it can be about creating inter-activity between the brand and customers. At the 2010 FIFA World Cup in South Africa, a small Dutch brewery gained significant worldwide media coverage. During a match between the Netherlands versus Denmark thirty-six young women wore orange mini-dresses in the colour both of Holland, but also the brewer Bavaria, and with their logo. This gained media coverage – but also got two of the ladies arrested for organising 'unlawful commercial activities' as Bavaria was not an official World Cup sponsor (Evans 2010).

Not all events have large budgets. Our next case study is an example of needs must, where artists were able to use their creativity as a means of attracting 'bums on seats' to their shows.

Sponsorship

Sponsorship is an area that has grown significantly in the past thirty years, both in terms of revenue and range of events, from a limited small-scale activity to a global industry (Meenaghan 1998). Sponsorship is important for events, as a means of securing additional revenue streams and attaining access to new marketing communication opportunities. In return, event sponsorship provides many organisations with a cost-effective alternative to advertising. IEG (www.sponsormap.com) has noted a trend of an increase in sponsorship globally since the turn

Image 8.1 Dutch Dress courtesy of Bavaria Netherlands

CASE STUDY 8.1

Club Chic – gaining attention with little money to spend

Uitmarkt (http://www.amsterdamsuitburo.nl/uitmarkt/) held over three days is the opening of the cultural season in Amsterdam. Organised by the Amsterdam Uitburo, it is held in the last weekend of August. Typically artistes such as playwrights, painters and authors showcase their projects for the coming year. So a band might play a short set of its latest album, a writer make a recital of their current work and a theatre give a free performance. It is also has a famous book market.

Typically there are about 450 performances with some 2,000 artistes, and the event attracts approximately 500,000 visitors, making it a major cultural event.

As a small fringe performing group, Club Chic could not afford to rent a stage, and so they turned to guerrilla tactics to piggyback on Uitmarkt. They piled into an old car with a frog green canvas roof that could be rolled down, with details of their performances on the car. They would drive to a part of the Uitmarkt, stop and pull down the canvas roof, put on their music, and then their drag-queens, juggler, magician and strongman would begin their show and start immediately to engage those standing nearby. Their theme was to re-create the 1920s cabaret style. The police would come along to move them on, typically the crowd would tell the police to let the group continue, but eventually they would have to leave. They would pack up, drive to another part of the event and the process would be repeated.

Their activity did not just allow them to reach the people they performed to, but also attracted the attention of some media, giving them more publicity. For example, the *Echo*, the free paper of Amsterdam, interviewed them, and *Nieuws Van De Day*, the regional paper of Amsterdam and its suburbs, dedicated half of page 5, with an accompanying photograph. The headline was 'Club Chic brings the atmosphere of 1920s cabaret to Amsterdam.'

On the eight evening performances they had in a small theatre prior to this campaign, there were some empty seats. For every one of the following eight performances they were sold out.

of the twenty-first century. For example, in 2008 there was a 15 per cent increase in sponsorship budgets, though as the recession started to kick in by 2009 this had slowed to a 3.9 per cent increase. In particular IEG notes that with the 2008 Olympics, Asia was recording the highest growth. We can assume that with London 2012 Europe may experience even more growth. Indeed, the ESA (www.sponsorship.org) estimated that the value of the European sponsorship market covering fifty countries was 23.33 billion euros in 2010.

This sponsorship spending growth is driven by a number of trends:

1 As noted in Chapter 2 there has been a fragmentation of both media and stakeholders. Consumers are now communicated with via a range of channels depending on their personal preference, such as satellite television, the Internet, text message, video games and social networks. As a result, events are one of the few remaining areas where consumers might come together at the same time.
2 Advertising in particular has been in long-term decline, and sponsorship is seen by many as a cost-effective and efficient means of addressing this marketing gap.
3 At the high end, such as mega-events, global companies see such events as a means of getting their brand across to global audiences.

Typically, this growth in sponsorship is often associated with high-profile sporting, Arts and cultural events. The implication is that sponsorship is attractive where events will gain media attention, or are so large that the footfall of visitors reaches a critical mass. However, we have also witnessed a growth in event sponsorship at the smaller, more local level, where sponsors still want tangible benefits such as media coverage, but are also using it as a means to put something back (often into the local community) as part of being seen as socially responsible. There are different layers to the purpose an organisation can have in sponsoring an event.

Sponsors have a variety of reasons why they want to sponsor an event organised by a third party, but essentially we can identify two main motivations:

● To promote or sell the sponsor's specific products/services/brands.
● To enhance the corporate reputation of the sponsor.

The former is essentially a tactical means of increasing sales of products; the latter is more strategic, addressing the corporate or brand image. These motivations are not mutually exclusive, though a sponsor may focus more on one than the other. For some sponsors, both are achievable. Thus Anheuser-Busch InBev's sponsorship of the FIFA World Cups means that only their brands will available at the stadia for each game. So Budweiser is the official beer of the World Cup and sales should increase, but at the same time Anheuser-Busch InB*ev* will also benefit from corporate advertising and brand opportunities.

However, as noted by Walliser (2003), there is no global consensus of the meaning of sponsorship. Indeed he highlights differences in English-, French- and German-speaking countries on the meaning of sponsorship. There are, though, clear traits to most sponsorship:

● It is a marketing tool designed to meet clear objectives.
● It is a risky undertaking with no guarantees on either side.
● Central to it is the relationship between sponsor and sponsored event.
● Both sponsor and sponsored event hope to gain from the relationship, so they exchange a value.

One of the concepts said to be central to the impact of sponsorship is congruence. Drengner *et al.* (2011) explain that this is where there is a fit between the event and the sponsor's brand. One obvious form of fit is where there is a clear link between the product of the sponsor and the event activity: for example, sponsors of the Cambridge Rock Festival (http://cambridgerock festival.co.uk) have included Radio Caroline and the Classic Rock Society. Another form of fit is with the event audience and the brand, so for example international jeweller, Cartier, sponsored the Hurlingham Polo Association's International Day (http://www.guardspoloclub.com/tournaments/cartier-international-day-teams-by-invitation) for twenty-seven years, which being hosted at the Guards Club, Windsor, attracts royal visitors and many rich patrons: exactly Cartier's clientele. As noted by Drengner *et al.*, congruence can also be based on the sponsor's message: thus they cite Red Bull's sponsorship of the Fleutage (http://www.redbullflugtagusa.com). This is an event where, in a series of US cities, human-powered machines jump off a pier into a lake. The link is that Red Bull's strapline is: 'It Gives You Wings.'

However, we should not automatically assume that there has to be congruence. There are thousands of successful sponsorships where this is not the case. For example, since 2005 Xchanging, who provide business processing, procurement and technology services, has been the official sponsor of the live televised University Boat Race between Cambridge and Oxford (http://theboatrace.org). For many brewers and distillers of alcohol, congruence is more difficult to find, and so they are more interested in events that attract a large number of attendees or media coverage. Thus the leading European-wide rugby tournament is the ERC Heineken Cup (http://www.ercrugby.com/eng/heinekencup/index.php), and the premier football cup in the UK, the FA Cup, is currently sponsored by brewer Budweiser (www.thefa.com). The size and nature of the live or televised audience may be as important as congruence.

For mega-events, sponsorship can be quite a complex process. For example, there is a range of different tiers of sponsors at the Olympics. At one level there are the International Olympic Committee's (IOC) Worldwide Olympic Partners, such as Coca-Cola and McDonald's. Then there is the London Organising Committee of the Olympic and Paralympic Games (LOCOG) first tier, paying about £40 million each (*The Guardian* undated). These are referred to as 2012 Official Olympic Sponsors: Adidas, BMW, BP, British Airwaves, BT, EDF, Lloyds TSB. Below these are some twenty-eight London 2012 Official Olympic Providers and Suppliers. For example, Westfield, a shopping centre in Stratford in East London, is the Official Shopping Centre Developer of London 2012. Sponsors get the package they pay for, though they all imply some level of exclusivity in their field of operations.

Sponsorship carries a risk, and events need to assess what could go wrong with their sponsors. Many professional football clubs, for example, have found that their own sponsors have gone into administration. In 2008 West Ham United allegedly lost up to £8 million when their airline sponsor, XL, collapsed (Hughes 2008). So sometimes commercial disaster has an impact. But it could also be negative publicity by association. For example, Phonak, the Swiss hearing aid specialist that sponsored a cycling team, would not have been happy when one of the team, Floyd Landis, won the Tour de France but was stripped of his title for testing positive for an illegally high testosterone use (de Mesa 2006). As a result it is reasonable to expect that, for example, LOCOG will have conducted an issues audit of what sponsors could do to tarnish the name of the Olympics.

Sponsorship raises two related issues: the law and ethical behaviour. A variety of countries and transnational bodies such as the European Union have progressively passed tougher and tougher legislation on advertising and sponsorship of events, concerning for example alcohol, tobacco and children. Traditionally tobacco companies have sponsored a number of events, especially in America, and have been particularly associated with sports such as cricket and motor sports, but changing laws have meant that fewer events are now sponsored by tobacco companies. For example, tobacco companies sponsoring sporting events has been banned in the UK since 2003, and many other countries have similar bans. Yet, there are still events sponsored by tobacco companies, although attendees may not necessarily realise this. For example, Urban Wave parties are underground parties with DJs which are funded by Camel (http://tobaccocommons.com).

There is also the ethical issue of ambush marketing. Here Bladen *et al.* (2011: 185) note: '*An ambush marketer creates marketing communications at or near the event to convince stakeholders that they are an official sponsor, even though they are not.*' In effect, they try to commercially hijack the opportunity an event provides without actually paying the event any money. At the 2009 golf championship, the British Open, held at Turnberry, Scotland near the coast, non-sponsor Hugo Boss had a sailboat emblazoned with the fashion label's logo which could be seen on the waters around the course and which cameras picked up in the background of the action (Taylor 2009). Ambush marketing is not just about rivals gaining attention outside an event, many sports professionals have personal sponsorship deals. For example, in the run-up to the 2003 ICC Cricket World Cup some Indian players threatened to boycott the competition because of the clash between the official and their personal sponsors. This also became an issue in the run-up to the 2011 competition (Rao 2011). During the 2011 Rugby World Cup in New Zealand, England player Manu Tuilagi was fined £5,000 by the International Rugby Board for wearing an OPRO gumshield, when OPRO was not an official sponsor (Kitson 2011; Sale 2011). While the player denies it was an orchestrated marketing campaign, it did bring OPRO a lot of global media coverage.

Advertorials

This is a very grey area between marketing and public relations, which essentially camouflages an advert. An advertorial is where print advertising space is purchased, usually in a newspaper, but is written to read like a feature article. As noted by Cameron and Ju-Pak (2000) it is a growing trend as marketers look at more effective ways of spending their advertising budget. In a sense it is an attempt to combine the control that advertising offers, with the third-party endorsement that editorial coverage brings, by trying to persuade the reader that it is an independent feature article. Typically an advertorial is for a whole page, or sometimes a half-page, and normally at the top of the page will be written 'Advertising Feature', but the advertiser hopes that the reader does not see this. Harrison-Hill and Chalip (2005) suggested that advertorials in sports magazines could be a way of promoting events such as motor rally sports. Robinson (2002) found that the impact on consumers of an advertorial was greater if it read more like an article than an advert. As a result, although usually commissioned by a marketer within their advertising budget, typically it is the public relations professional that provides the copy.

New Zealand based agency Write Agency (www.writeagency.com) provided powerful copy describing in attractive terms the King St Great Race Ball. A different approach is suggested by Chain Media (www.chainmedia.com/advertorial) who suggest that an organisation hands out advertorials to attendees at an event. Our next case study demonstrates how an advertorial may boost event attendance.

CASE STUDY 8.2

Advertorials

North American based marketer Julia Hidy (http://juliahidymarketing.com) believes that advertorials ought to be used more often to promote events:

'When placed in a magazine that has a print and an online version, the advertorial can be viewed and searched for keywords before and even during an event. I've recommended placing advertorials to my clients since, when placed in the right publication, I've found them to be such useful lead generators to connect with highly qualified clients.

Advertorials can be an effective way of getting responses. For example, a print ad we would normally receive 10 to 25 leads, but an advertorial for a global supply chain virtual conference drew in 650 pre-qualified leads.

Very often an advertorial would not be used alone. The mobile POS advertorial (page opposite) was used, along with a print and online ad and four press releases, to draw attention to a large trade show, the National Retail Federation's Big Show in New York, held in January at the Jacob Javits Center. The placement of the print and online version of the advertorial was timed to take place in October 2010, one month prior to the likely announcement by the publication, *RIS News* (www.risnews.com), that Magstar Total Retail (http://www.magstarinc.com) would be mentioned on a top 20 US national software vendors' annual LeaderBoard listing in their November issue.

Since the POS Mobile advertorial appeared in the online version of the magazine, the text was fully indexed and would allow prospects to find the advertorial, and other press and editorial mentions that had been garnered earlier in the year. The advertorial was also included as one of six pieces of content posted onto an online press kit that went live for the Big Show in early January 2011.

The combination of the advertorial, top 20 trade magazine mention, and carefully timed release of each press release during the trade show event both boosted walk-in traffic at the show. Although the advertorial was not directly tied in to the event, it helped to influence more people to visit Magstar's booth and connect with the company. For example, the advertorial drew in 93 qualified leads on its own, which allowed the company reps to contact those individuals and invite them to visit them in New York at the NRF event if they seemed a bit resistant to set up a meeting otherwise.'

Events

We have noted above that Edward Bernays has been considered the 'father of public relations', but Harris and Whalen (2006) suggest that he should also be considered the 'father of event marketing'. This is because of his use in the early and mid-twentieth century of events and stunts to raise awareness of products. For example, they cite the long-term impact of the first Pillsbury Bake-Off in 1949, launched by President F. D. Roosevelt's widow Eleanor. This event is a US-wide cookery contest with a grand final held each year in New York with a $1 million prize, which gains media publicity for the flour manufacturer Pillsbury.

Media relations

The next chapter will deal with media relations in depth, but the premise of this book is that virtually every event communicator will have to deal with the media. For most, it could be a proactive process of trying to get their message out via the media, but others may need to respond to negative stories. The prime reason for dealing with the media is outlined by Getz *et al.* (2007), who note that the media is especially important for reaching key targeted audiences, and changing opinion towards festivals in Sweden and Canada. However, as noted at the 1996 Atlanta Olympics (Higham 1999), and the 1999 Rugby World Cup hosted in Wales (Jones 2001), such events can also bring negative publicity. Media relations is part science and part art, and, as we shall see in Chapter 9, focusing on writing and sending out press releases, is not enough: good media relations requires building relations by email, on the telephone, and face to face with key journalists.

Stunts

Stunts are designed to gain attention, which can be interpreted to mean several different related activities. For example, Morris and Goldsworthy (2008: 33) define stunts as pseudo-events: '*In which any action or content is essentially symbolic and which are organized to achieve publicity.*' Borkowski (2000: 87) views them more as visual events and defines a stunt as: '*A photo-opportunity is a mini-event. It transforms flat information into a three dimensional, living breathing entity.*' A stunt may be for a cause and have a clear message, so that pressure

Image 8.2 Courtesy of Julia Hidy (http://juliahidymarketing.com), *RIS News* (www.risnews.com) and Magstar Inc (www.magstarinc.com)

groups such as *Fathers 4 Justice* (www.fathers-4-justice.org) have had activists dressed in a Spiderman outfit climbing Tower Bridge in London. But a stunt can also be simply a photo-opportunity such as getting a celebrity to launch a new product. In March 2010 the Black Eyed Peas performed a surprise concert to 10,000 people in New York Time Square to launch a Samsung 3D television. What we can be certain of is that stunts are designed only to receive media attention – if photographers or television cameras don't turn up they have failed.

As a consequence you need to give a lot of attention to devising stunts which will interest a picture editor. Borkowski (2000: 7) refers to the idea of 'improperganda', the

> Setting up situations which are so intriguing and so bizarre that the press cannot resist them. It's about creating images which tell those stories directly, or which lead readers straight to the copy to satisfy their curiosity. It's about entertainment.

Creating such intriguing ideas is not an easy process, and it is helpful to consider what might make an amusing, stunning or intriguing picture. Moreover, the stunt needs to link with the story you are trying to get across. Key to devising a stunt, therefore, is time spent coming up with ideas which link with your campaign/story. Borkowski (2000) suggests that particular fields are good for stunts: circus, sex, animals, records, self-publicists, events, products and protest. You will note that several of these are directly or indirectly event related. Indeed, the world's premier cycling race, the Tour de France, started out in 1903 as a stunt by Henri Desgrange, the editor of *L'Auto-Vélo*, to promote the newspaper.

Practical checklist

- Be both 'loud' and 'quiet' in your use of MPR.
- Use visual events to create an MPR experience.
- View MPR as part of the communication function, rather than viewing either marketing or public relations as dominant.
- Consider guerrilla tactics if you are a small event.
- Do not ignore the responsibilities that come with sponsorship.
- Write in an attractive and positive style about your event.
- Encourage a creative atmosphere if you want to produce stunts.

Our last case study demonstrates that MPR is not just about activity, but involves a range of related activities, such as audience, product and promotion.

CASE STUDY 8.3

Taste festivals – raising event awareness

Taste of London (http://www.tastefestivals.com/london) is an open-air pop-up restaurant festival held each summer for four days in Regent's Park. Forty of the city's best restaurants dish up their finest in an alfresco gourmet feast, while 200 producers provide a bounty of the best food and beverages, ensuring that guests sample and shop for a range of produce in the laid-back atmosphere of a boutique food market. They also host a Best Taste Wine Awards.

The aim of marketing is to deliver tickets sales, and public relations does this, but also acts as a brand champion. Because of the importance of selling tickets, marketing drives public relations activity.

The event has a range of different target audiences, such as sponsors, the chefs, celebrities, exhibitors and attendees. Chefs, exhibitors and sponsors are more important stakeholders early on in the planning process, because they are what get people to come and enjoy the show. As it gets nearer to the event, the focus of communication turns to customers, so that they have all the information they need to enjoy the show.

The chefs and celebrities may want to use the event as a means of managing their own image. Meeting the needs of both the event and these participants can be tough. The issue is not the chefs and celebrities themselves, but that their managers will have clear objectives of what they want to get from the event. It requires, therefore, negotiation between what the event organisers want them to do, what they are prepared to do, and how much it will cost. This is especially the case with very famous chefs. However, the event organiser's media team can help chefs as well, so they might be able to get them on a daytime television show. The chef will be able to promote themselves, their book or whatever, but they will have also been well briefed on what to say about the Taste of London. Success is down to handling people.

Taste of London has a strong brand image, with 2012 being the eighth running of the event. It has a strong database and a loyal following, and so direct mail is one of the main channels used to promote the event. The website is one of the channels which is used from the start, and the organisers make sure they use SEO (Search Engine Optimisation) to drive traffic to the site. Advertising includes glossy magazines, the commuter newspapers in London (*Metro* and the *Evening Standard*), and even the sides of London buses. In more recent years they have made a lot of use of SMS (Short Message Service) and social media.

Taste of London often makes use of celebrities either to launch the event to the media, such as with a famous chef such as Jamie Oliver, or they use them to gain extra media coverage. For example, they might piggyback on what the celebrity is trying to achieve. In 2011 the Hollywood A-list actress Gwyneth Paltrow had just launched a cookbook; at the same time Taste of London had launched a VVIP ticket which would mean that the actress could be comfortable and not be hassled. Taste of London gained coverage, and benefited from the 'wow' factor, and Gwyneth Paltrow gained access to the right people to promote her book at the event. Such media coverage gained as a result helps grow the event brand.

Taste of London also makes good use of statistics, so that in 2011 press releases pointed out that 200,000 Michelin starred dishes were served, 20,000 glasses of Laurent-Perrier were consumed and 10,000 truffle based dishes were eaten. Such statistics come from information provided by the restaurants, and also the feedback forms from customers that outline what they did, ate and drunk.

The organisers also look at the dishes that restaurants offer, and then a trend might be identified – so in 2011 it was truffles, and in 2012 it was Peruvian food. Statistics around such trends and stories have very good media relations value, with the daily and commuter newspapers particularly liking such quirky stories. The food pages of newspapers always want to know what are the 'hot' trends.

All the marketing public relations activity is measured by its return on investment (ROI) and ticket sales, which are monitored closely both in terms so how many, and where they are sold. A lot of the promotional material, both advertising and online, has codes inserted so the organisers can track how well the campaign is doing.

Planning for next year's event occurs almost immediately after each one is over. The first stage is to conduct research both during the event and post-event. The marketing of the event is reviewed in a forty-page document, which includes a PR review which is discussed at a full-day meeting of everyone involved in the event. This then feeds into the planning of the next event. The actual promotional campaign starts out about 18 weeks before the event, the website is launched, advertising media selected, public relations advisers appointed and long leads with the media are started. Tickets are on sale from about 12 weeks.

Discussion questions

This chapter highlights that the use of publicity raises some key issues:

1　Should you decide which model of the relationship between marketing and public relations to use? Or is this a dangerous option which can narrow an event's options?
2　Gaining publicity is fairly easy. How would you use MPR to educate new event markets of the need for the event?
3　How would you select which is the correct mix of MPR tools to use for your event?

Further information

Other sources which might help you consider the issues outlined in this chapter include:

Websites

http://www.bulluk.com – Bull Creative is a marketing and PR agency.
http://www.youtube.com/watch?v=viMcNqtO0ys – Bavarian beer ambush at Football World Cup.
http://www.creativeguerrillamarketing.com/ – Guerrilla marketing blog that identifies interesting examples.

http://www.sponsorcouncil.org/ – the International Sponsor Council represents corporate sponsors worldwide.

www.sponsorship-awards.com – the Hollis Sponsorship Awards.

http://www.visualarts.net.au/advicecentre/resources/casestudies/sponsorship-case-study – interesting article on how an Australian charity event attracts sponsorship.

http://twitter.com/#!/PRexamples – microblog which updates PR stunts and campaigns.

Chapter 9

Using media relations

Introduction

Probably all event communicators will use media relations, through writing press releases, conducting interviews and telling a story through pictures. This chapter will first explain the value and importance of media relations. We will then address the core concept of news. If your event does not have a story, your target media will not be interested in your event. We will assess how to generate media coverage, followed by looking at the key tools and techniques of media relations.

By the end of this chapter students will be able to:

● Justify why media relations is appropriate for an event.
● Understand how to develop news for an event.
● Assess the appropriate use of media relations tools.
● Write a press release.

What is media relations?

Definition box 9.1

Defining media relations

Media relations is the means by which an event reaches its core audiences via a third party, the media. An event communicates its messages orally, visually or in writing in a way that is attractive to the media. Media relations is first and foremost providing what the media want, and in so doing the hoped-for pay-off is that the event gets the oxygen of publicity that it requires.

A range of terms is applied to media relations practitioners, such as spin doctors, flack and press agent. Each of these somewhat derogatory terms suggests that media relations practitioners exist on the edge of, or sometimes beyond, acceptable behaviour. So promoters and agents have been accused of manipulating the public, as with Max Clifford who represents celebrities and boxing promoter Don King. However, as we shall see, media relations has a positive role to play in promoting events. A more neutral term is public relations officer (PRO), and perhaps Edward Bernays got it right when he suggested that the role of a public relations practitioner was to put an organisation's position in the best light possible. Hence, the need to find good news stories and angles.

The use of media relations raises important questions for our three public relations approaches. Richard Bailey (2009) suggests that the sort of mutual understanding required by the Grunigian paradigm is simply not achievable within media relations. Rather, media relations is clearly a core part of any persuasion approach, where your event in a crowded market seeks to be heard. The media are the gatekeeper you use to reach your primary target. The media relations practitioner is first and foremost an advocate for their event. In order to get your message out you need to build relations with journalists, and work and respond in the way they expect, not how you want to. There are rules to the game, and to be effective you (and often your boss) need to learn these.

Why choose media relations?

There is a potential danger in using media relations, and this is getting carried away with the process. You, and especially your boss, need to be very clear why you are using media relations. I have seen a number of practitioners get caught up with seeing their own name, or that of their organisation, in the papers or being broadcast. They can view a press release, and the resultant media coverage, as an end in itself, but it is important to realise that although a tactic, media relations must help you meet a strategic goal. If it does not, then don't waste time writing the release.

Another key point to be aware of with media relations is that it is not like a tap that is switched on or switched off. While this approach, especially in the run-up to an event is common, it is not the most effective way of building long-term relationships with journalists. Media relations is not just about you sending out a release and letting the journalist get on with it: rather, it is a continual process requiring commitment and resources. For example, often journalists will want to get back to you with requests for further information or wanting to do an interview. If journalists find that you are reliable, media friendly and articulate they may come to you for help, even when you have not sent them a release. You make think that such requests are a pain and require unnecessary extra work, but in fact they are the best-case scenario you should be aiming for. If journalists regularly contact you, the impact of your event and organisation will be enhanced significantly in both the short and long term. If you want to invest in media relations the rules of the game are that it needs to be given a high priority. You get only one chance with each journalist.

Media relations helps individuals make informed choices. As Moloney (2006) notes it helps us decide what products to buy, which causes to support and what politicians to vote for. Michael Bland (Bland *et al.* 2005: 55) observed that the general role of media relations is to: *'Enhance the reputation of an organization and its products, and to influence and inform the target audiences.'* This could apply to almost any communication tool, but there are two main reasons why you might select media relations. First, it is relatively cheap – indeed media relations is often referred to as 'free' because unlike with advertising there is no purchase of airtime/print space. Of course it is not really free: there are costs, usually in writing, distributing and evaluating the release. The second reason is that the media are a gatekeeper, and as such any third-party endorsement they might give to your event can enhance its credibility. When you see an advertisement you probably think: 'Well of course they would say that', and almost instinctively give less value to the message you are receiving. Yet, if you read something in your daily newspaper, you are more likely to believe what you are reading. Media relations can provide a cost-effective and powerful means of raising awareness of your event.

However, this does not mean that media relations is a panacea. The prime issue to consider is that media relations does not always work in the way you want, because there is limited handling of the message. Once you have sent your release you have largely given control of it to a journalist. The release could go straight into the virtual dustbin, only the less interesting bits could be used, a journalist might contact someone else for comment or they may write a critical piece. The rest of this chapter will hopefully help you identify and avoid the possible pitfalls, and maximise the impact of your media relations.

What is news?

The absolutely key thing you must do is identify news. If you do not address this then journalists simply will not be interested in your press release. This requires a slight shift in your thinking: rather than considering first what message you want to get across, you need to consider what is the news you are imparting that the journalist might be interested in? The rules of the game are that they might give you some 'free' coverage if they get something in return.

On day one of journalism school students are often exposed to two well known axioms about news, and they should guide your approach to promoting an event. The first is a quote from Harold Evans, who was the editor of *The Sunday Times* from 1967 to 1981, and has an almost legendary status in British journalism. Evans stated:

> News is people. It is people talking and doing. Committees and Cabinets and Courts are people; so are fires, accidents and planning decisions. They are only news because they involve and affect people.

This tells us that we should always be thinking about the human interest. Your event may be happening on a particular day at a particular venue, but what will be the effect on the people attending that event? Answering this is the source of your news stories.

The second quote is more a saying: *'Dog bites man is not news: man bites dog is.'* This statement sums up what journalists are looking for. It includes conflict (man versus dog), pain (for the dog), it is unusual (have you read of this before?) and it involves emotion (presumably why the fight).

When you first think about news you probably have in mind what you see on the television news bulletin, or the front pages of your daily newspaper. But news is more than headlines, and much of what you focus on for your event can be packaged as news. It is possible to construct a simple checklist to help you to identify a story. For example, we can apply it to an event such as Sky Ride Plymouth, which is part of a wider UK-wide scheme (www.goskyride.com) to encourage people to have cycling fun on traffic-free roads. It was:

- *Timely* – in the run-up to London 2012.
- *Significant* – the Plymouth event kicked off the whole UK series.
- *Close* – the 8-km route in the centre of the city.
- *Of human interest* – there were 8,000 participants.
- *Unusual* – first time the series had visited Plymouth.

- *Conflict* – none in this instance, though roads were shut (which could have angered local residents).

However, what is considered news is not static, it evolves. For example, the BBC's current political editor, Andrew Marr, writing in 2004 identified a growing trend in news gathering when he suggested that many journalists are now interested in 'shopping'. Rather than stressing 'hard' news, such as politics and economics, he felt that much news was in reality a form of advertising because the focus was on gossip, products and celebrity. This suggests that event managers in these fields might find it easier to attract media coverage than those organising political events.

While a number of your news stories will be based on forthcoming activities, it is also possible to create news angles. Typical approaches are:

- *Anniversaries* – your one millionth customer.
- *Stunts* – in May 1999 FHM projected a 60-ft nude image of television presenter Gail Porter onto Parliament.
- *Events* – for example, many solicitors run free advice sessions on particular legal issues.
- *Opening* – getting a celebrity to open your shop, building or school.
- *A first* – to get a qualification, to use a technology, to offer a product.
- *Job creating* – a major local and trade story – it says you are successful.
- *Awards* – has an award body given you anything? This is something food retailers and restaurants use a lot.
- *Winning a competition* – winning a trade competition can be good publicity.
- *Charity donations* – especially if this ties in with the people concerned – say a photo opportunity of an official handover of a cheque.
- *Seasonal* – giving advice on issues such as dieting around New Year, on love around Valentine's Day (14 February) and on getting into your swimming costume in the summer.

Creativity may get a small event media attention. Apparently a UK national newspaper sent a reporter to the World Orienteering Championships in the 1970s primarily because the organisers pointed out that one of the competitors was a pilot of the famous plane, *Concorde*. This may be apocryphal, as I have not been able to confirm this story, but the logic of why it would work is clear: it had an unusual human interest angle.

If you are a local community event it can be difficult to get beyond local media coverage, and to do so you have to think of something that is quirky, different or fits in with wider news stories. In the wettest summer on record, the Thruxton Flower and Produce Show in September 2012 (http://www.thruxtonvillage.com/flower-produce-show/) gained front-page national Sunday newspaper coverage because they had introduced two new categories, Largest Slug and Heaviest Snail. They also helpfully pointed out that these entries would be kept away from the others. Given that slugs and snails are major foes of gardeners, this story piqued the interest of readers.

In our next case study the organisers of a long-established event wanted to increase the number of attendees. Their public relations advisers came up with an idea which fitted with the organiser's specialist advice, but gained significant media attention and provided a spectacle for those attending.

CASE STUDY 9.1

Using stunts to generate media coverage

Hatch Communications (www.hatchcommunications.co.uk) was tasked by Burgess Pet Care and the Bradford Small Livestock Society to carry out a sponsorship maximisation PR campaign for the 89th Burgess Premier Small Animal Show, the 'Crufts' of the small animal world. Held annually in January, it is the biggest show of its kind in the UK, but only drew in 3,000 visitors in 2010.

The show was renowned for attracting animal exhibitors, but had no connection with family pet owners. Hatch decided to create a spectacle that would attract new visitors and provide a platform for standout media relations, driving awareness and engagement in Yorkshire. Hatch therefore introduced the UK's first ever Rabbit Grand National. This was a mini version of horse jumping, specially designed for rabbits. The team flew in specially trained Swedish star rabbits to the UK, along with their owners, to battle with the best of British bunny jumpers.

Burgess Pet Care was keen on promoting animal welfare, and a key message for them is that rabbits spend too long in hutches, and rabbit jumping is a great way to show the amount of space and exercise they actually need. Burgess Pet Care mentioned that it had seen this type of event before in Scandinavia. Hatch then spoke to jumping organisations in Sweden and Denmark, and as result made the event a bit shorter and more consumer friendly.

The Rabbit Grand National, made possible by Burgess Pet Care's involvement in the show, was pre-promoted as the star attraction and used as a hook to create national and regional media interest, encourage exhibitor sign-ups and ultimately attract a wider variety of visitors to the show. A press release was sent out in December, 'Swedish Rabbit Stars Jet into Yorkshire', which gained significant coverage over the Christmas period. And then in January another release was sent out which focused on how the Grand National would work, the dates and how to get tickets, and led to a huge response from journalists wanting to know more. Accompanying the press release were images of rabbits jumping, and this was used a lot in the press coverage to show high they jumped.

Media interest was extensive and included:

- 6 pieces of national coverage, including ITV *Daybreak* – in the 'Something Cool Before School' segment, the *Vanessa Show*, BBC Radio Five Live, the *Sunday Telegraph Magazine*, BBC online and *Telegraph* online.
- 61 pieces of regional print and broadcast coverage.

Hits to www.smallanimalshow.co.uk increased by 400 per cent in January 2011.

The budget was small, but the return on investment was huge. Kirsty O'Connor from Hatch Communications said: 'We knew it was a good story, and it was something we passionately believed would deliver, but we never anticipated this much coverage. With so much doom and gloom in the news, journalists once in a while want something different. They particularly like animal or human interest stories, and this was so unusual that it had journalists intrigued to hear more.'

Public attendance at the show increased by over 300 per cent compared with the previous year, to 10,000 visitors. This was the highest attendance in the show's 89-year history. The impact was not just quantitative: feedback from the public was very positive. A lot of people came because their children were interested in having a pet, so they were able to see over 200 varieties of rabbit. The races were held three times a day, and people came to the area half an hour early, and were twenty people deep, and so there were talks about the rabbits and people got to meet them. This was an added bonus for Burgess Pet Care, who were able to deliver pet ownership messages to the audience during these times.

The children enjoyed the rabbit jumping because it is not something you see often. It was unusual and triggered an interest amongst people. The majority came because their children wanted to see the rabbit jumping.

Generating good media coverage

There is a tendency when considering how to get media coverage to immediately start with the tools you will use. However, Hitchins (2008) rightly cautions against this and suggests that a framework is required first. He identifies techniques which help create media interest, the tools are only used once the processes are in place. Research conducted by Hitchins (2000) constructed a template for such a framework:

1 Create news vehicles such as surveys/forecasts.
2 Take advantage of opportunities of media preoccupations (hot topics).
3 Campaigns.
4 Slogans (such as headlines).
5 Talk to the particular needs of each of the media.

Having addressed the basic framework, the tools of the trade include:

- Press releases.
- Interviews.
- Feature articles.
- Pictures.
- Press conferences.
- Open and Awareness Days.

- Stunts.
- Letter writing campaigns.
- Piggybacking.

We will below cover the most important ones you are likely to use.

Writing a press release

Assuming that we have identified a strong news story, there are a number of ways that a release can be constructed, but I suggest that a coherent framework is required. This is made up of:

Layout

- The words 'News Release' or 'Press Release' at the top, typically centred, or you might have headed paper.
- The date.
- Who it is to be given to (i.e. news desk or picture editor) (increasingly this is now on the email not the actual release).
- An embargo time (a strict limit on when the information can be used). Use only rarely – most releases are 'For immediate release.'

Structure

Press releases normally follow a simple formula:

- An attention grabbing headline in bold or slightly bigger type (but do not try to be too clever – just sum up the story to the journalist, as a sub-editor will probably re-write it).
- An opening paragraph of the five Ws: Who?-What?-When?-Where?-Why?.
- A second paragraph outlining your case very briefly.
- Subsequent paragraphs, either making additional but less central points, or quotes of the opinions of a spokesperson.
- Finish with the words 'ENDS' – the journalist knows that the story is now finished.
- Always have 'Contact Details', which should have contact name, telephone number(s) and email for further information. To help control the process only have one person as contact (yourself normally).
- Lastly, include 'Editor's Notes', listing background facts or the existence of photographs, etc. Does not include opinion. It should always include what is in the jargon (though not in your release) referred to as the 'boiler plate' – a short sentence about the event/host organisation and any main sponsors/partners. In effect, this is the corporate message they want to get across.

General rules

Journalists receive dozens of press releases each day. To stand out your press release needs to be easy to read, and there must be a news story contained, tailored to the needs of their viewers, listeners or viewers:

- The most important paragraph is the first one. In a maximum of 35 words you need to explain the – Who?-What?-When?-Where?-Why? The journalist will then decide whether there is a story or will bin your press release.

- Occasionally you cannot fit all five Ws into 35 words. When this is the case, I would start the second paragraph with the Why?
- Paragraphs should be in order of importance to the story. This is sometimes referred to as the 'inverted pyramid' (see, for example, Gordon 2011). If it adds nothing to the story, don't include it.
- Use quotes when you can, but try to make them snappy and interesting (typically I use two). If you have a sponsor or event partner, normally they would expect to be quoted (agree the release and their quote with them).
- Write in such a way that a non-expert can understand what you are saying – avoid jargon or complex language.
- Paragraphs should only be 40–50 words in length, but do not be afraid of one sentence paragraphs.
- Use double or 1.5 line spacing to allow journalists to make notes.
- Different countries have different norms, but as a rule get it on 1–2 sides.
- Typically your release is likely to be 250–350 words in length. Any less and you probably will not explore the story enough; any more and the journalist may stop reading.
- If you are going to break the rules, know why you are doing so.

Timing

With a little bit of practice most people can write press releases. The more difficult bit is getting it to the right person at the right time. To achieve this you must:

- Find out the deadlines of your target media.
- Do not send it too far in advance of their deadline or your embargo, but neither should you leave it to the last minute. For a daily publication 10 days should be fine, for a weekly then 2–3 weeks, and for monthlies this would normally be 2–3 months.

The release opposite is a good example of how to construct one.

CASE STUDY 9.2

The Burgess Premier Small Animal Show
29th–30th January 2011
Organised by the Bradford Small Livestock Society

Jet-setting bunnies hop to Yorkshire for the UK's first Rabbit Grand National

Yorkshire is host to an unusual sporting spectacle next weekend as the UK's first Rabbit Grand National is held at the Yorkshire Event Centre in Harrogate, on 29–30th January 2011.

British bunnies, including competitors from across the region, have been in training to take on serious International competition from four of Sweden's finest jumpers, who are flying in with their owners for the event.

The rabbit jumping attraction is taking place at the Burgess Premier Small Animal Show, the 'Crufts' of the small animal world, attracting more than 3,000 gerbils, guinea pigs, hamsters, mice, rabbits and rats. Open to the public, the event showcases a trade area which will house a range of stalls selling craft, food and pet products as well as the new Showcase Square Activity Zone, where children's activities will be taking place throughout the weekend.

Show organisers are thrilled to stage the Rabbit Grand National and expect the title of champion to be hotly contested. Thirteen rabbits will take part in the timed display and tackle the course, which is based on horse jumping, but designed to be rabbit friendly. The current world record for the highest jump was set in 1997 by Danish rabbit, Tosen, who jumped almost a metre, and the long jump record was set by another Danish rabbit, Yabo, who hopped an amazing three metres (10ft) in 1999. It is hoped that next weekend's show could be the venue for some more record breaking bunny hops.

Demi Smith, from Wakefield, who is responsible for bringing the competition to the UK, and who will be competing with her rabbit Harley, said: 'The Swedish contingent may feel they have the competitive edge, as the sport originated in Sweden in the late 1970s, but we're confident that we can keep the title on home turf! The rabbit jumping is a fantastic addition to the show and one that is sure to attract a great deal of interest as the craze has captured the imagination of so many small animal lovers.'

Naomi Chatterley, marketing manager at Burgess Pet Care and Small Animal Show sponsor, said: 'Rabbits are natural hoppers of course, and because of their agility, the rabbits love it. It's fun for owners and rabbits alike. These rabbits have been specially trained for rabbit agility and travelling, and while we wouldn't encourage just anyone to do this with their own pet rabbit, it does demonstrate to people who attend the show, or who might be thinking of getting a pet rabbit, just how much exercise and space they do actually need.'

Naomi added: 'We have been working hard to make sure the conditions at the event are a home from home for the stars of the show. Their demands have been quite modest, with just one or two special requirements such as deluxe double-sized pens.'

The rabbit Grand National will take place at intervals throughout the weekend in the main Showcase Square Activity Zone. Visit www.smallanimalshow.co.uk for more information. Tickets to the show are just £7 for adults and £3 children, a family ticket is £18 for two adults and three children, entrance for children under five is free. Tickets can be purchased on the door. The show is open from 9.00–17.30 on Saturday and 9.00–16.00 on Sunday.

ENDS.

Notes to Editor

For further information please contact Kirsty O'Connor on (details removed).

About Burgess Pet Care

Burgess Pet Care is a small family-owned Yorkshire business that makes high-quality food for all small furry pets. We work with expert nutritionists, behaviourists and vets to ensure we are leaders in the field of pet nutrition and care. Our products include Burgess Excel, the UK's No. 1 vet recommended food for small animals, as well as Supadog, Supacat, Supahamster, Suparat, Supagerbil, Supaferret.

About Burgess Premier Small Animal Show

Previously the Bradford Championship Show, the newly named Burgess Premier Small Animal Show is the UK's longest running and largest small animal show in the UK. The Small Animal Show brings breeders (or 'fanciers') of gerbils, guinea pigs, hamsters, mice, rabbits and rats under one roof once a year and has been doing so since 1921.

The show is organised by a dedicated committee and run, not as a profit making business, but as a popular tradition and a show held in high regard in the small animal world.

You will have noted from Harold Evans's quote that news is about people, but it is also by people. As a result it is the norm to have a quote from someone involved in your event. Many students assume that the quotes they read in the newspapers are the basis of the journalist talking to the respondent. This may indeed be the case, but probably more common for news like events is that they take the quote from the press release. It is therefore important that you select the correct person to speak publicly on behalf of the event, check that they are happy with what they are saying and that the quote you write on behalf of them adds colour and flavour to the event.

Examples of event press release quotes

Lindy Hume, Sydney's Festival Director, said: 'I'm enormously proud of my third and final Sydney Festival. In 2012 Sydney Festival stepped forward in some exciting new directions and delivered a power-packed program of Australian and international performing arts with the broadest possible physical and emotional impact.

We were particularly thrilled with the response to our program hubs in Redfern and Parramatta.'

> Source release: Sydney Festival 2012 Celebrates Australian creativity, 2 April 2012 (www.sydneyfestival.org.au)

Exhibit Curator Pat Sparkhul commented: 'Pulling from the Festival of Arts Permanent Collection, this show features some of the finest watercolour artists that have exhibited at the festival. We're honoured to have the opportunity to showcase these spectacular pieces.'

> Source release: Festival of Arts Presents: Collections from the Water Show 27 February 2012 (www.lagunafestivalofarts.org)

The 2011 tournament champion Catriona Matthew, from nearby North Berwick, commented: 'It's good to have a different format every so often. It's quite special that the sponsors and their guests get to play more than just the normal Pro-Am, and having a few celebrities is an additional positive.'

> Source Release: Professionals and Celebrities Compete at Aberdeen Asset Management Ladies Scottish Open, 26 April 2012 (www.ladieseuropeantour.com)

As a rule of thumb I always have a quote from someone, and I typically aim for two, and very occasionally have three. You need to make clear their name and job status such as event organiser. Quotes are normally only two sentences, occasionally three, in length. For an event there are often obvious people who should be quoted, such as the owner/organiser, but also there may be partner bodies and they need to have their say. If there are partner organisations check with them all parts of the release, not just their quote and boiler plate.

Your prime purpose is to provide what the journalist wants, our next case study gives you an insight to what an event journalist is looking for.

CASE STUDY 9.3

A journalist's perspective

Event magazine (www.eventmagazine.co.uk) is the UK's leading publication for the event industry. It focuses on all sectors of the live events arena, specifically exhibitions, experiential campaigns and creative events. *Event* focuses on the events created by the world's leading brands and features everyone from the event agencies, venues and suppliers responsible for creating these events.

Approximately a third of *Event*'s online stories originate from press releases, while the rest come from attending events, gossip from other event managers and national news angles. The editorial team will regularly Google the key terms it covers, such as 'events', 'event suppliers' and 'venues' to see what stories are out there.

Event reporter Louise Ridley offers some practical advice on how you can maximise the impact of your press release, and build long-term relationships with key media. Louise suggests:

'Press releases are very important for *Event* as they are a great source of news. Indeed, even if we hear about a story from other sources, we still try to contact the event and get a copy of their release because it is a reliable form of getting news.

The first consideration for using a press release is that events should use it as a form of news. We are looking for all the information about the event, what happened, when did it happen and who is involved with the event as attendees or partners. In short, we need a breakdown of what happened in detail such as number of people, types of equipment/features and any other interesting facts.

What we do not want is events spending too much time on what we call the bumpf, don't tell us that you event was, for example, extravagant we were not there so we do not know whether it was. Rather, show us what it was like by providing as much detail as possible of what happened, that will allow us to make our own conclusions. One of the main Do Not's to avoid is to undersell your event by not providing enough detail.

In terms of writing the release the important information should be at the top of the release. We don't have time to read lots of paragraphs to find out what has happened. We have to make our decisions quickly, often before we reach the bottom of the release.

We would normally like a quote, and a good quote adds to the story. We do not include phrases such as 'we are delighted', 'we are happy to work with our partners', or that 'the event went well'. We assume that all events would say this, so avoid these. What we are looking for is something that adds to our understanding of the event, such as an opinion, something more subjective or something that only the event manager would be in a position to know. For example, that a particular section went well this year, or next year you will do something different instead.

We like to talk to event managers because everyone gets their release, but by talking to them as well we get exclusivity by asking our questions.

A press release is not a one-off, and a good contact for us keeps us updated with what they are doing, and this helps us get to know their company. It is important to build relationships and inviting us to events is a useful way of achieving this. Meeting event managers, if we both have time, is also useful as it helps us put a face to a name. We want to know what people are doing. A basic point is that event managers should ask us what we want, such as how and when do we want information delivered and each publication will be different. We have a rule that we only cover an event online if it is up to two days after the event has finished. If it is three days afterwards we do not use it. It also helps to ask what type of stories a publication is interested in.'

One controversial question is whether you should 'call round' after the release has gone out. Typically a senior manager will say 'What's happened to that release?' and the press officer will be dispatched to phone round the journalists to check. Almost to a person they will be mightily annoyed to receive such calls. Unless you have further news that has just come to light to add to the release, do not chase up journalists after you have sent the release. However, the experienced and clever press officer takes a very different and more successful approach. Produce your release, but do not send it: rather, phone named journalists and talk to them to sell the idea. And only if they appear interested should you send the release: this is a relationship, not press release, based approach. It is more intensive, but by talking to them prior to sending the release you have increased the chance of the story being taken up. In addition, you will gain valuable intelligence on the interests of journalists on your list.

Being interviewed

Being interviewed, or organising interviews for others, is a key part of the role of a press officer. Interviews may be the result of a release you have sent out, or may be a 'cold call' by the journalist because they have worked with you in the past. There are fairly simple rules in providing journalists with what they want. The press release primarily provides information and fact; the interview may add facts and information, but also provides a lot of opinion. However, if a journalist has one 'bad' experience with you, they are unlikely to come back to you next time they have a story requiring comment.

The biggest lesson to learn is that every single time you speak to a journalist assume it is an on-the-record interview. You may think it is a chat, but if you say something interesting or controversial you may find it being reported. Your role with interviews is either to set them up for colleagues, or to be the spokesperson yourself. The three types of interview you are most likely to be involved in are with print journalists (typically on the telephone), radio (telephone, studio or outside broadcast) and television (outside broadcast or studio). Broadcast interviews can be either live or recorded. Although more daunting for the novice interviewee, live interviews actually give you more power because your message cannot be edited.

Key is knowing exactly what you want to say, and then making sure you say it. Do not wait for the question you want to be asked – it may never come. Watch politicians: they are very astute about getting across their message, with tricks such as 'You may think that but actually the key issue is . . .', where they deflect the question and get across their message. Of course, this is easier for politicians than for an event – some questions cannot necessarily be deflected – but it does stress the point of knowing what you want to say. When you first start it is a good idea to jot down the three key messages/points you want to get across. And make sure that you do get them across, almost irrespective of the questions asked. Moreover, always remember that you are the expert, and normally know far more than the person doing the interview.

If you are organising the interview for a colleague, make sure that you get from the journalists the details such as:

- What are they looking to cover in the interview? They are unlikely to give you the questions in advance, but you can get an idea of what the interview will be about.
- When and where do they want the interview conducted?
- Is the interview live or recorded?
- How long will the interview be?
- Who else is going to be interviewed (this is particularly important to ask when a live studio-based interview)?
- When is it going to be broadcast or to be published?

Interviews with print journalists

Journalists frequently phone up to ask for background information or a comment they can use. You do not have to respond immediately. Indeed, you may not be the person they need to speak to – there may be an expert who is more appropriate. Whatever the situation it is perfectly acceptable to say that you will get back to them on this. Therefore, you need to be clear what they are looking for, and more importantly what their timescale is. Gather your thoughts and then phone them back by the time they need the information. If you don't deliver what you promise, they will probably never contact you again.

Broadcast interviews

Whether they are live or pre-recorded, Table 9.1 suggests that there are some basic hints for dealing with television

Most of the tips for the preparation and purpose for television interviews apply to radio interviews. However, the listener cannot see you, and the key to getting across your message is sound and painting a picture with words. Table 9.2 shows what you need to do for this type of interview.

Writing feature articles

After you become experienced with press releases, the next level up is writing a feature article, typically of 600–2,000 words. Where press releases impart hard news, feature articles are primarily about opinion, though the hook can often be about current news stories. Used properly they are a more subtle and potentially more effective means of promoting your organisation/event. Here, you are writing in journalistic style as an expert in a field.

Table 9.1 Conducting a television interview

Key areas	Tips
Preparation	Turn up early so you can get briefed in advance. Chat to the reporter while you are waiting for them to set up, since often they will regurgitate your points as questions as a result
	Never ever drink alcohol before appearing
	If in the studio, watch the stories prior to your appearance: you might be able to relate your answer to one
Appearance	Avoid horizontal stripes: the pixels cannot handle them
	Do not have anything in your hand
	If in the studio, sit upright and put your hands in a comfortable position
	If they offer make-up, take it: you can look shiny and heavier on TV
The camera	Always look at the interviewer not the camera
	Do not allow the cameraman to use angles you feel unhappy with

Table 9.2 Conducting a radio interview

Key areas	Tips
Preparation	Having crib notes in front of you (you cannot do this on TV)
	Sit in a comfortable position so that your diaphragm is not constricted: this helps you speak better
Sound	Have nothing in your hands, and keep bulky/noisy things out of your coat
	Always turn off mobile phones
Body language	Have a note saying 'Breathe': it can help overcome nerves by making you slow down
	Smile and be happy and upbeat. Silly as it might sound, such positive body language will come across in your voice.

Types of feature

- *Case studies* – perhaps where you have done something particularly well.
- *Research studies* – data you have that point to advice for others to follow.
- *Backgrounder* – basic details about your organisation/event, good figures and statistics or practical advice in a field.
- *Link to current news.*

Even more so than press releases feature articles need to be about human interest. For example, Neil Campbell wrote a feature for *The Chap* magazine (23 April 2012) referring to a new sub-cultural trend, Steampunk, which could have an impact on music and art events in the future.

Different types of publication will require different types of feature. You are probably best off starting with a trade publication where you will be writing for a publication and audience you understand well. The most demanding (and difficult to secure) are national broadsheet press.

You can develop feature ideas by:

- Keeping a file of possible ideas – for example, news stories, facts and interesting case histories.
- Making a shortlist of your event interests that you believe you can write about and which will engage the reader.
- Reading features, lifestyle sections and a range of publications to get an idea of the kind of stories they develop as articles.
- Considering whether your idea has a particular angle. Is it fresh and is it timely?

When you write an article the feature editor will want a more detailed written synopsis (effectively a plan). This should include a title, an introduction that sets the scene, your premise, the core facts/arguments, supporting material such as examples, quotes, statistics, and a conclusion.

When writing your feature, use a stand first to set the scene – this is usually one short sentence after the title but before the main text which sums up the article or puts it into current context. The lead paragraph needs to be punchy and interesting and in essence should sum up the angle you are taking. The main body should include key facts, argument and quotations. The feature editor expects a professionally written piece, so avoid puffery, and at most include only one or two quotes from your organisation – you get a mention at the end typically in the form of contact details and website address. The conclusion should sum up your point of view, and normally should link very closely with the lead paragraph. Feature editors nearly always want photos to go with copy, therefore try and get some pictures taken to accompany your text.

Using pictures

An old axiom states that a picture is worth a thousand words. The good press officer thinks about combining words and pictures to make a more effective message. Journalists are always looking for pictures to help illuminate news stories and feature articles. If your event has occurred before, you are in a powerful position to use previous action photographs to accompany your press releases. For example, the annual Street Machine Summernats Car Festival (www.summernats.com.au) uses pictures both of the cars in their different competitions, but also of the crowd experience. This gives a sense both of the action, but also what the impact is on those attending. With a more B2B audience the International Film Festival on Tourism Films (www.tourfilm.cz) takes a slightly different approach, which stresses the high quality of what attendees get. Those events aiming primarily at a B2C audience are more likely to stress emotion and excitement and being part of a crowd, whereas B2B are more likely to stress the rational message of the quality of the experience.

You should build up a stock of background pictures. For example, of your senior personnel, organisation's activities and what happens at your events. Unless you have a very good amateur, always pay professional photographers to take these background pictures. You also need to introduce an organised library system so you can quickly access pictures. When you are emailing out a press release, as a basic principle attach a picture (usually in jpeg format) and a caption of what/who it shows.

Letter writing campaigns

For certain types of event, letter campaigns to local and sometimes national newspapers can be a very useful way of raising attention. Here 'Letters to the Editor' from people may point out the importance of your event. This is especially so if your event is for a cause, charity or campaign. Indeed, pressure group Save Our America's Forests (www.saveamericasforests.org) suggests that letter writing campaigns can be particularly effective at promoting political events designed to mobilise support.

The importance of letters to the editor is not just initiating a letter writing campaign yourself: monitoring of newspapers may allow you to identify and respond to a potential problem, such as local concerns over parking caused by your event. A slightly different example was that of a resident in Auckland, New Zealand, who complained about the lyrics of rap-collective Odd Future who were subsequently dropped from the Big Day Out tour show in Auckland (Nzherald 2011). Scanning the media enables you to gain feedback and instantly rebut criticisms.

Targeting your media

You may have the most brilliant story and a well written release, but unless it goes to the right media at the correct time all your efforts will be wasted. Targeting is central to your success in generating media coverage. Figure 9.1, the Media Terrain, identifies the different types of media that may help you reach your key audiences. Although there are seven different categories, these can be based around three types of media: print (newspapers and magazines); broadcast (radio; television); and the Internet. While the detail in different countries will be distinct, this provides a framework for identifying which medium to select.

Newspapers and magazines

Local newspapers offer a very good way of promoting your event, and they are always looking for local angles. They will cover anything as long as it is local. This can mean the story is local or that there is a local slant on a national story. For example, your organisation might be organising a golf tournament for charity, or a member of your staff might have achieved national recognition for some work or non-work activity. Not all countries have a tradition of a national press, but as with the UK there are newspapers whose focus is national and

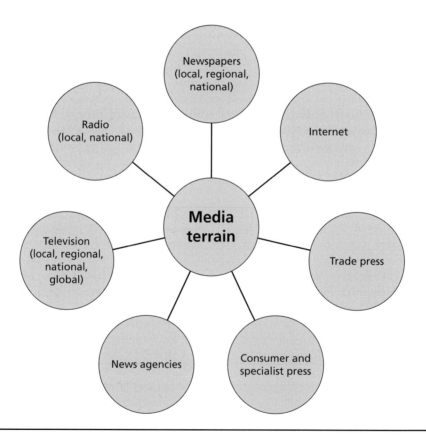

Figure 9.1 The media terrain

international. These are the most difficult to get coverage from for your event, in part because of competition to get it, but also because they want a national story.

The trade press is a colloquial term for publications, typically but not always in magazine format, that are concerned with all matters relating to a particular profession. As a consequence the readership is practitioners in that profession/industry, not consumers. The content will, therefore, cover in detail a range of aspects of an industry, such as who is doing well, what is happening and what are the developing trends. For example, the trade press for events includes *Event Magazine* (UK), *Australia Special Events Magazine* (Australia) and *Mid-Atlantic Events Magazine* (US). Depending on your event field other trade press might also be relevant, such as *Sport Business*, *Canadian Musician* and *Politics Magazine*. Your trade press will be read by competitors, suppliers but also buyers, and so it can be a good way of getting out good news stories about your organisation or event which will impress those who understand your field. This might help recruit staff, shape your reputation and generate new business.

Broadcast

Countries have different traditions for radio broadcasting. Some have mainly a very local radio system, some only a national one and others have a combination of both. Do not target just the news desk – your event might well interest the producer of a specialist programme.

Probably the hardest to get coverage from is television, especially at national level. Again, as with radio, countries have different traditions: in the US public broadcast is a fairly low-key local affair, but in many European countries it is at national level. When you send out your release to a broadcaster, if they like the event they will put it on their forward plan. And then, on the day, they will decide where they send their outside broadcast crews, which makes their attendance more of a lottery if a big news story comes along, such as a major accident or terrorist attack.

Internet

We deal with the Internet in Chapter 11. It is worth noting here, however, that it can act as a megaphone allowing events to repeat messages sent out by other media, but it is also a discrete communication channel. In particular, it enables your event to reach a younger audience, and one with a higher level of education and income. The uses and gratifications literature (Luo 2002) suggests that those online are particularly interested in gaining information and in being entertained.

News agencies

While you would normally try to contact journalists direct, a complementary route is to send your release to a news or picture agency, who may then try to sell the idea to media outlets you do not know exist. News agencies are commercial operations of journalists who supply news to broadcasters and print publications, and they may use your release to achieve this. For example, when professional diver Professor Splash dived 30 feet (10 metres) into 12 inches (30 cm) of milk at the Royal Cornwall Show in June 2012, it was agency photographers who took the pictures that were used the next day in the national newspapers. Internationally Reuters, the Press Association and United Press International are well known. But you are more likely to deal with those that are regionally based near you, such as South West News Service, and others that specialise in particular fields such as Snowdon Sports.

Practical checklist

- Practise writing releases – practice makes perfect.
- Construct a mechanism for capturing news stories. This might be a dedicated meeting, walking around talking to people, or a regular agenda item.
- Keep a log book that records which media you spoke to and the result.
- If you or some of your colleagues are being interviewed regularly by broadcast media, consider getting training – it will pay off.
- Have a press page on your website with your latest press releases.
- Produce 'action' photographs, not just head and shoulders.
- Press release pictures tend to be more action and people based; marketing brochures can be more product feature based.
- Keep a record of where the originals of your pictures are.
- Work on your database of contacts – build this up.
- Target key journalists, and seek to build a relationship with them. Do not rely just on press releases.
- Monitor what happened to your release. Learn by noting how journalists wrote it up.
- Arrange to meet journalists or invite them to your event.

Our final case study exercise sets a range of problems for how you could use media relations for the market leader in a crowded event field.

Case study exercise

CASE STUDY 9.4

Promoting the Apple Festival

Brogdale Farm (www.brogdale.org) based near Faversham in Kent is the home of the UK's national fruit collection. This includes over 3,500 named apple, pear, plum, cherry, bush fruit, vine and cob nut cultivars, which means that it has more varieties of fruits than any other collection in the world. The orchards cover more than 160 acres, and in 2012 Brogdale celebrated its Diamond Jubilee (50 years).

Brogdale offers courses, workshops, seasonal walks and daily visits, and the venue hosts meetings and parties indoors and outside. It has a number of events from spring (April) through to autumn (October). The large events are the Festivals, which last a whole weekend, such as the Cherry (July), Cider (September) and Apple (October) Festivals. The small events are Days, such as Soft Fruit Day (June), Plum Day (August) and Nut Day (September).

The Apple Festival took place over the weekend of 20–21 October 2012, and was open from 10 a.m. to 5 p.m. each day. Attendees got the opportunity to taste and buy some of the 2,200 apple varieties grown. Some of those available for tasting included old or unusual ones not normally available, such as Greasy Pippin, Old Fred and Smiler.

Activities include:

- Fruit tasting.
- Children's Storyteller.
- Alpacas (Saturday Only).
- Hook an Apple, and Splat the Maggot.
- Live music.
- Feature Classic Car.
- Craft and local produce stalls.
- Orchard tours, tractor trailer tours, and walks.

Prices are:

- £8.00 Adults (£7.00 Group Rate – 10+ people)
- £20.00 Families (2 adults & children)

The target audience is those interested in gardening, especially fruit, and families looking for something to do outdoors. Brogdale is in Kent, and so geographically fairly easy to get to by car from London and the rest of the South East.

Your task:

1 There are hundreds of apple festivals throughout the UK. How will you make this one stand out?
2 What sort of broadcast shows might be interesting in piggybacking on to the event (so broadcasting some aspect of their programme live from the venue)?
3 When would you send out your first press release?
4 What types of print publication would you target?
5 What quirky or interesting features from this event might be attractive to the media?

Discussion questions

This chapter highlights that the use of media relations raises some key issues:

1   What are the requirements for setting up your media relations operation?
2   In what circumstances would you use a press release?
3   How would you evaluate the effectiveness of a press release?
4   What is the best way of spicing up the media relations of an established event?

Further information

Other sources which might help you consider the issues outlined in this chapter include:

Websites

http://shaa.com/ – boxing promoter and entrepreneur.
http://www.youtube.com/watch?v=wOptT637vSY – event manager being interviewed for an
   in-house video.
http://www.youtube.com/watch?v=JVMpDb57l6Q – event manager being interviewed at World
   Sports Destination Expo.
http://scouts.org.uk/supportresources/593/public-relations-activity-
   badge/?cat=7,64,172&moduleID = 10 – The Scout Association public relations activity
   badge.
http://www.entrepreneur.com/article/159484 – creating a stunt.

Chapter 10

Corporate public relations – building your reputation

Introduction

Given that many event organisers do not automatically consider the importance of Corporate Public Relations (CPR), this chapter will start by explaining what corporate reputation is, and why it is important for events. This will include an assessment of corporate identify and image, and what impact they can have on key stakeholders. We will then address the core areas of CPR activity: issues management; acting in a socially responsible way; crisis management; government relations and internal communications. Throughout we shall link these activities to key strategic issues.

By the end of this chapter students will be able to:

- Define corporate reputation.
- Identify the core audiences for CPR.
- Assess the importance of corporate reputation.
- Evaluate the main tools of CPR.

Defining corporate public relations

The driving philosophy behind CPR is the importance of reputation management (Hutton *et al.* 2001). CPR tools include community relations, issues management, crisis management, corporate social responsibility, investor relations, corporate advertising and lobbying. Ultimately, CPR focuses not on promoting a specific individual campaign, but the overall reputation of an organisation (Fombrun 1995; Griffin 2008; Cornelissen 2008). The purpose of CPR is to assess all factors which might favourably or adversely impact upon the corporate reputation of an event. This also includes those who associate with your event, such as artistes and sponsors. In essence, you are trying to shape what people (irrespective of whether they attend or not) think about your event, and sometimes your partners.

Although CPR is responsible for a smaller slice of the public relations budget than MPR, at some 30–40 per cent (Moloney 2006) it is considered more strategic and consequently of greater importance than MPR. Viewed as the domain of senior management, CPR addresses the image of a company as a whole. The focus is primarily on corporate logo, name and overall branding/impression. What we are looking at is the reputation of an event, host organisation and sponsors, and how to manage this. The term 'corporate' comes from the Latin word for body – a corporation is a group of individuals acting as one. However, we need to bear in mind that we are not talking about just a company's reputation: it can also apply to non-commercial organisations such as governments, charities and NGOs (Non-Governmental Organisations). The reputation of an event depends as much on the strength of its corporate brand/image, as it does on the quality of its products and services.

Corporate reputation

Event communicators are very good at north/south visibility in terms of customers, suppliers, artistes and the like (see Figure 7.1), but not necessarily so good at east/west visibility in terms of political, economic and social audiences which might come from the side to undermine their event. Reputation may appear an intangible and woolly concept, but a number of commentators, prime amongst whom is Fombrun (1995), believe that corporate reputation affects the bottom line of company profitability. Indeed, Fombrun suggests that the value the stock market ascribes to companies largely reflects the reputation of that organisation. For events, the concept of corporate reputation raises an issue which is not relevant to other fields: Is the reputation we are referring to that of an individual event, a series of events or the host/owner of the event? The answer is clearly all of these, and this complicates how we understand event reputation management.

Definition box 10.1

Defining corporate reputation

Corporate reputation is what people think of an event. They do not even have to have attended it in order to have an opinion, though the views of some audiences might be more important than others. There need not be one single view on an event's reputation, but a simple test is to state an event name and see what the initial response is. Corporate reputation is a hard-to-pin-down concept, but it can be good, bad or indifferent and can be shaped by ethical behaviour, corporate governance and the event itself. It is influenced by all deliberate and unintended communication to and from an event.

The corporate reputation of an organisation includes its image and branding. Whilst there is no clearly agreed single definition (Gotsi and Wilson 2001), the focus on reputation implies that public relations is used persuasively to shape the opinion of both narrowly defined key audiences and wider public opinion, so communication is both narrowcast and broadcast. The assumption behind this approach is that a concept as intangible as reputation, can actually have a tangible effect on an organisation's operations, revenue and bottom line (Fombrun 1995; Gray and Balmer 1998; Fombrun and Van Riel 2004; Griffin 2008). In essence, corporate reputation is designed to develop a competitive advantage for both commercial and not-for-profit sector organisations (Doorley and Garcia 2007). The ultimate aim is the long-term survival of that event/organisation.

The remit of reputation management is essentially strategic, and so seeks to reach beyond just consumers (Oliver 2007; Griffin 2008). So while consumers can indeed be a target, they are not always, and there are others such as local politicians, residents' groups and expert commentators, who may be more important at certain points of the event cycle. For example, during the legislative process of what became the 2010 Bribery Act, a vital audience of many corporate hospitality event hosts was, probably for the first time ever, individual politicians, government ministers and senior civil servants. While generally such lobbying would be done collectively and not by individual event managers, the fear was that the terms of the Act could literally wipe out the corporate hospitality industry in the UK. However, following lobbying, further legal guidance was issued which took concerns into account (Parry 2011). Another common scenario, especially for a new event, is the importance of gaining the support, or at least acquiescence, of local residents, because without it the event might not actually happen. Recognising the importance of reputation management opens up the event communicator to new audiences.

A wide range of tools is used including issues management, community affairs and corporate social responsibility (CSR). This emphasis reflects Regester and Larkin's (2008) view that corporate reputation is influenced more by what an organisation does than by what it says. The implication is that corporate reputation is not merely the concern of the public relations department, but of the whole organisation (Gray and Balmer 1998). Indeed, Lewis (2001) notes that corporate reputation is influenced not by individual public relations activity, but by the actions and policies of the whole organisation. This is especially so with a transient body like an event. The importance of organisation policy is not a new idea, Arthur Page was associated with it when he joined AT&T (American Telephone and Telegraph) in 1927, but it is only in the last twenty years or so that it has been widely understood in strategic terms. The corporate reputation tools that the event communicator uses are designed to change the opinion of all stakeholders of an event.

Genasi (2002) suggests that there are five main reasons why corporate reputation is growing in importance:

1 The death of deference – people are far less accepting of the actions and views of those in power, politically, commercially or socially, which creates new challenges for communicators.
2 More media channels and outlets – changes in the breadth and quality of media bring massive challenges to those who manage reputation.
3 Me, first and foremost – the role of the individual in society has grown, so that commercial and non-commercial organisations have increasingly to listen to the views of individuals.
4 Fast news – reputation managers now swim in a reputation fish bowl. Positive and negative views about an event or its hosts and sponsors can be circulated globally very quickly.
5 The importance of money – organisations need to gain the trust of consumers.

This suggests that there is a range of social and technological changes that means consumers will expect more from events. At the same time they have more opportunities of gaining information about an event, which shapes their view of it.

There are plenty of anecdotal examples of business leaders talking about the importance of reputation. One typical example is from Alan Greenspan (1999, cited in Hannington 2004: 1), when Chairman of the US Federal Reserve, and so probably at the time the single person with the greatest impact on the world economy. He recognised the importance of reputation. He stated

In today's world, where ideas are increasingly displacing the physical in the production of economic value, competition for reputation becomes a significant driving force, propelling our economy forward. Manufactured goods often can be evaluated before the completion of a transaction. Service providers, on the other hand, can usually offer only their reputations.

This means that, primarily, consumers are not buying into the components of your event *per se* but rather their perception of whether you will deliver what they want. Lose your reputation and you do not have a viable event.

It may be more difficult for some events to have a good reputation – perhaps because they are associated with celebrity and seen as fluffy, or they damage the environment in some way. However, for most events a good corporate reputation is shaped by being a good event to work for, having clear leadership and strong actions and deeds, and not just words. The International Olympic Committee's (IOC) reputation suffered after allegations of corruption in the allocation of the 2002 Salt Lake City Winter Olympics (Wenn and Martyn 2006). Subsequent to this the IOC made significant changes, including to its governance, so that the selection of Olympic venues was not in the hands of a small unaccountable group. Now, more than ten years later, the IOC has a much improved reputation.

CPR's target audience

As implied above, the audience of CPR is primarily a small number of important decision makers, and also secondarily a larger body of consumers and even non-attendees who are part of the background noise of reputation. Figure 10.1 shows not only the types of target audience CPR includes, but divides them into two groups with differing levels of priority. Where marketing's audience is often prioritised based on numbers, this is not the case with CPR.

We are primarily focusing on powerful bodies who are either affected by our event, or who in turn can affect it. At the same time we cannot ignore consumers, though they are likely to be a secondary audience. What Figure 10.1 suggests is that choosing our audiences shapes the strategy we take. Those events which emphasise a small number of key audiences are likely to

Target audience

Select audiences
Pressure groups
Government and government agencies
The media
Expert opinion formers
Event sector – suppliers and competitors

Mass audiences
Consumers
Potential consumers
The general public

Strategy

Reputation focused
Happy employees
Impression management
Dialogue
Policy development
Engagement with external audiences

Product focused
Supply chain
Identify consumers' needs
Deliver what consumers want

Figure 10.1 Key CPR audiences

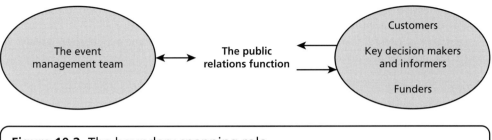

Figure 10.2 The boundary spanning role

follow a reputation based strategy. Those events which focus on mass audiences take a product focus, in effect they use MPR.

To facilitate reputation building with external audiences the public relations professional plays a boundary spanning role. As Figure 10.2 shows, rather than just promoting what the event wants to say, the boundary spanner also assesses what others think of the event, and if need be recommends changing event policies, behaviour and messages. An event needs to take into account the impact on its reputation of its words, and especially its actions.

Issues management

We start deliberately with issues management, because there is limited evidence that events take this seriously as a core part of their public relations. Yet effectively managing potential issues is probably the single most important thing that can shape an event's reputation. When issues are not handled well, they frequently become crises. In part, therefore, issues management is about how we avoid a crisis. Event managers are generally very good at handling internal audiences, contractors and consumers, but not necessarily other stakeholders, who may in fact be more important even though they are not actually attending the event. For example, you might persuade consumers that yours is an excellent event to attend, but local residents may be so concerned about the resulting noise pollution, or whatever, that they get their local councillors involved, and before you know it you might be faced with the reality of the council or other statutory bodies threatening to close your event. Face-to-face conversations with local resident associations or councillors early on in the process may solve such potential problems. And you might then convert potential opponents into allies.

The Taste of London Festival (www.tastefestivals.com/london) conducts issues management with key audiences. For example, each year it invites the Mayor of London, Boris Johnson. At a different level it has meetings with local residents and the Regent's Park community. This might address respecting residents' concerns, and helping to take care of the park. There are a lot of people and bodies the event organisers need to keep friendly with.

The difficulty for us is that where it is fairly easy to know when an event has suffered a crisis, the inherent nature of successful issues management is that we are not often aware of what has happened. Issues management is often played out away from the public gaze in private meetings, it is therefore often a hidden ground. The case study at the end of this chapter, Beach Break Live, is a good example of how an event has learnt its lesson well and now employs an impressive issues management strategy.

Before we can assess issues management we need to identify what is an issue, and what might be the source of one. L'Etang (2008: 75) defines an issue as: *'A topic of debate, trend or a recurring theme that moves from the private sphere to the public sphere.'* So an issue has a meaning or importance to someone, and they seek to get it addressed.

Issues may be general to all industries and organisations, and some may be more specific to events. The possible sources of issues include:

- *Proposed legislation* – such as relating to ambush marketing or licensing hours.
- *Litigation* – unhappy customers or negligence from event staff.
- *Poor corporate governance* – for example, how the IOC allocated the 2002 Winter Games.
- *Organisational change* – changes in the management of the Dew Tour (http://www. allisports.com/dew-tour);
- *Political change* – the Arab Spring of 2011 may make some countries such as Egypt more attractive as an event host.
- *Economic necessity* – especially tourism based events.
- *Demographic change* – an ageing population has different leisure interests.
- *New technologies* – the development of hybrid and online events.
- *Changes to leisure time* – when and how people want to be entertained and relax.

Table 10.1 suggests that we must approach the concept of issues management at two different levels. As an event organiser we may face some specific issues, such as relations with residents, staff and funding. Yet we must also be aware that events can be a means of addressing issues that face an organisation, such as managing change, encouraging social responsibility and generally addressing overall reputation.

Issues management is widely considered to be first associated with American public relations practitioner, W. Howard Chase (Jacques 2008). In 1977 Chase and his partner Barry Jones developed their Issues Management Process Model so that companies could identify and respond to emerging issues before they became public knowledge. Jones and Chase (1979) felt that most companies responded after the fact, and brought public relations in as a tactical tool to 'fight fires'. Issues management was a response to criticisms of business activity, and they felt that companies needed to act as advocates, recognising the impact within wider public

Table 10.1 The relevance of issues for events

Issues facing events	Issues that events can help address
Ownership	Demonstrate social responsibility
Stakeholder relations – especially local communities	Address staff morale
Quality of staff	Manage change management
Evaluation systems	Corporate governance and transparency
Generating sufficient funds	Consumer relations
Participant relations	Enhance expert credibility
Suppliers and contractors	Community relations
Legal and political requirements	Mobilise support for campaigns

policy of their actions. Chase believed that within any company there exists a group of individuals with the network of relationships that could alert the organisation early on as to when an issue was brewing. Initially, issues management was American led and focused on the business community, but it has now broadened so that non-profit organisations, high-profile individuals/celebrities and events now need to consider what issues might affect them. The concept of issues management assumes that society has an impact on business, organisations and events, and therefore the concerns of society needed to be taken into account.

Issues management is not crisis management: rather, it is about identifying a small number, say 3–6, of issues at any one time which may have an impact on an event. While it is often assumed that events management is only about what could go wrong, it can also help identify opportunities. For example, talking to consumers could identify a new event market. Regester and Larkin (2008) suggest that effective issues management requires a different approach to considering problems. They suggest that as a boundary spanner the public relations person is in a position to interpret both what the organisation wants to achieve, and also what external stakeholders want. To achieve this they advocate outside-in thinking, so instead of starting with what the event wants, they believe that the event communicator should consider what outside stakeholders think of the event, and what they want from it, and then consider how to deliver this. This requires not only identifying key audiences, the importance of policy formulations and societal norms, but also taking into account ethical concerns.

A typical method, as recommended by Regester and Larkin (2008) to issues management is a step-by-step approach:

1   Anticipate issue and establish priorities.
2   Analyse issues.
3   Recommend an organisational position on the issue.
4   Identify publics/opinion formers who can help you achieve your position.
5   Identify desired behaviour of publics/opinion formers.

The event communicator needs to use a risk audit to identify the key issues they might expect to face, such as local opposition to the event occurring, attitudes of local council officials and the vagaries of the weather. Having identified the possible issues they may face, the event communicator needs to consider how they will manage them. Figure 10.3 suggests an easy step-by-step way of managing any issues facing your event.

Acting socially responsible

Acting in a socially responsible way is typically equated with corporate social responsibility (CSR), which is a specific tool designed to demonstrate that an event is adopting this approach. However, it can be a wider concept which addresses how an event responds to the society in which it exists. So on the one hand social responsibility is important because it demonstrates how an event interacts with others, but events themselves can also be a means by which other organisations can be seen to be socially responsible. For example, McDonald's has introduced it McDonald's Community Awards (http://www.mcdonalds.co.uk/ukhome/Sport/Football/Inspiration/fa-community-awards.html), where it seeks to support grassroots football in the UK.

There will indeed be events which are inherently philanthropic in nature, where the organisers want an event to address ethical issues such as global warming. However, for most event organisers the decision to be socially responsible is probably a response to one, or more, of three forces:

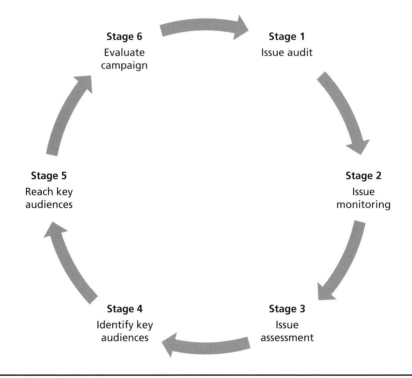

Figure 10.3 The event issues management process

1 Avoiding government legislation or intervention – this is in effect fear of political action if an industry, or event industry, does not put its house in order.

2 Consumers may demand a more socially responsible event from organisers. In particular, there has been the growth of an educated, higher income group of 'articulate consumers' whose purchase decisions are not just based on price.

3 Acting responsibly is perceived to have a positive effect on the reputation of an event.

Events are part of the society in which they operate. The assumption behind acting in a socially responsible way is that events need to consider their corporate behaviour as part of their role in society. However, we can also consider the impact of wider political-economic developments shaping whether social responsibility is at the forefront of business and organisational behaviour. Figure 10.4 identifies different political-economic orthodoxies within the Western world. While there can be grey areas between them, they set the scene for the political and economic work in which events sit. For example, Milton Friedman is probably best known for the phrase: *'The business of business is business.'* When this neo-liberal approach was dominant, subscribing politicians did not expect businesses to put much back into society. However, events play a role in this approach, for mega- and hallmark events are a means of getting access to markets. Conversely, the stakeholder approach encouraged social responsibility by businesses, which in turn encouraged the sponsoring of community events. Indeed, Foley *et al.* (2009b) suggest that events are a means by which socially disadvantaged groups can be helped.

Another way of viewing issues management is offered by Peach (1987), who likens the effect of an organisation on the communities within which it operates to a stone dropping into a

Liberalism	Keynesianism	Neo-liberalism	Stakeholder perspective	The future?
Nineteenth century, early twentieth century	1930s–1980s	1960s–1990s	1990s–early 00s	Early 00s onwards
Emphasis on market economy	Use of government to help manage the economy Associated with John Maynard Keynes and F. D. Roosevelt's New Deal	Reduce state interference in the economy Associated with Milton Friedman, Ronald Reagan and Margaret Thatcher	Transparent business practice, takes into account a range of perspectives Associated with the Third Way of Bill Clinton and Tony Blair	The Green Agenda? Crusty conservatism of David Cameron?

Figure 10.4 The impact of political philosophy

pond. As Figure 10.5 shows, level one equates with the neo-liberal view that businesses should behave legally and pay their taxes. Level two recognises that it may be to an organisation's benefit to be considered by others as acting in a socially responsible way to some degree. At this level they seek to minimise negative effects and act in the spirit of the law. Level three is less common, but Peach argues that it is not a luxury – it should guide the company into a new way of thinking about all aspects of its activities. Here, companies recognise that they have a responsibility for a healthy society. This last level is consistent with the stakeholder perspective, which raises the question of how applicable this model will be in the near future.

CSR is one of the fastest developing trends in the commercial world. Our first case study highlights what may well become a growth area for events.

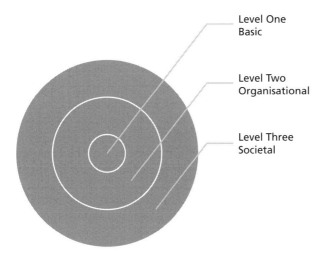

Level One
Basic

Level Two
Organisational

Level Three
Societal

Figure 10.5 Impact of a business on its environment
(Adapted from Peach 1987: 191–3, cited in Kitchen 1997: 129)

CASE STUDY 10.1

Using corporate social responsibility within events

MCI (www.mci-group.com), a communications and event management company with offices in forty-five cities worldwide, has introduced a number of CSR policies about its own behaviour, and has a CSR Director within the organisation. The assumption is that MCI should grow its business sustainably and responsibly in a way that supports communities and safeguards the environment. The focus of this activity is clearly on the external impact of MCI's own activities, but it also advises clients on how they can implement CSR for their events.

For example, at the UN Global Compact Leaders Summit 2010: Building a New Era of Sustainability, MCI performed audits and verifications of the sustainability performance of the hotel, venue, caterers, food and beverage suppliers and transportation suppliers.

MCI makes clients aware of its relevance, and will advise how events can implement a CSR initiative or strategy for an event. Clients may initially be interested, but at times, however, the detail of what can be done and then the costs associated with the said activity may see the item shift to a lower priority on their agenda. For example, there are very simple and not very costly measures, such as using recyclable materials and local produce, but when you start to expand into the more detailed areas of CSR, which can have a significant cost associated to their implementation, clients can at times pick the easy option at less cost. Often it comes down to objectives – for example, if they are looking to achieve a form of accreditation and it has its own agenda item, then CSR within events is taken far more seriously by clients.

Handling an event crisis

Many practitioners believe that events management can be equated to crisis management, that something will always go wrong. Yet, at the same time most event managers do not strategically address how to avoid, prepare for and manage any crises their event may suffer. There can be a direct relationship with issues management, that issues which are not managed properly become a crisis. However, some crises have nothing to do with issues: for example, if you have an event and there is a terrorist attack, a major transport system malfunction, or a World War II unexploded bomb is found, people may not be able to get to your event. You have not caused the crisis, but you have to respond to it.

Some crises may have a slow build-up, which allows you to plan and respond with sufficient time for a considered response. For example, if your staff are unhappy with their terms and conditions, you should find time to address this before they announce a strike during your event. However, other crises such as those created by fire, earthquake or plane crash, are all sudden, giving you little time to respond. The timing, and how much notice you have, can

Table 10.2 Types of event crisis

Type of crisis	Event application
Act of God	Adverse weather conditions Traffic crashes and jams Public transport delays
Negligence	Failure to meet legal standards or duty of care Failure to meet event operation standards Absence of insurance, risk assessment and other required policies
Victim of criminal behaviour	Criminals on site, such as pickpockets Terrorism

therefore determine how you prepare and what you do. Table 10.2 outlines some of the types of crisis you may have to respond to.

The perception of who is at fault will influence how successful you are at handling a crisis. If you are perceived to be at fault, due to negligence by you or your staff, such as not following your emergency plans, then this will make it more difficult for you to handle the crisis. However, if you are considered the victim of criminal action by others, or it is what insurance companies refer to as an 'act of God' you will have the goodwill of most of the people affected. For example, severe weather conditions meant that the 2007 New Year (Hogmanay) celebrations in Edinburgh, had to be cancelled at the last minute, disappointing some 100,000 expected attendees, plus those hoping to attend a concert headlined by the Pet Shop Boys. However, it was widely recognised that the organisers had no option.

We will assess three approaches to crisis management: crisis planning; the importance of corporate culture; and relationship building.

The orthodox view, and the normal starting point for handling a crisis, is to construct a crisis plan. Such a plan will identify what can go wrong, suggest actions to avoid this, but will also recognise that this will not be 100 per cent successful. The plan identifies who should do what in crisis situations, such as key spokespeople, and how information will be filtered to targeted internal and external audiences. It will also identify who needs what training such as media handling, and whether any equipment is required. One of the key areas is to assess how those who could be affected, such as staff, participants and spectators, gain their information about an event. A crisis plan is not a panacea guaranteeing success, but it helps an event prepare should things go wrong.

Looking at constructing a crisis plan for a youth sporting event Kronin (undated) identified five steps:

1 Identify the roles of those involved with handling a crisis.
2 Access accurate information.
3 Create an algorithmic approach to medical management.
4 Promote standards for documenting the incident.
5 Review the crisis.

Kronin recognises that this is designed for amateur sport for young people, but it does indicate the importance of identifying key systems around communication, health care and clear responsibilities. To this we can add for many entertainment based events crowd management.

The second approach is to suggest that while a good starting point, plans alone are not enough. An event needs to consider its communication culture. Francis Marra (2000) found that organisations with crisis plans did not always handle a crisis well, and that conversely some without a plan did. In order to explain this apparent paradox Marra suggested that how they communicated in normal circumstances had an effect on how they handled a crisis. A closed organisation that did not normally communicate well, such as by avoiding transparency, would behave the same way in a crisis, whilst an organisation with an open communication culture would reach stakeholders during a crisis. An event's normal day-to-day handling of communication is a strong indicator of how well it will perform during a crisis.

A third approach suggests that whilst a plan and communication culture are important, they do not necessarily take into account what an organisation has done to shape wider opinion of them. Coombs (1999) suggests that relationships shape perceptions of the crisis and of the organisation in crisis. So if your event has a strong reputation with the local community, built up over a number of years, you are more likely to come out of a crisis with your reputation intact, even if you are culpable. However, if your previous reputation was poor, this will reflect badly on how successful you are in handing the impact of the crisis. The relationship building approach to crisis management is a long-term approach, where events seek to build a 'favours bank' with key audiences, which they can 'cash in' during a crisis.

During a crisis situation, handling the media can be vital, and they are likely to focus on the impact of a crisis in the following order:

1 People
2 The wider environment/communities
3 Property
4 Money

You might be primarily concerned with the financial effect on your event, but the media normally will not be, and you need to recognise this.

At the beginning of a crisis the media will normally be neutral towards you – they will just want to get the story. First questions from the media might include:

● What happened?
● Why did it go wrong?
● Who is accountable?
● What is the situation right now?
● What will you do to stop this occurring again?

To manage your crisis effectively you need to address information flows and relationship building. You should monitor what the media are saying, and respond or rebut them if necessary. At the beginning of a crisis you should avoid an information void – if you say nothing then the rumour mill takes over. If the media feel you are being obstructive, or are wholly at fault, their attitude will become hostile. This does not mean that you say anything or make things up, but you can clearly state, for example, your sympathy for any victims, that you will find out what went wrong and make sure it cannot happen again.

Government relations

An event manager cannot ignore the many public policies and regulations that affect them.

Known as government relations, public affairs or political lobbying, this is where organisations seek to influence decision makers either to change public policy, or alternatively to stop public policy being changed. Critics suggest that lobbying is 'influence peddling' (Malvern 1985), essentially buying political support and access. But where there are competing interests, it provides a means by which your voice can be heard.

A useful definition of lobbyist was provided by future American President John F. Kennedy when he was a senator in 1956:

> Expert technicians, capable of explaining complex and difficult subjects in a clear understandable fashion. They prepare briefs, legislative analysis and draft legislation, they frequently can provide useful statistics and information not otherwise available.

This means that a lobbyist is a bridge between an organisation and the political world, a boundary spanning role. Lobbying might not appear something of relevance to an event, but as noted by Hall and Rusher (2006: 220): *'Events are hosted in a political world.'* Like it or not, you may be affected directly or indirectly, short or long term, by the wider political system. Typically this would be local government, but the principles of lobbying are the same irrespective of the level you lobby at, be it local, national or transnational government.

The core to lobbying:

● Access to decision makers and influencers.
● Gather information (monitoring).
● Persuade (meetings and briefings).
● Build coalitions.

This means that what you have to offer politicians and officials is access to information, and other ways of looking at a problem.

Each different country will have different approaches to, and rules concerning lobbying, but in essence you need to identify who makes the decision that affects you, and who influences who makes the decision. So looking at the UK the decision maker might be the relevant Secretary of State who sits in the government and his senior officials; those that influence them are MPs, colleagues from the same political party as the minister and other interest groups. The targets of UK lobbying include:

● Westminster (individual politicians).
● Whitehall (government ministers and senior civil servants).
● Local and regional government.
● European Union.
● International bodies.

Possibly belatedly, the events industry in the UK is now lobbying, and our next case study exercise highlights the specific impact of politics on part of the events industry.

CASE STUDY 10.2

Impact of legislation on events – the 2010 Bribery Act

The Bribery Act created four separate offences:

1 Bribery of another person.
2 Being bribed by another.
3 Bribery of foreign public officials.
4 Failure of a commercial organisation to prevent bribery.

'Bribery' is defined broadly to cover any financial 'or other' advantage offered, promised or given by one person to another, where the intention is to induce or reward someone to perform improperly a 'relevant function or activity'. Those offering cash or other benefits provided improperly in a purely commercial, 'business to business' setting could also be caught. This means that an event manager could be convicted not only of themselves bribing someone, but also of turning a 'blind eye' if colleagues do so. It was the term 'improperly' which raised concerns regarding whether corporate hospitality would be determined as bribery.

Individuals convicted of bribery offences could face up to ten years imprisonment and/or an unlimited fine. A director convicted of a bribery offence could also be subject to a director disqualification order under the Company Directors Disqualification Act 1986 which could prevent the individual from being a company director for up to fifteen years.

According to Powell (2011) the Director of the Serious Fraud Office has stated that 'most routine and inexpensive hospitality would be unlikely to lead to a reasonable expectation of improper conduct'. However, lavish or extraordinary hospitality may lead a jury to reach the conclusion that it was intended to induce the recipient to act improperly. The effect of this advice is that the impact on corporate hospitality is likely to be fairly minimal.

Your task

1 Why was this legislation introduced?
2 Why might other countries consider similar legislation? Which countries might these most likely be, and why?
3 What can the events industry do to prevent negative legislation being introduced?
4 Why is the political sphere important to the events industry?
5 How might you campaign to build support for new legislation that would help the events industry?

As a postscript, there is some evidence that this legislation has had some commercial effect. Research conducted by Ernst and Young (King 2012) suggests that 18 per cent of companies have reduced their level of corporate entertainment since the introduction of the Act.

For most event communicators the main political audience will be those within and associated with local government. One reason for lobbying local government is to seek funding. Generally within a worldwide recession this is more difficult. In addition, the event organiser needs to understand the priorities of local government. So in the UK Allen *et al.* (2005) noted a shift in funding away from supporting cultural or sporting events towards those that deliver economic benefits, such as bringing in tourism, creating jobs and the like. In the UK, local authority grants are usually shaped by Local Area Agreements and Local Strategic Partnerships. These identify local priorities, such as children and young people, community safety, health, older people, economic development and environment. For example, Tamworth Borough Council has two strategic priorities: the first is to create and sustain a thriving local economy, and the second is to create a safe environment for local people (http://www.tamworth.gov.uk/council_and_democracy/performance/council_vision,_priorities_and.aspx). Events which could help achieve either of these aims are more likely to secure local council support. Typically, local authorities will seek to fund only those events which support their priorities.

Lobbying events

On 2 July 2005 over 1,000 musicians took part in ten concerts in different parts of the world. Whilst those attending each concert, and the estimated three billion watching on television, will have enjoyed the entertainment, the sole purpose of this event was political. Live 8 was set up by British musician Bob Geldof to bring people together to fight extreme poverty, with its subtitle 'The Long Walk to Justice' clearly stating its aim. This was a lobbying event, organised at short notice (only being announced on 31 May), to pressure the G8 summit of world leaders being held on 6–8 July in Auchterarder, Scotland, to do something. This was an example of an event used as a lobbying tool.

Events such as public meetings, rallies and protests can be used as a means of lobbying political influencers and decision makers. So pressure groups and other interested groups may use meetings to mobilise support for their views. One of the most significant occasions was in 1963 following racial and civil unrest in America. It led to a coalition of organisations organising a civil rights march on Washington DC on 28 August. An estimated 250–400,000 attended the march, and they enjoyed musical performances by artists known to be 'political', such as Joan Baez and Bob Dylan. There were also a number of speeches, with the most famous being Dr Martin Luther King's 'I have a dream' speech. As with Live 8 this had an overtly lobbying agenda, in part to mobilise individual citizens but also to bring pressure to bear on politicians.

We have given here two large well known examples, but in fact most lobbying events are small meetings with a few dozen people discussing something of interest to them, or a rally of a few thousand people protesting. Lobbying events are happening all the time, but normally as part of the background noise of civic society.

Definition box 10.2

Political event management

Political event management is the use of events by political actors, such as individual politicians, political parties and pressure groups. Such events include meetings, rallies, stunts, conferences and campaigns. They are designed to help achieve the objectives of a partisan interest, often at the expense of a political competitor. Such events can be aimed at external audiences and designed to achieve publicity, secure funding or win campaigns. For internal audiences political events can aid planning, motivate and direct external action. Political event management is a means to securing political objectives, not an end in itself.

In different political and electoral systems, party meetings and conferences are used for different roles. In despotic countries they tend to be little more than toothless rallies: for example, the December 2011 ZANU PF Annual Conference in Bulawayo, Zimbabwe, was really a rubber stamp of the rule of despot Robert Mugabe. In liberal democratic societies the public relations role still exists, but there is less control over the delegates. In the UK there has been a long tradition of the major political parties taking it in turn to host their annual party conference in September/October each year. Jackson (2009) has referred to party conferences as 'A festival of politics'. What this means is that this is where politics meets pomp and circumstance in public. Typically most political activity occurs behind the scenes, in private meetings, but a party conference provides an experience for those participating, attending and watching on television. Party conferences are evidence of experiential marketing and relationship management in action, where citizens come face to face with the party brand and image.

UK political parties organise a range of conferences, but their annual conference is the main event. There are a number of roles that they are designed to meet. Ostensibly they are often assumed to be about policy and ideas development, but this role has been decreasing. Conversely, their role as a means of the party managing their media image has significantly grown. Indeed, Jeremy Paxman (2002), the BBC news presenter, stated that they were 'empty vessels'. By this he meant that there was no policy substance, just public relations puffery. But as part of the experiential and relationship management approaches, they do provide a means for activists to meet old acquaintances and make new friends, socialise and have a good time. A party conference acts as a physical means of bringing together people from within one party, to confirm that they are not alone in believing that they are right. The emotional and motivational aspects are now probably more important than any other.

Internal communications

Internal communications (IC) is also known as employee communications, internal relations and internal marketing. It is a contested area, which human resources (HR) in particular feels is in their remit, and in which occasionally the IT manager may want to play a role – for example, through intranets. This is a growing area. Lots of larger companies now have a dedicated internal communications department, smaller companies usually make it part of someone else's job, and there is now a growing internal communications agency specialism. There is in the UK a professional body, the Institute of Internal Communication (IoIC) (www.ioic.org.co.uk), which defines internal communications as: *'Any communication designed to build a shared understanding and foster a sense of community within a clearly identified and discrete group.'* This definition reflects the need to include communication within membership organisations and similar groups, as well as employee communication.

There are two clear attitudes towards internal communications. The first views it as internal public relations, so that it is about communicating what senior management wants to achieve. This is essentially one-way, top-down vertical communication. It may be necessary at certain parts of the event cycle, such as at the beginning of planning and on the day of the event when going through health and safety and other briefings, but its long-term use tends to turn staff and volunteers off. A much better approach for event communicators is to view internal communications as a means of improving information flows, and so making better decisions. Internal communications is closely associated with the idea that employees work more effectively if they feel they are well informed.

Where many industries may lag far behind on internal communications, events have traditionally recognised the importance of dealing with employees, contractors and volunteers, precisely because they impact on the event experience. Van der Wagen (2007) stresses that good communication is essential at two stages: during event planning; and on-site. She believes that the intranet can be a useful tool for the first, and on-site she prefers two-way communications, typically in the form of face-to-face and radio contact. Bowdin *et al.* (2010) suggest that the size of the event will have a bearing on the form of internal communications used. For a small event they suggest that a mobile phone or even a loud hailer will suffice; but that large and therefore more complex events need a clear communications plan which outlines key staff mobile telephone numbers, possibly includes pagers and radio assignment numbers, on-site locations and clear lines of responsibility. In really complex events, such as a major exhibition or music festival, contractors may also be included in the plan.

The big mistake when using internal communications is to feel that having said the message once, that that is enough. Rather, you need to communicate your messages many times, using a range of different techniques. These certainly should include face to face, such as team meetings, but also newsletters and e-newsletters, intranets, notice boards, email, social activities and teleconferences. One technique suggested to some managers is the idea of managing by walking about (MBWA), where senior managers make sure they are physically accessible to staff regularly. These techniques are designed to help an event tell its story to its staff, which will in turn affect the external relations these staff have.

Center and Jackson (2003) suggest that internal communications needs to impart clear messages that are about news, event policy and announcements, but must also include the subjects staff consider important, such as recruitment, pay and conditions and staff development. Moreover, they suggest that channels need to be ones that staff trust, that staff need to be told before outside agencies, such as the media, and they need the bad news as well as the good. For example, public relations agency McEwan Partners points out that a key part of its internal communications strategy for the Royal Bank of Scotland Information Technology Division was regular 'meet the managers' events (http://www.mcewan-partners.co.uk/casestudies.html). One of the big recent debates is the use or over-use of email. Pre-Internet, many offices had an excess of memos (the memo culture) that were sent round to staff. Email has ended this practice, but event managers can be over-reliant on it (the email culture). I would suggest that too much use of email, without the balance of other channels, is a matter of internal public relations. The event manager should not just think 'Job done' as they press 'Send':

internal communications is much more than providing anodyne information. To be effective it must be a two-way process.

Practical checklist

- Introduce east/west vision to the targeting of your events.
- Always consider the reputation of your organisation/event.
- Remember the importance of reputation to your sponsors/partners.
- Create a small list of key decision makers and influencers you need to target.
- Invite key decision makers and influencers to your event.
- Create a crisis plan.
- Assess your communication culture through a communications audit.
- Keep an eye on the local and national media for issues and political developments which might affect your event or event field (positively or negatively).
- Irrespective of the size of your team instigate regular formal and informal communications mechanisms.

Case study 10.3 shows how ignoring issues management could have been terminal for an event, but that the organisers survived, learnt their lesson and are now an example of best practice.

CASE STUDY 10.3

Learning the reputation lesson

Beach Break Live (BBL) is an annual music festival aimed at the UK student market during the summer vacations (www.beachbreaklive.com). BBL is now at its hopefully final outdoor venue at Pembrey Country Park on the coast of Carmarthenshire. The 2012 event over a 'long' weekend in June was the sixth time it has been run.

The first BBL festival took place in 2007 on farmland overlooking a beach in Polzeath, Cornwall. Inevitably as this was the first BBL, the organisers Ian Forshaw and Celia Norowzian had a number of logistical issues: for example, transporting the 1,000 attendees to a remote site and stewarding, but their real problems were of a public relations nature. Given the peculiar nature of the site, the sound of the music travelled across the hills to local residents, who complained to the local council. Officials from Health and Safety within the local council visited the site and insisted that either the music was turned down, especially late in the evening, or they would exercise their regulatory powers to shut down the event.

Having learnt the hard way about the power of local residents, in 2008 Ian and Celia sought to address this by booking a nearby field as the venue, which did not have the peculiar acoustic problems of the 2007 site. They also made certain that they spoke to local residents and councillors, and as a result there were no major public relations problems. This second year the number of attendees increased to more than 5,000. In 2009 they had a major problem, when at the last minute they had to move from the venue. Having continued to engage with the local council they had their necessary licenses, but then an unexpected planning bylaw issue came to light. They had already had the foresight to have a back-up outdoor venue and so with literally days to go they moved the event to a site in Kent, some 300 miles away from Cornwall.

In 2010 they found their present site on the beach in South Wales. They had learnt by this time that once you get to 10,000 attendees you are creating a small town, probably bigger than the actual one nearby. To address this Ian and Celia had to learn the politics behind such events, and so stress the economic benefits locally, and actively seek to work with local people and their elected representatives. Although in this first year local residents were not sure about having the festival nearby, the activities of the organisers at managing issues so crises did not develop assuaged local concerns for 2011 and 2012. They sought to find out from the key local politicians what was wanted of them, and then to deliver this, and they created a joint working group with local people.

An issue of paramount importance to BBL is working with the local area to ensure it has a positive effect. This includes dedicating time to working with local stakeholders, including the council and responsible authorities (police, ambulance, fire and health and safety), residents' associations, the parish council and local business, to establish how to run the event in harmony. Key concerns are typically excessive noise, traffic congestion and pressure on local facilities. To mitigate these issues BBL has:

- Designed the site layout and acoustics to manage noise pollution.
- Used coach travel from universities and introduced a park-and-ride service to reduce traffic problems.
- Ensured that guests will be on site in the evenings – to prevent problems occurring on the beach at night.

To help make a positive contribution to the area BBL:

- Sources supplies (whenever possible) from local businesses – from beer and burgers to stages, sound equipment and event staffing.
- Organises training and provides opportunities for local people interested in getting into events management and related industries.

- Promotes the location as an area of outstanding natural beauty and introduces students to the area as an amazing holiday destination (creating tourism now and in the future).
- Actively seeks and works with local activities and businesses to provide surfing, coasteering and other outdoor pursuits.
- Works with local charities and community projects.

BBL's corporate reputation is not just influenced by successful issues and crisis management, but also by promoting from day one an ethical ethos based on sustainability. For example, carbon emissions are one way in which BBL attempts to reduce its impact on the environment. BBL also helps raise awareness of how others can reduce their impact by introducing fun and interactive activities like its Great Eco Race. The festival also uses renewable energy on site where possible, uses recycled products and then recycles its own.

Discussion questions

CPR opens up a new area for many event communicators, and this chapter highlights that reputation raises some key issues:

1 How would you justify to your boss, partners or sponsors that you should invest resources in what appears to be an intangible concept: reputation management?
2 Event communicators are set up to reach mass audiences, so how would you adapt your structures and practices to target small numbers of important individuals and groups?
3 What is it that addressing corporate reputation adds to your event?
4 What is more important: that your event must use CPR tools, or that events can be a means for organisations to enhance their reputation?

Further information

Other sources which might help you consider the issues outlined in this chapter include:

Articles

Melo, T. and Garrido-Morgado, A. (2012) 'Corporate Reputation: A Combination of Social Responsibility and Industry', *Corporate Social Responsibility and Environmental Management*, 19 (1): 11–31 – covers the impact of social responsibility.
Surma, A. (2006) 'The Rhetoric of Reputation: Vision not Visibility', *PRism* 4(1) http://praxis. massey.ac.nz/prism_on-line_journ.html – identifies the importance of ethical practice on reputation.

Books

Kelly, R. (1989) *Conservative Party Conferences: The Hidden System*, Manchester: Manchester University Press – explains how Conservative party conferences work.

Websites

www.regesterlarkin.com/ – global reputation management consultancy.
www.sbs.ox.ac.uk/centres/reputation/Pages/default.aspx – source of academic research.
http://issuemanagement.org/ – US based Issue Management Council.

Chapter 11

Promoting your event online

Introduction

This chapter is different from Chapters 3 to 10 as we are not considering marketing or public relations separately. Rather, we are considering how marketing and public relations are used alone and together within one communication channel. Throughout this chapter we will weave in data from a content analysis (see Appendix) conducted of 209 worldwide event websites[1] to assess how web technologies are being used.[2] We will first briefly explain the meaning of the Internet, and we will then assess its key characteristics. The chapter will address the concepts of Web 1.0 and Web 2.0, and then evaluate how events have used web technologies.

By the end of this chapter students will be able to:

● Construct a clear rationale for using web technologies.
● Assess the core components of the Internet, and their implications.
● Evaluate current debate about the application of the Internet.
● Identify how events are using the Internet.

Why should an event be online?

The Internet is a relatively recent technology which has, along with mobile (cellular) telephones, become a core part of social and commercial communication. As recently as 2006 Rogers was able to suggest that for one part of the events industry – conferences – the Internet would be only a niche tool because of the supreme importance of face-to-face communications. Yet the ubiquitous, and for some dominant, role that the Internet now plays in communication makes such a view seem outdated.

Yet, it would be wrong to assume automatically that we must have an online presence, or the very latest Internet technology. The event communicator should not accept that just because everyone else is getting on a bandwagon, they robotically should too. You need to decide clearly that a particular web application will help further the communication objectives of your event, otherwise you are wasting resources that could be used more effectively elsewhere. Although the concept of the digital divide (Norris 2001) may appear less relevant than ten years ago, there are still people – based on their age, income, education and where they live in the world – for whom the Internet is largely irrelevant. If your event is aimed at one of these communities, then the Internet is at best a secondary channel. Conversely, there are some audiences – typically younger people and students in the West – for whom the Internet might be the first appropriate channel for reaching them. The Internet is merely a technology, not an automatic panacea, and you need to decide whether it is right for you, your audience and your event.

One of the core debates concerning the Internet is whether it has acted as an evolutionary or revolutionary influence on events. Certainly, it has transformed many of the everyday tasks for both event organisers and attendees alike. It makes searching for venues, suppliers and event ideas far easier, quicker and typically cheaper. There is now also the ability to register delegates online, book accommodation and promote events via the Internet. There is even the suggestion that the content of events is changing, as attendees experience it physically and virtually at the same time. However, are event communicators doing exactly what they used to, but just using a new technology, or are they doing completely new things, with the nature of events changing as a result? In short, are we moving from word of mouth to word of mouse?

What is the Internet?

The Internet has a variety of meanings, and we need to be clear how we are using the term. Simply put, it is a global computer network of networks that allows information to be shared from computer to computer (Joinson 2003). Because it can be used to achieve a number of different functions, such as a meeting place, market or source of information, the Internet is versatile. The Internet is a hybrid technology capable of being both an unmediated interpersonal communication channel to build relationships, and a broadcast mass media (Barnes 2001). Conceptually the Internet enables us to identify, reach and converse with individuals, so narrowcasting, but it also allows us to reach and mobilise crowds, so broadcasting. As Cox (1999) notes, crowds are powerful and they can be mobilised more easily in interest clusters through interactive environments such as forums, blogs and social networking sites. The Internet is comprised of a range of modalities which are all essentially based on web technology. We can identify eight separate modalities which event communicators and/or their stakeholders regularly use.

Definition box 11.1

What is web communication?

Web communication is essentially a means of promoting a message online, which can either be purely informational, such as this event is happening at such a time and place, or persuasive, explaining why you should attend. It is a flexible means of getting across and reinforcing messages to both large amorphous and small targeted audiences. It is merely a technology, and while this imparts cultural impacts, what matters is the content of messages. Web communication which applies digital technologies can be private, public, a monologue or a dialogue.

Websites

A website is the term for a series of web pages hosted on a server and available via a network. Each individual web page is merely a document that is available to the viewer. The web designer has to use a software package such as HTML (HyperText Mark-up Language) to construct each page. The web author is the person that writes the text/content on the web page. Such a simple description of a website does not tell us how it is used. Some websites are little more than an electronic brochure (Jackson 2003), so that it is essentially a static document used like a flyer, leaflet or newsletter that does not utilise the discrete architecture of the web. What the web offers, however, is the ability to create interaction in a way not normally possible outside direct face-to-face contact.

Intranet

An intranet is a website which is a private network within an organisation for employees (Callaghan 2002). As well as letting people know what is happening elsewhere in the organisation, say proposed organisational events, they can often encourage social activities outside of the workplace. They could include web pages, forums, bulletin boards/calendars and news pages. Intranets can be the means by which collaborative work is encouraged, or can host video conference meetings between geographically disparate parts of an organisation. You may find them especially useful for mega-events or large organisations with events where staff cannot easily speak to each other face to face.

Extranet

An extranet is essentially the same as an intranet in terms of its functions, features and purpose, but it can be accessible to selected audiences external to an organisation, such as suppliers. Typically they would be given a password to access it, and this allows them to know what is happening within the organisation, and so can better meet its needs. For example, participants, food, drink and equipment suppliers may be allowed to gain access to the event or organisation's extranet.

Email

Email is simply a means of sending a message electronically in digital format from one computer to another. It is a means by which event communicators can inform, persuade and seek to mobilise colleagues, participants, attendees, suppliers and interested third parties. Email is essentially a private message, the electronic form of a posted letter, but it can be sent to thousands of people at the same time, and so an e-direct mail industry has quickly grown up. It has developed its own style of writing and norms, and is especially applicable for short messages of only a few paragraphs, but more detailed content can be attached in the form of documents. Many commentators focus on more high-profile online channels such as social networking sites, but by doing so they may be missing the quiet steady workhorse online that gets things done. Downes and Mui (2000) suggested email would be a 'killer app' that would fundamentally change communication, society, business and politics for ever. The jury is still out on their prediction, but in the long run, especially if you are following a relational approach, email is probably likely to be your most persuasive tool.

E-newsletters

E-newsletters are an application of email, in the form of a newsletter offering information and sometimes special offers. It is e-direct marketing, and acts as a 'reminder facility' (Ollier 1998) whereby stakeholders regularly 'hear' from an event. They can be in a variety of formats, such as a full electronic newsletter as an attachment, hyperlinks to websites, or a very common approach is to have a short taster paragraph and then the reader needs to click to the full story. Software is available that allows the sender to know exactly what the receiver has done with the e-newsletter – Has it been opened or not? Which pages/stories have gained most traffic? Has it been deleted? Jackson (2008a) found that the use of an e-newsletter before and during an election campaign could make the difference between being elected or not, so it is potentially a persuasive channel. E-newsletters need not be used just as a one-way route from sender to receiver: with the touch of the reply button the receiver can send back their solicited or unsolicited views. Indeed, if you send out an e-newsletter you are tacitly inviting subscribers to respond.

There are two keys to an effective e-newsletter. First, your database needs to have the correct people on it, and you must continually manage and update it. This means that you need to note how subscribers respond to the e-newsletter and what impact it might have on their relationship with your event. For example, do they buy tickets for your event or take up an offer? Second, you should have something interesting to say that adds value. Do not just promote your events, but have stimulating stories: the reader of an e-newsletter is looking to get material, such as offers, that they cannot get elsewhere (Chaffey 2003). E-newsletters are not a hard sell – rather, they are a means of exchanging ideas, views and news over a period of time. An e-newsletter can be used pre-, during and post-event.

The recommended approach by the Direct Marketing Association (www.dma.org.uk), the trade body representing direct marketers, is that there are different accepted practices for postal and e-direct mail. Offline it is possible to 'buy' mailing lists and then send material through the post to those you think might be interested in your events. Training companies have typically used this method to reach business audiences. Online, however, the equivalent of this is spam, and so e-direct marketers cannot just buy a list and email out. This is frowned-upon behaviour, and in some countries it is illegal. Rather, the DMA suggests e-marketers get permission to send an e-newsletter, so people opt in to receive it regularly.

Our first case study explains the importance of databases and content to using e-newsletters in building relationships.

CASE STUDY 11.1

Using an e-newsletter – building long-term relationships

WildWise Events (www.wildwise.co.uk) delivers an exciting, diverse programme of courses, camps and events for adults, children and families to inspire and inform them about the natural world. It creates public and bespoke courses and

---

events covering bushcraft, nature awareness and outdoor education for the general public, environmental organisations, schools, corporate and private client groups.

WildWise has been providing an e-newsletter since 2010, which was set up as a method of communicating and establishing relationships with people who attended events. It was a way of organising information, rather than being a random and unscheduled communication. So it is a regular and organised form of communicating to prompt, remind and provide people with a flavour of what is coming up.

Most of WildWise's events are in the summer, so in the winter the e-newsletter is sent out bi-monthly, but in the summer months it is usually monthly and no more than six weekly. Each e-newsletter has information on some of the next events coming up, and normally a week or two before the last of these happens the next e-newsletter is sent out. Content is therefore based on a rolling pro-gramme of events.

Subscribers want to find out what is going on in an easily accessible way, without having to trawl through the website. As a result WildWise uses a template with a few general paragraphs, and then has links to each event with a short 10–15 word description. In addition WildWise also provides offers, normally at the beginning of the year, not available elsewhere, which means the e-newsletter provides added value.

The email address of everyone who comes on a course is collected, and then they are asked if they would like to receive the e-newsletter. Most people agree to do so. This is the main way that the number of subscribers is built up; only a few subscribe direct from the website. The list is mostly comprised of parents and other adults who attend events and public courses. Businesses and schools are normally contacted directly.

It is difficult to assess the impact of the e-newsletter on event attendance, but WildWise is able to analyse a range of statistics on how many open the e-newsletter, how many click-through and what are the most popular pages. Typically there is about a 45 per cent open rate. A number of subscribers come to events year after year, and this where the e-newsletter may have an impact in helping to build long-term relationships.

WildWise wants to increase the number of subscribers, and is also considering having two e-newsletters, with one targeted at local people and another at those based farther afield.

Weblogs

Weblogs are different from websites, being essentially a published real-time online diary. There are two types of weblog: those that emphasise the diary and comment aspect, and those that emphasise hyperlinks (Blood 2000). The former allow a blogger to promote their ideas, whereas the latter act as a filter, looking at what exists on the World Wide Web that might be of interest to visitors. Increasingly weblogs contain both personal views and links to other interested weblogs. Weblogs are very diverse in that there is no one dominant style or activity, but common to all is that they share information. They offer a subtle means of promoting an event, often indirectly because they are considered experts in a field, interesting to read or are prolific posters.

There are a few weblog experts who post about a range of event based issues, such as www.eventmanagerblog.com and www.theeventexpert.co.uk. As Table 11.1 shows, blogging is a fairly minority activity for events. The blog of the Sydney Festival (http://blog.sydneyfestival. org.au) provides mostly a behind-the-scenes peek with lots of pictures, and does not appear to encourage dialogue. A different approach is taken by http://www.4deserts.com/sahararace/ blogs, where the posts are made by individual competitors, so there appear to be no imposed boundaries – posters say what they think. These two blogs are opinion pieces from the authors. A completely different approach, that of a filter, is taken by http://www.walesrallygb.com/blog/ wrgb_blog.php, which provides links to interesting stories. Weblogs do not appear to be a major promotional tool for events, because their impact does not justify the amount of work they require.

Microblogging

Microblogging sites, such as Twitter, Tumblr and Plurk, appear to be a response to the limitations of blogs. McFedries (2007) suggests that the requirement of writing lengthy and considered posts on weblogs is a 'hard slog'. In contrast, microblogging is a 'quick-ping' medium, which allows people to post brief updates of up to 140 characters. Therefore, microblogging has lowered the barriers in terms of thought investment by users (Java *et al.* 2007). Twitter has become popular because users, who are referred to as tweeters, can send and receive messages via a wide range of delivery mechanisms. Users of Twitter can be classified as followers and followed. Some tweeters have more people follow them than they follow, so they are largely broadcasting messages. Others have more reciprocal relationships with users and may both follow and be followed by a distinct community, or may simply follow a wide array of tweeters in order to gain news and updates without personally communicating a great deal. Inherently, Twitter appears to have encouraged a hierarchy of users (Java *et al.* 2007).

There is in the history of Twitter a clear link with events. It was an event which helped to raise the profile of Twitter, when at the South By Southwest Festival in Austin, Texas in 2007 Twitter usage rose from 20,000 to 60,000 tweets a day. In an open and large venue Twitter encouraged attendees to communicate with each other. It was a means by which they kept in touch.

As Table 11.1 notes, Twitter is a major online communication channel for events. As with weblogs there are general event management Twitter accounts. Several of these are from publications and magazines, such as http://twitter.com/#!/EventNewsBlog and http://twitter. com/#!/eventprofsUK, which provide a range of news links and snippets of information that might be of interest to those working in the industry. A typical approach from an event is the V Festival (http://twitter.com/#!/vfestival), which every few days tweets either directly about the event itself, such as the availability of tickets, or promoting the artistes. For annual events Twitter raises issues during their quiet times, so seven months before the MTV European Music Awards its account (http://twitter.com/#!/mtvema) was giving factual information, and trying to get a debate going of what followers wanted from the event. It is likely that the ease of tweeting as opposed to posting a blog makes Twitter more attractive for many event managers.

Our next case study explains how Twitter and Facebook are used by a local community event as a promotional tool that encourages dialogue. It is interesting to note contrary to what we might expect the former has proved more interactive than the latter.

CASE STUDY 11.2

Building online relationships

The Orkney Storytelling Festival (www.orkneystorytellingfestival.co.uk) is organised by the Orcadian Story Trust to preserve, promote and develop the traditional culture of the Orkney islands through stories and storytellers. The festival includes a series of events of local and international storytellers. In part, the festival seeks to encourage Orcadians in their local culture, but it is also timed to extend the tourist season.

The festival was resurrected in 2010, and was based on an event that had not happened for a decade. From the outset the organisers created a website, Twitter account and Facebook page as a means of letting people know what was happening. Although the festival is in October both the Twitter account and Facebook page are maintained year round to retain people's interest in Orkney, the festival and storytelling.

The Twitter account is managed by two people, both of whom have other accounts. Content on the Twitter account is very eclectic and is added to in a random way. It might include announcements concerning the festival, discussions about storytelling or general material about Orkney – for example, that the puffins have arrived. The content is deliberately interactive in nature because this encourages all sorts of linkages, such as between storytellers. It is felt that if followers know more about the people behind the festival and the storytellers, they might be more likely to attend.

There are more than 500 followers, who include individuals, other festivals and storytellers, and assuming they are real accounts the Orkney Storytelling Festival normally follows their followers as well.

The effect of the Twitter account is difficult to gauge, but there have been at the festival attendees who have sought the organisers out, and asked whether they are the ones who manage the Twitter account. It certainly raises awareness of Orkney, the festival and storytelling.

The same two people manage the Facebook page. Those who sign up on Facebook are different from those who follow Twitter: while there are storytellers at the event, and other storytellers, they are predominantly local people. Content is less regular than the Twitter account, but it is used more for promoting local events and making announcements. It is far easier for users to find out about local events than scrolling down Twitter. Facebook is also where people access photos as they are not yet on Flickr, so people do not access pictures via Twitter.

The organisers do not do blanket invitations because they feel it would be annoying for those in North America and elsewhere who could not come, but people do sign up and say they are coming.

Twitter and Facebook have similar roles in engaging individuals in the festival and storytelling. However, they are also distinct: Twitter is less specific, whereas on Facebook the organisers need something specific to say, so Twitter is more frequent, and seemingly (though not necessarily in reality) more trivial. Moreover, the organisers deliberately do not cross-fertilise content, so Twitter is used more to promote the festival, and Facebook has details of the specific programme.

Although the signal is not always good (there is no 3G in Orkney), Twitter and Facebook are used to enhance the experience of attendees at the event. There is a live Twitter feed and pictures on Facebook which receive responses.

Social networking sites (SNS)

The first SNS was created in 1997 (boyd and Ellison 2007), but only really took off with Facebook in 2004. SNS is a means by which events can reach out to new audiences, engage in dialogue with them and allow stakeholders to communicate with each other directly. Inherently it should be interactive in nature. Popular SNS include Facebook, Bebo and LinkedIn, and we should also note file sharing sites such as Flickr and YouTube. Facebook claims that it currently (2012) has 800 million active users worldwide (http://www.facebook.com/press/info.php?statistics).

As Table 11.1 shows, social networks, primarily Facebook, have become very popular channels, and this implies either a lot of events have jumped on the bandwagon or they get real value from these websites. As with Twitter, there are Facebook pages provided by industry publications, which provide up-to-date industry news. Such general sites include http://www.facebook.com/pages/Conference-News/110867218948494?sk=info and http://www.facebook.com/pages/Conference-and-Meetings-World/110579492314051?sk=wall.

While clearly the content analysis is only of those events with websites, Table 11.1 suggests that the Internet is a major communication and promotional channel for events. Email is clearly the most popular, followed by social networks, primarily Facebook, and then Twitter. E-newsletters are popular amongst just over a third of the sample. The only publicly available modality which is not popular is weblogs. However, just the availability of these modalities does not give us the full picture. A lot of smaller events tend to use Twitter and social networking sites only in the run-up to their event, and not year round, though larger events tend

Table 11.1 The use by events of Internet modalities

Modality	Presence %
Email details	95.2
Weblog	13.9
E-newsletter	37.3
Twitter	55.5
SNS	63.2

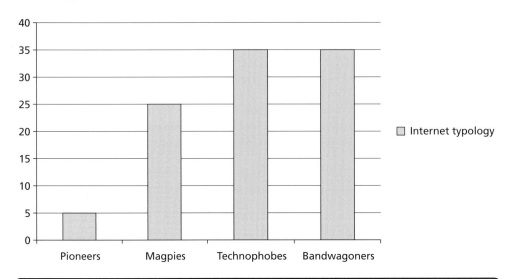

Figure 11.1 Event online typology
(Adapted from Jackson 2008b)

to build up the brand. Moreover, a key issue is to what extent events are using these modalities as a part of a clear communications strategy, and how many are doing so because everyone else is.

Although a different field to events (politics) Jackson (2008b) provides a typology which might apply, which is presented in Figure 11.1 He suggests that only 5 per cent are *pioneers* who have a clear vision as to why they are using web technologies. Another 25 per cent are *magpies*, who use the Internet to gain competitive advantage. The rest are either *technophobes*, who use little of the Internet, or *bandwagoners*. If this typology applies to events, then just over a third has a clear idea as to why they are using these modalities.

Characteristics of the Internet

It is not enough for the event communicator to know the different modalities of the Internet: to utilise the Internet effectively they need to understand the peculiarities of each. Overall, the Internet has core characteristics which shape how it can best be used.

User-led

The Internet implicitly suggests a slight shift in the power balance between the sender and receiver of a message (Ollier 1998). Typically, when promoting your event offline you decide who receives your message, and what you want to say. With the web, the user has more opportunity to decide what information they access. Moreover with search engines if they don't find what they want immediately they can be off to other websites. As a web author this means that you need to think not just about what you want to say, but also what the visitor wants to know. This is not to overstress the power change, but the Internet is more user-led than most other communication channels.

Table 11.2 Navigability of websites

Feature	%
Contact details	95.2
Search engine	24.9
Enmeshing	96.7
Online help	11

This characteristic has a clear bearing on the feel and content of an event website. The first issue for the event communicator to address is page navigability: namely, once a visitor is on the site how do we encourage them to move around in a way they feel comfortable with so that they stay longer. Typically, a host would provide a means to contact the site, and how to find out what is on the site. Table 11.2 suggests that our content analysis found that event websites only partially addressed the core components of navigability, with only the provision of contact details being standard. Rather surprisingly nearly 5 per cent of events did not want to be contacted by visitors. Only a quarter provided a search engine. For example, professional cycling event www.tourdownunder.co.au tries to makes the site attractive through a range of colourful images, easy to follow buttons, clear headings and an easy to use search engine. Our data suggest that the navigability of event websites can be improved to enhance the visitors' experience.

Out of our four measures that encourage navigability, our content analysis found that events only had two as standard. This implies that many events have not yet fully understood the needs of visitors.

Interactivity

Inherently, it is argued that because the Internet is user-led it also means that it automatically encourages interactivity, with the receiver of the message offering their feedback. Indeed, a consensus exists that the most important and unique aspect the Internet offers is interactivity (Hoffman and Novak 1996; Bell 1998; Ward 2001). However, as Sadow and James (2000) point out, a consensus does not exist of what exactly interactivity means. One of the classic definitions of interactivity is provided by Rafaeli (1988: 111), who suggested that:

> Interactivity is an expression of the extent that in a given series of communication exchanges, any third (or later) transmission (or message) is related to the degree to which previous exchanges referred to even earlier transmissions.

For Rafaeli interaction requires that a conversation has to take place, and while this could be face to face, it could also be via web technologies.

Addressing interactivity specifically via the Internet, McMillan (2002) produced a typology with three levels of interactivity. The first is whether the visitor actually accesses the web page. The second is how the user interacts with the system – perhaps the software by which they access the site. The third is user to user, where there is a conversation between the sender and receiver of an online message. This implies that interactivity is not a single concept, but can vary in intensity and nature.

A different approach is provided by Stromer-Galley (2004), who distinguishes between interactivity as a product of technologies (what is provided), and interactivity as a process of communication (what the outcome is). The former considers the architecture provided for interactivity, and the latter assesses how this architecture is actually used. Consequently, she suggests that it is with the latter that we have evidence of real interactivity and dialogue.

The application of interactivity online has led to the idea of co-production of content, where technology is used to encourage participation, so instead of the website being a hard sell, the host seeks to provide a rich experience for the user which draws them in. Pre-internet, James (1991) developed the idea of the produser within education and learning, but it is a concept which has been applied to the Internet (Lilleker and Jackson 2011), the idea being that the visitor does not just consume a website's content, but that interactivity enables them also to contribute to that content. This raises a question we shall now turn to: Should you consider your website visitors as passive recipients of your message, or as engaged with you in co-production of the content of your site.

As we shall shortly see not all events encourage interactivity, but of those that do a typical one is The Sun-Herald City2Surf (www.city2surf.com.au). This encourages interaction through Facebook, Twitter and clips on YouTube, but it also does it in other ways: for example, merchandising can be bought, the highest fundraisers are mentioned, and competitors can sign up for the after-party. However, this interaction is fairly controlled by the web host, and there is no evidence of co-production of content through forums or allowing visitors to upload their material. The Hornbill Festival in India (www.hornbillfestivasl.com) is more unusual, possibly because it is comprised of a wide number of community events. As a result the website includes videos and stories clearly provided by participants and visitors, which adds a level of credibility and interest to the site. A slightly different approach is taken by the Korea Food Festival (http://koreafoodfestival.or.kr/2012_english), which allows prospective and actual visitors to ask questions and post comments. A high-risk approach is to have a forum, because you can never be sure what members will post, and it takes up time to moderate. V Festival (http://www.vfestival.com/social/forum) has a fairly vibrant forum with ten different subject areas that allow for discussion about the acts and other aspects of the event.

Writing on the web – a journalistic approach

Writing on the web is very different from authoring a newsletter, press story, poster or flyer. Where in a brochure you can afford to take your time to get across your point, on a website you have to get straight to the point or your visitor will be off somewhere better. For example, Morris (2000) suggested that where a printed promotional document might have a 1,000 words, a website should take 100. Each website has to be short and to the point, utilising multimedia such as graphics and images to help get across the point.

Non-linear arrangement of information

In a website, unlike a brochure, information is presented in a non-linear way. While the visitor will often arrive at the home page, after that they choose which page they visit and in what order. It is they who do so, not the web host. However, one way of trying to control and direct how visitors access your information is to use hyperlinks within the site. Enmeshing is the means to use such links to guide the visitor to where you want them to go next (Ollier 1998). Our content analysis found that events are very good at trying to direct visitors, with 96.7 per cent using enmeshing as a deliberate tool. For example, the One World Film Festival (www.oneworld.cz) on a page of 110 words looking at its Programme and Events has six hyperlinks.

Both synchronous and asynchronous

The Internet creates a changed timeframe for communicating, allowing for both asynchronous (not concurrent) and synchronous (live) communication, depending on what the receiver prefers (Grieco and Holmes 1999). The receiver could access a message, and respond to it, at a time to suit them.

Web 1.0 versus Web 2.0

In recent years one of the biggest debates about the application of the web has been whether to use a Web 1.0 or Web 2.0 approach. Web 1.0 sites are those where the sender of the message concentrates on promoting their message, so although some interaction is expected, such as a response to an email, the emphasis is on controlling the process. The term Web 2.0, believed to have been coined by O'Reilly (2005), challenges this presumption. He suggests that the concept relates to an architecture of participation, that the Internet structurally encourages conversations. This analysis in part reflected the development of new technologies such as Facebook, YouTube and Twitter, but perhaps more importantly referred to changing communication strategies, that people wanted to encourage greater use of interaction because this gave the website intrinsic value. Where Web 1.0 is about the provision of information through essentially top-down vertical communication controlled by the website host, Web 2.0 gives greater value to user generation of content through non-hierarchical horizontal communication. Jackson and Lilleker (2009) suggest that what may actually exist is a Web 1.5, where the web host struggles to find a balance between wanting to control their message and encouraging user input. Events probably want to use their online presence to control their message, but individual web users now expect to interact with sites. The genie of dialogue is out of the bottle.

Figure 11.2 presents a framework for understanding whether Web 1.0 or Web 2.0 is being used by event communicators. The position that each event website occupies reflects two factors: use of the architecture of participation and the democratic structure. The former reflects to what extent the tools for interactivity exist, such as Facebook, weblogs, forums and allowing visitors to upload material. But Web 2.0 is not just about the existence of such technologies, it is also how they are used. Which model is present reflects the level of control that the web host wants to exert, so the tools might be present but does the event communicator take part and respond? So, for example, say an event forum or Facebook page identifies a concern about the toilets. Evidence of Web 2.0 would suggest that the event organisers would engage by explaining the situation and if need be doing something about the toilets (and being seen to do so). An event following a Web 1.5 approach would allow the complaints, but would not respond (and quite probably later would remove the complaints). It is therefore not enough to have interactive tools: what matters is how the event organisers use them.

Figure 11.3 represents this idea in a slightly different way, but indicates exactly where we would expect to find each approach. Moreover, this figure suggests that the likelihood of an event applying Web 1.5 for its website is conceptually twice as likely as pure Web 1.0 or Web 2.0.

Adapting Jackson and Lilleker's model for assessing the existence of Web 1.0 or Web 2.0, Table 11.3 suggests that while events want to use their web technologies to promote a clear message by presenting details of the event, where it has come from and what is happening recently, there is some evidence for Web 2.0. The preferred architecture for participation is primarily Twitter and Facebook, and perhaps the most significant statistic is that on 40.2 per cent of the websites studied, visitors were allowed to offer their own information. This suggests

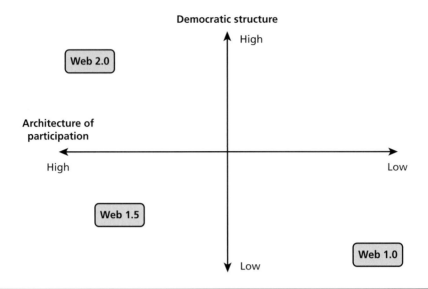

Figure 11.2 A web conceptual framework
(Adapted from Jackson and Lilleker 2009)

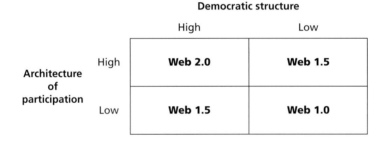

Figure 11.3 The application of Web 1.0, Web 1.5 and Web 2.0 to events

that while event managers want to get across their message, many appear willing to encourage some co-production of content. Therefore, a significant minority of event website visitors are produsers not just passive receivers of messages. Perhaps they suspect that the potential attendee who feels themself an online produser, is more likely to actually attend because they feel part of that event.

E-marketing

E-marketing has now become a central part of the marketing mix, a specialism in its own right. You need to be very clear what you want it to achieve, so to get across your message quickly a content-led website might be most appropriate. To build stronger relationships with

Table 11.3 The existence of Web 1.0 or Web 2.0 in event websites

Web 1.0	%	Web 2.0	%
Event programme	94.7	Weblog	13.9
Event history	52.2	Microblog	55.5
Virtual tour	1	Social networking site	63.2
First timer's guide	1	Online forum	6.2
News	56.5	Questionnaire polls	2.4
Testimonials	13.9	Flickr	5.7
		RSS feeds	12.9
		Videos uploaded	50.7
		Visitors can upload material	6.7
		Visitors can share information	40.2

consumers, e-newsletters are an obvious approach, whereas to create a buzz or a sense of belonging to a community an SNS or a discussion forum might be appropriate. You need to be very strategic about the need for, purpose and use of, a web application.

It is vital to drive traffic to your website, both in terms of first getting visitors to your site and then getting them to return. Visitors may hear about your site because you contacted them directly, or they may have heard about the event offline and found your website address to find out more. Here, traffic is driven by your offline activities, but what you do online is crucial. The way in which many people hear about an event is by using a search engine, such as Google, Yahoo! and Bing. Typically someone might type in to a search engine 'something to do on a wet and windy Tuesday in Plymouth', and then see what comes up. When I typed in this phrase to Google, I found in the first page water based events (Plymouth is on the coast), 'what's on' guides and a travel guide to New Plymouth, New Zealand. I did not look beyond page two. Given the propensity for most of us to rely on search engines to find something new, or what we require only occasionally, event marketers need to know about SEO (Search Engine Optimisation). When someone tries to find out about an event, or type of event, where is your event in the page ratings? If you are not in the first two pages of any search engine your event website is unlikely to be viewed. SEO, therefore, utilises techniques to increase your page rating and hence how often your site is viewed. For example, you need to make sure that all your online modalities are integrated, the message that goes out in one automatically goes out in the others.

Having encouraged a visitor to access your site you need to ensure that your website is 'sticky' (Jackson 2003). This means that you offer features which encourage the visitor to return, for the occasional visitor to become a frequent visitor. Typically this could be with news stories, special offers, competitions, event features and photograph updates.

Online promotion

The data from our content analysis help explain how the 7Ps are used online by events. The Internet is inherently a promotional tool, and we would therefore expect a high level of promotion on event websites. Table 11.4 suggests that one of the first uses of an event website

Table 11.4 Use of promotion by event websites

Promotion feature	% of websites
News	56.5
Testimonials	13.9
Video of previous event	43.5
Pictures of previous event	78
Sponsor's details	78
Link to sponsor's website	73.7
Weblog	13.9
E-newsletter	37.3
Microblog	55
SNS (Social Networking Sites)	63.2
Flickr	5.7
RSS (Really Simple Syndication)	12.9
Videos uploaded	50.7
Links to organiser's other events	15.3

is to use it to promote the sponsor. In terms of content we see a predominance of visual images of previous events. In terms of channels, social networking sites and microblogs are very popular. Event websites are clearly a promotional tool, but the fact that no single feature is present in more than three-quarters of sites does not imply that it is the prime purpose.

Online place and processes

Having noted in Chapter 5 that place/distribution is generally easier for events because they are normally centred on a geographic venue, the Internet has had an impact on event ticketing. Up to the 1980s tickets were sold over the counter or by post through a venue box office: essentially paper based and cash oriented. As a result little information was gathered from customers which could help event communicators tailor their message more effectively. Then, with the increased use of credit cards from the late 1980s, there was a corresponding increased use of telephone box offices. As software became more sophisticated, ticketing moved away from just sales to part of marketing through customer relationship management.

E-ticketing has revolutionised ticketing, so that the event generally save on costs, allows accurate monitoring of sales, and because it is usually outsourced there is one less problem to consider. For the buyer it is about convenience. Our data found that despite the apparent sense of a ubiquitous use of e-ticketing, in fact just over half, 52.2 per cent of our sample, used e-ticketing. The focus on e-ticketing is not just relevant to place, but also to the idea of processes within a wider 7Ps approach. The data suggest that there is only limited evidence of processes being used by event websites.

E-pricing

The Internet raises interesting pricing issues. As noted above, it may reduce costs through e-ticketing, but as Chaston (2004) notes e-pricing can include online auctions, rapidly changing prices and with some products such as Adobe we have zero-pricing. Obviously not all events incur a cost, but of those that do it was normal to have an easily to find button with how to get tickets and what they cost. A typical example was the music festival, T in the Park (www.tinthepark.com), which offers six ticket prices based on a combination of how many days visitors intend to stay for and whether it includes camping.

E-product

Some products are, on any spectrum, inherently offline, so for most people the local greengrocer will be primarily a physical offline business you have to visit to buy your vegetables. Others, such as financial services, could be both physical and online; and some such as Amazon are wholly online. Events are mostly offline though there is the potential for an element of online product. As Table 11.5 shows, for most events the online product equates to a programme of activities, and possibly a news page updating new activities of the event and a narrative explaining the event's history. So websites promote and explain the product. There is limited evidence of a website being a major tool for generating new income in the form of merchandising and very few offering an Internet product of the event. Thus the London International Technology Show (www.litshow.com) gave special offers from exhibitors. However, one interesting figure which may represent a growing trend is that over one-third, 36.4 per cent, used the Internet, such as a microblog or SNS, to enhance attendees' experience of the event during the event. So the Diwali Festival in India (www.diwalifestival.org) provides recipes, poems and songs which accompany the festival. This latter figure supports the idea of a hybrid event using the Internet to add value to an event.

Physical

Table 11.6 shows that a website provides an opportunity to offer some sense of tangibility of the event, yet the data do not suggest that events are fully taking advantage of this. Most events,

Table 11.5 The event e-product

The product	% appears
Event details programme	94.7
Event history	52.2
First timer's guide	1
News page	56.5
Online product of an event	7.7
Online experience during the event	36.4
Merchandising	21.1
Corporate hospitality	3.3
Webcam	1.4

Table 11.6 The illusion of tangibility by events

Feature	% present
Virtual tour	1
Testimonials	13.9
Videos of previous events	43.5
Pictures of previous events	78

78 per cent, offer pictures of previous events, and just under half, 43.5 per cent, offer videos of previous events. Yet only 13.9 per cent offer any form of testimonial from happy consumers; so the home page of the London International Technology Show has a testimonial from an exhibitor. Only 1 per cent use the technology available to offer a virtual tour. The data suggest that there is a lot more that events can do to address the issue of intangibility.

E-public relations

This is essentially the same as offline public relations in terms of overall principles. Where it often differs is in the detail of practice. It is still aimed at key audiences, though these may be different in nature being global, 24-hours and often only virtual (so we do not necessarily meet them physically). E-public relations can still be applied to a wide range of activities, including media relations, issues management and crisis management, but there are some differences. Haig (2001) notes that most offline public relations is via a gatekeeper, typically a journalist, but e-public relations is direct. Traditionally public relations content is information based, and while this is still true online, we also have the potential of interactive communication. It is for this reason that Gordon (2011) stresses the importance of social media changing the nature of public relations.

Our debate in Chapters 8 and 10 on MPR and CPR is replicated online. Haig (2001) views online public relations as part of marketing as a means of selling products, whereas Phillips and Young (2009) stress the application of the Internet to reputation management. Similarly, there is a different view on the application of the approaches to public relations. Grunig and Hunt's two-way symmetrical approach has been criticised for being difficult to realise, but conceptually it is more achievable online. Kelleher (2007) believes that interactivity has encouraged the building of relationships. Logically if persuasion is considered to be dominant for offline public relations we would consider this to be the case online, too. Indeed, the idea of equalisation (Rheingold 1993) implies that smaller organisations can use the Internet as effectively, if not more, than bigger organisations, so levelling the communication playing field. The detail of online public relations practice is different, but the overall principles are the same for offline public relations.

While not overtly addressing e-public relations, Table 11.7 provides a sense of how events used their links. The majority of events recognise the importance of promoting their sponsors, and this probably represents a very high proportion as not all of the sample would have had sponsors. A significant number of sites recognise that local information concerning how to get to an event, accommodation and what to do there, is quite important to the overall event

Table 11.7 The use of links

Feature	%
Links to sponsors' websites	73.7
Links to participants' websites	37.8
Links to other events	13.9
Links to the organisers' other events	15.3
Links to local accommodation	52.6
Links to local tourism	32.5
Links to travel information	56.5
Links to local weather information	10

experience. Just over one-third promote participants sites, but very few develop a community of events.

Practical checklist

- Create a website that encourages people to return with regularly updated content.
- Provide testimonials from happy attendees.
- Consider using e-newsletters as a means of building relationships.
- If you use an external web designer make sure you can update content without incurring extra costs.
- Use software that allows you to analyse what subscribers do with your e-newsletter.
- Remember content is king online – and think what the user wants.
- Give a high priority to driving traffic to your website – learn about search engine optimisation.
- Consider using SNS to enhance the attendee experience during the event.
- Use links to other websites to enhance the visitor/attendees' experience.

Our last case study shows how a range of different Internet modalities can be used to complement one another, so that the whole is greater than the sum of the parts.

CASE STUDY 11.3

Integrated web communication

Yael Rose has been organising The Chocolate Festival (www.festivalchocolate.co.uk) since 2009. There are four open-air street events held each year in Brighton, Oxford, London and Bristol. There are two sister events, The Tea & Coffee Festival and The Cheese & Wine Festival held in central London.

The Internet is very important for the marketing of The Chocolate Festival in two key ways. First, the most popular way that attendees hear about the festivals is through online listing websites such as *Time Out*. The second most popular means of promotion is their own website, which is also a means of selling and where everyone gets information about the festival. Yael strongly suggests that you cannot have an event without having a website – a website is the business card of the twenty-first century.

The Chocolate Festival has a website, a weblog as part of the website, a Twitter account, Facebook page and posts visual content through Flickr and on YouTube. The weblog helps to show that the website is changing, and that there are things on it which are topical so that it is not a static site. Sometimes Yael tries to create a buzz, such as if there is any news, or when a competition was held to find Britain's Best Drinking Chocolate. Because the blog is part of the website rather than a discrete weblog site, it is not possible to quantify the effect of the weblog.

Twitter is a good way of getting the word out, but also of getting feedback, and there are over 3,000 following the Twitter account. Twitter appears more than Facebook to be about people and what they are doing. So it is easier to have a conversation, and often this leads to meeting people who are important for the business who otherwise Yael might not meet. A lot of people tweet to say that they will be coming, and they share this with their friends, so it acts like word of mouth.

Facebook is a means of gaining presence. It is not really used to generate a conversation because it seems less set up to encourage this than Twitter. Things that might be of interest are posted, such as videos. Quite a lot of people like the Facebook page. They used to use PINGG, but could not tell what effect it had, so stopped using it, though some bloggers have said they did not know when the festival was now on, so it may have had an effect. Normally people are invited to attend, and this might lead to 20–30 RSVPs out of 3,000 Friends. However, as this is a non-ticket open-air event it is impossible to know how many of these people attend, so it is difficult to measure the effect of Facebook on attendance.

While there are some people who visit the weblog and sign up for Twitter and Facebook, some of the names on Facebook and Twitter are different. It is likely that they are different sets of people, because people communicate differently, and so The Chocolate Festival can communicate through the online channel people prefer.

Although content on the blog is completely different, stories tend to go to both Twitter and Facebook. Though the Twitter account can be managed from a mobile phone, and so there are more tweets and you can re-tweet, if Facebook was accessed from a mobile phone there would be more posts on this. There is a clear connection between Twitter and Facebook, but Twitter is more likely to be used for business purposes to reach journalists and exhibitors, whereas Facebook is more likely to reach the public.

During the event itself, festival organisers try to encourage use of Twitter and Facebook to enhance the experience attendees have while at the festival. All the marketing material has the Twitter account and Facebook page address, exhibitors are encouraged to tweet and before scheduled events such as demonstrations the organisers might tweet half an hour before they start.

Discussion questions

The rapid adoption of the Internet raises some key issues for events:

1 If you consider the Internet to be either a revolutionary or evolutionary technology, how might this influence your approach to it?
2 On what basis will you choose which Internet modality you will select for your event?
3 Is a Web 1.0, Web 1.5 or Web 2.0 the most appropriate approach for events?
4 How would you develop a hybrid event?

Further information

Other sources which might help you consider the issues outlined in this chapter include:

Books

Scott, S. (2007) *The New Rules of Marketing and PR: How To Use News Releases, Blogs, Podcasting, Viral Marketing, & Online Media To Reach Buyers Directly*, New York, NY: John Wiley – addresses how to conduct online public relations.

Articles

Gonzalaz-Herrero, A. and Smith, S. (2008) 'Crisis Communications Management on the Web: How Internet-based Technologies Are Changing the Way Public Relations Professionals Handle Business Crises', *Journal of Contingencies and Crisis Communication*, 16 (3): 143–53 – addresses how to manage crises online.
Gregoire, K. (2012) 'Tweet Me, Friend Me, Make Me Buy', *Harvard Business Review*, 90 (7/8): 88–93 – looks at how SNS can be used as a sales tool.
O'Reilly, T. (2007) 'What is Web 2.0?: Design Patterns and Business Models for the Next

Generation of Software', *Communications and Strategies*, 1(1): 17–38 – the originator of the term Web 2.0 explains his thoughts.

Websites

http://www.socialnomics.net – site with lots of videos with statistics of online usage.
www.workcast.co.uk – agency that provides online events.
http://www.xtmotion.co.uk/ – web designers who specialise in producing event websites.
http://www.searchengineoptimising.com/seo-guide – advice on search engine optimisation.

Chapter 12

Conclusion

Introduction

The final chapter highlights some of the key ideas which have been covered throughout this book for improving event managers' understanding, and use, of marketing and public relations. The case studies have provided practical illustrations of the ideas and theories emphasised in the chapters. We start with a case study which pulls together some of the material we have covered across chapters. The rest of the chapter will consider five themes which run throughout the book, and will help you better promote your event.

Our final case study addresses how a non-profit organisation uses events within its communication function. It stresses the importance of relationship building, creating memorable experiences and shows how events are a key strategic tool designed to enhance an organisation's reputation.

CASE STUDY 12.1

Using marketing and public relations

The Hansard Society (www.hansardsociety.org.uk) is the UK's leading independent, non-partisan political research and education charity. It aims to strengthen parliamentary democracy, and encourage greater public involvement in politics. The society regularly holds a number of events to promote the discussion and debate of topics connected to its work. Very often these events are held within the Houses of Parliament, or other well known political buildings.

In terms of the Hansard Society's overall communication strategy its regular and one-off publications are the main way in which it engages with its audience. However, the society's events are very important both to launch and promote its one-off reports, and also to help build the Hansard Society's corporate reputation.

Typically events tie in with emerging issues within UK politics. For example, in February 2012 an event was held which looked at political lobbying, just as this had become a major issue following recent scandals.

Through its events the Hansard Society reaches different audiences within politics, and draws in speakers such as MPs and other high-profile people. Having an event with a high turnout, high-profile speakers and high-profile attendees shows that the Hansard Society is addressing key issues, and so enhances its reputation.

The society uses a range of tools to market its events, but the most successful are digital media. The society does not rely so much on formal channels such as advertising. The most effective is Twitter, with over 3,500 followers generating a huge amount of traffic, though it was only in 2011–12 that it had a real impact on marketing directly and promoting a dialogue. Luke Boga Mitchell, Coordinator Scholars, Communications & Events suggests that: *'The reason Twitter is so successful is because we can engage in conversation with everyone. For every event we speak to attendees and others before, during and afterwards through Twitter.'* The Hansard Society also encourages speakers, especially if they are well known, to tweet about the event, and many people find out about the events from the speakers, and then contact the Hansard Society to attend.

A regular e-newsletter is sent out promoting events, publications and other activities, and for events on large important issues they might email all MPs and peers. The Hansard Society also promotes its events on other sites that attract an audience of those interested in politics, such as www.4mp.org, which is for those who work for an MP.

All of the Hansard Society's events use online promotion, and the society is exploring other tools such as Google+.

The events tend to be part of a series, not one-offs, so there may be 2–3 over a two-year period on the same topic. As a result, the first event has to be a memorable experience, which enables the society to build relationships with those interested in this topic. Part of creating a memorable experience requires getting lots of people to attend the first event.

The Hansard Society uses media relations in the form of emailing press releases to a specific group of journalists interested in a set area. Events are not used specifically to increase membership or other aspects of the society, but every event is established to boost the overall reputation of the society. However, the wider reputational aspects are secondary: the main focus is on the content of the event. Get this right and everything else flows from it.

The centrality of the communication function

This book started with a discussion about different interpretations of the relationship between marketing and public relations. We conclude that viewing them as competitors or totally separate functions is not helpful: rather, a more appropriate attitude is to view an event's internal and external relations as part of an overall communications approach. Marketing and public relations are part of a wider whole. Figure 12.1 outlines an event communications model which essentially rejects the approach of Kotler and Mindak (1978), and as updated by Pickton and Broderick (2001). Their five models described the range of relationships to be found between marketing and public relations, although they did suggest that marketing would probably become dominant. I suggest a normative model where we do not think in divisive terms of marketing versus public relations, but rather focus on the wider picture, namely the communication function. We then look at the different tasks required to complete this, and just select the appropriate ones, irrespective of who performs them. So the emphasis is on the inherent functions of the communication function.

Communication is important to how events promote themselves to key audiences, but at the same time events can be used by others for communication purposes. Throughout this book, therefore, we have witnessed this duality to understanding marketing and public relations within events.

Textbooks traditionally start with the meaning of events and some typology for explaining the different types. I suggest that the communication needs of organisations and audiences can shape the nature of events delivered, and moreover that communication should be reflected in an events typology. Therefore, events are also assessed by why and how they communicate.

It may come as a surprise to some event managers, but they are all inherently and explicitly in the communication and persuasion business. Event organisers, and especially those responsible for marketing and public relations, need to reach and persuade them they want a range of internal and external audiences. Irrespective of who with and when an event manager is communicating, there are core lessons:

Communication functions

Promoting the event   Designing the event product

Reputation building   Income generation   Motivating staff

Crisis management   Supply chain management

Database management   Media relations

Communications training   Boundary spanning

Research   Environmental scanning   Leadership

Making decisions   Evaluation   Producing sales material

Building relationships   Managing online presence

Figure 12.1 The event communication model

Conclusion

1   *Use the full range of direction of communication available.* Too many event managers rely almost exclusively on top-down vertical communication. This may be appropriate in many circumstances, but certainly not all. The wise event manager introduces some form of bottom-up communication to get feedback from staff, consumers and others with an interest in the event. Moreover, do not focus just on vertical communication: horizontal communication, especially if facilitated by social media online, can encourage communication between audiences, leading to a greater sense of ownership of, and belonging to, an event.
2   *Think about the receiver of a message, too.* Many organisations are guilty of considering only what they want to say and get out of communication. However, a message is likely to be more effective if the sender considers what the receiver might also want to hear, and how they want to receive the message. This might not necessarily mean a fundamental change in the actual message (though it might): rather, it necessitates a clear recognition that the audience matters. Inherently, this makes it more likely to be persuasive.
3   *Select the correct channel to deliver the message.* Do not assume that all channels available to you are equal. As noted by Daft and Lengel (1986), depending on the circumstances, audiences and what information you have to convey, different channels will be more appropriate.

As an event communicator you want to persuade your audience. We covered in Chapter 2 a wide range of persuasion theory, which then shaped our later discussions on marketing and public relations. Whatever event function or task you are involved in, persuasion is maximised if:

1   *An audience's needs are assessed.* Those audiences who have an obvious interest in an event subject area are communicated to differently from those who are not. With the former we should focus on the detailed content of the event and topic/interest it is addressing; for the latter, heuristic shortcuts such as celebrity endorsement are used to encourage attendance.
2   *The construction of attitudes is understood.* Factors such as beliefs, values and social norms shape what we want and are able to do. It is worth remembering, however, that as Cialdini suggests, it is possible to address behaviour directly without having to shape attitudes first.
3   *Persuasive messages are constructed.* The two-millennium old orthodoxy of rhetoric is that persuasive communication is based upon three factors: source, message and receiver characteristics. The evidence, however, implies that for the vast majority of cases event persuasion is influenced most by choosing a credible source, and crafting the delivery and content of the message.

Combining the lessons of how to communicate and persuade we can construct a fairly simple step-by-step model (Figure 12.2), to help the event communicator be more effective. The first step is to conduct research to assess your key audiences. Are they likely to be interested in your event, or do they have a view (positive or negative) of you which will determine what in step two should be your decisions on what to communicate to them? This could be a rational content based argument, or a more emotional heuristic approach. This will then shape the final step of what is the precise mixture of channels you choose to deliver your message. This model hopefully provides a logical means of encouraging each audience to act in the desired way.

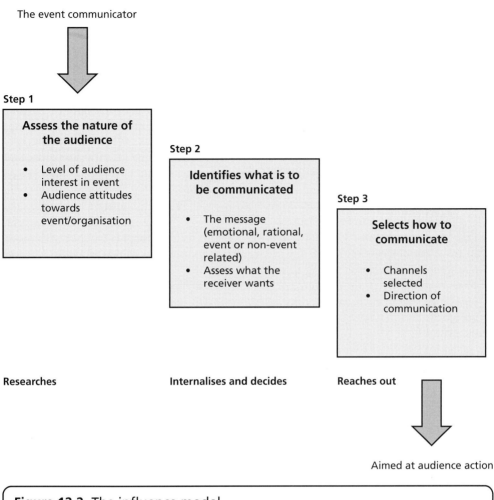

The event communicator

Step 1

Assess the nature of the audience

- Level of audience interest in event
- Audience attitudes towards event/organisation

Step 2

Identifies what is to be communicated

- The message (emotional, rational, event or non-event related)
- Assess what the receiver wants

Step 3

Selects how to communicate

- Channels selected
- Direction of communication

Researches   **Internalises and decides**   **Reaches out**

Aimed at audience action

Figure 12.2 The influence model

The growing importance of providing an experience

Four chapters of this book dealt with marketing and, although we covered a very broad range of activities and skills, you cannot be expected to master them all. Rather, as an event marketer your role is to manage the process, so you might be excellent with the databases that you handle personally, but 'buy in' from colleagues or external specialists market research expertise, media relations or whatever it is required. This means that you must have a basic breadth of marketing knowledge so you can manage those who deliver these functions for you, but you will also probably specialise in some narrow areas of marketing activity as well. The event communicator requires both some depth as well as breadth of knowledge.

Because the event marketer will be both doing and managing, it is important to remember the importance of marketing strategy. This might seem pretty obvious for a large well known event that is regularly repeated, but appears to be far less common for one-off or small events. Yet I would argue that it is important for all events to have a strategy, because at the very least it means that the reason and purpose of the event must be clear and justified.

We addressed a number of different ways of creating an event's strategy, and the simplest way of creating the strategy for your event is to ask five questions:

1   *Where are we?* This encourages the event manager to assess what lessons have been learnt from previous events, the strengths and weaknesses of your event(s)/organisation and what impact the wider environment might have.
2   *Where do we wish to go?* This encourages the event manager to identify clear goals and objectives of why they want to have an event. All events should have a clear rationale as this directs effort.
3   *Who are our key audiences?* Who do we need to reach in order to achieve our goals, such as staff, consumers and the media?
4   *How do we reach them?* This encourages the event marketer to identify the channels needed to reach the audiences, or what are often referred to as routes to market, such as direct marketing, media relations and meetings.
5   *How do you know if we have arrived?* Consistent to all approaches is the importance of measuring and evaluating how successful your event has been at reaching its aims and objectives.

The orthodoxy is that the consumer is the core concept for marketing, and the event marketer must understand the impact of the different types of consumer. However, event marketing raises three peculiarities unique to the industry:

1   For most marketers the concept of consumer is simple, those who buy or receive the product, but participants such as artistes and officials display consumer-like behaviour.
2   What the B2B and the B2C consumer want from events will normally be very different in terms of product and price, and how you will communicate with them may well be different, too. Many events will specialise in one or other audience and this will shape the nature of the event. However, in order to maximise their yield, many other events try to reach both audiences at the same event, so you may have at a sporting event executive boxes for the B2B market, and terraces or seats for the B2C market. This is a complication most other types of marketers are not faced with.
3   Not all consumers actually pay to attend the event: for example, a marathon, summer fair or public meeting.

One constant theme that this book has identified is the importance of collecting data. Although the promotional side of events may be the fun, exciting, high-profile aspect of the job, success is based upon making informed decisions. Collecting intelligence from consumers and others may appear a very dry function, but it is vital. The event marketer needs to create a means of accessing, analysing and applying feedback and information from appropriate internal and external sources.

We assessed three different marketing approaches: transactional; relationship; and experiential. All three can be applied by events marketers, though the first is most applicable to one-off events, and the latter two to events designed to be repeatable. As we assume that most event managers want repeatable events, the expectation is that event marketers will apply the relational and/or experiential approaches. An event which is promoting itself is likely to want to build up a relationship with suppliers, participants, sponsors, the media and attendees over a period of time. This is a logical and sensible approach common to many other products. Experiential marketing adds something new, and inherently event linked. Experiential marketing might be the way you promote your event – for example, a flash mob stunt might gain you attention. However, it represents a much more fundamental evolution in marketing. Experiential marketing has encouraged more marketers to use events to promote their products or enhance their corporate reputation. Experiential marketing, therefore, has changed the environment within which events, and event managers, exist.

Figure 12.3 suggests that an event experience is not suddenly created: rather, it is at the end of a process. The initial starting point is to work out what your role in event marketing will be: which activities will you run and which will you manage directly, outsource or delegate to others? The next two stages require us to understand what the consumer might want, by collecting data and then constructing messages and products which might meet their needs. The fourth stage is based upon you assessing what your objectives are. The final stage, then, often using some form of creative process such as brainstorming, tries to merge what you want to achieve with what consumers might want from a product or experience.

The event world view

The four chapters which dealt with public relations suggested that understanding the role and impact of public relations is based upon a different world view from marketing. A public relations practitioner who visits an organisation or event for the first time does not just consider the 'hard' aspects of the product, but also the 'soft' side: What does reception look like? What image is it presenting? When you telephone or look at the organisation/event website what does this tell you about them? In short, what would an outsider think of an organisation/event? Thus public relations is also concerned with the overall intended or unintended image and reputation. One important trick for the event communicator is to view the world not just through north–south visibility focusing on suppliers, artistes and attendees, but also east–west, considering

Figure 12.3 Developing the event experience

Conclusion

other audiences such as politicians, statutory authorities and pressure groups who might not attend your event but can have an impact on it.

Many event practitioners take too narrow a view of public relations. This book strongly suggests that the event communicator should apply the tactical use of public relations, namely MPR, but at the same time consider the more strategic application of CPR. We can simplify MPR as what you say, and CPR as what you do. MPR is therefore the application of techniques to get a message across. CPR is a longer game designed to shape key audiences' views of an event. Moreover, where MPR mostly targets consumers, CPR aims to reach not just consumers but also a wider range of audiences. If there is one single change in event communication I would hope this book encourages, it is that event managers should consider their long-term and wider reputation to be of equal importance to their short-term profile. For example, issues management opens up potential long-term advantages which MPR alone cannot provide.

Figure 12.4 suggests that at least two different routes are open to the event communicator for using public relations. There is the narrow route, when the prime use of public relations is to help the event communicator reach consumers who might attend their event. And there is the broad route. This differs because although it may reach consumers they are not the only audience targeted. Rather, other potential audiences such as funders, regulatory bodies and opinion formers are the target as well. Moreover, where the narrow route is marketing led, whose main purpose is to get people to attend (consumers, participants and staff), the broad route aims to provide a different function: that of changing people's view of the event, whether they attend or not. These two routes are not exclusive. An event could run them in parallel, but they would have fundamentally different though ideally complementary purposes.

Although this book promotes the importance of building reputation, we cannot ignore the centrality of media relations to promoting an event. Assuming you are going to use media relations, and this has resource implications for you, then the most essential lesson to learn is

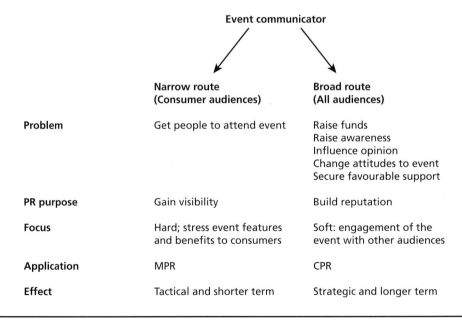

Figure 12.4 Event use of public relations

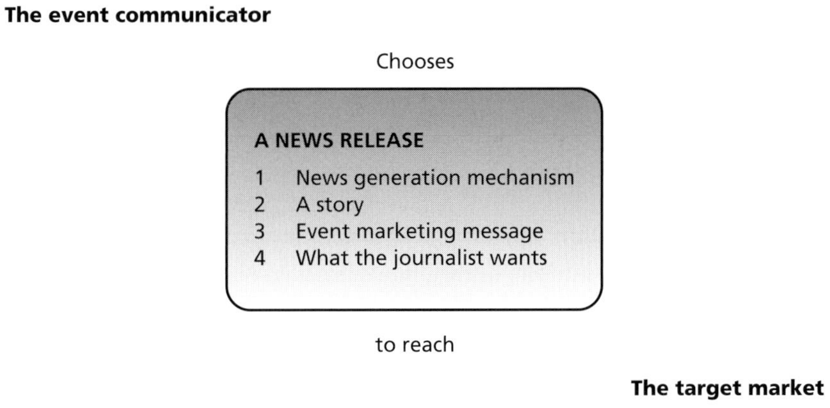

The event communicator

Chooses

A NEWS RELEASE

1   News generation mechanism
2   A story
3   Event marketing message
4   What the journalist wants

to reach

The target market

Figure 12.5 The media relations mix

that news is everything. Figure 12.5 shows how you can create a mechanism for selecting your media relations mix. You will need to develop internal systems for identifying what is news about your event, and then present this to journalists in the way they want it – that there is a story their viewers, listeners or readers will be interested in. Media relations is a two-step process. To get your marketing message across to your ultimate audience you need first to present it in a way that journalists want. The story comes first, and then you weave your marketing message into this. To be successful, news needs to be viewed from the journalist's perspective, and in this way you may construct a win-win situation for you and the journalist.

Much of our understanding of public relations theory is framed by Grunig and Hunt's four models of public relations: press agentry; public information; two-way asymmetrical communication; and two-way symmetrical communication. These models have elicited much comment, but for our purposes they provide a simple framework for understanding that one size does not fit all: that for different types of events different public relations styles are appropriate. We need to be very careful of press agentry because used improperly its unethical nature can affect event reputation, but for many entertainment, political and sporting based events the hype aspect of press agentry can be applicable. For events trying to change behaviour – for example, road shows that want people to think about social issues such as binge-drinking – the factual aspect of public information may well be applicable. Two-way communication is more relevant for events that wish to engage with audiences. The key question is whether such interaction should benefit only the event, or its key audiences as well. However, it would be too simplistic to suggest that these four models are exclusive: an event may apply a combination of these depending on the circumstances in which it finds itself.

We assessed three different schools of thought explaining public relations: Grunigian paradigm; persuasion; and relational. While these are not necessarily exclusive, we suggest that the Grunigian paradigm is more of a normative theoretical construct, that is an ideal to strive for rather than a description of event reality. Events exist within a competitive world – there may be direct competitors in our field or just other events on at the same time in different areas of interest. As a consequence the persuasion approach applies to nearly all events, for they want to get their voice heard in a crowded market place. The event communicator is, therefore, seeking to get across their message in the best possible light to get people to attend. The relational approach is also applicable for events, and provides a means of using CPR. It reminds us of the importance of targeting key individuals and groups, and how this can help shape the long-term reputation of an event. The event communicator can use different public relations approaches depending on the problems they face, and their event's objectives.

Online communication

A consistent theme from nearly all of those interviewed for case studies was the growing importance of online communication. In part, the Internet is seen as a sales tool, so that several of the interviewees have found the distribution of their events transformed by e-ticketing. Perhaps even more important has been the use of websites as a promotional tool, so that they contact attendees through media relations, direct mail and email and direct them to the websites, where up-to-date information is available. Because it is cost-efficient and effective, for many events their website is their 'go to' promotional channel. At the same time, event organisers have pointed to Web 2.0 tools such as Facebook and Twitter as means of reaching and conversing with key audiences. This suggests a dramatic and continued expansion in the use of the Internet by events organisers.

However, the content analysis of global event websites paints a slightly refined picture. The interviews highlighted what events thought they were doing online, but the content analysis analysed what they are actually using their websites for. The main difference between the perception and reality concerns interaction. This is a generalisation, but events are not necessarily using the Internet as a medium that encourages conversations as much as they could. Undoubtedly, many events have engaged online with potential and actual attendees, but this Web 2.0 use of the Internet is probably no more or less interactive than in other industries. Rather, as suggested by Jackson and Lilleker's (2009) model, events are likely conceptually to adopt a Web 1.5 approach. The interactive tools are present, but event web hosts are reticent in encouraging too much uncontrollable dialogue.

When considering promoting an event online there needs to be clarity on the meaning of the Internet. We identified eight different modalities, but the five events that are most likely to use are: websites; email; e-newsletters; microblogs; and social networking sites. Though I would suggest we can divide these into three different levels of use:

- *Primary tools* – websites, email, e-newsletters.
- *Secondary tools* – microblogs, social network sites.
- *Marginal* – intranets, extranets, weblogs.

This classification slightly contradicts the case studies, which would probably have Twitter and Facebook as primary tools, but probably reflects that not all are using them as coherent, integrated and strategic communication tools. It is likely that any new event would focus online on the primary and/or secondary tools, probably ignoring the marginal.

Each modality has different applications, and event communicators must know why and how to use them. I suggest that websites are good informational sources, typically fitting with a transactional marketing and persuasion public relations approach. Email and e-newsletters are likely to be most persuasive because they work over a period of time, and so fit with relationship marketing and both persuasion and relational public relations approaches. Microblogs and social networking sites are more likely to encourage conversations, and so also fit with relationship marketing and persuasion and relational public relations approaches. Event communicators need to 'pick 'n' mix' the correct online tools for each different task: one web technology does not address all communication issues.

We looked at how events used online marketing and public relations, and one area that elicited some interest was the idea of online events. However, it is highly unlikely that these will take off because of the importance of direct human contact that events inherently encourage. Rather, of more relevance for the event communicator is the idea of what event marketing agency George P. Johnson refers to as 'hybrid events', so that events use web technologies such as Twitter and Facebook to add value to the event experience. We should expect more and more events to use online channels as selling and promotional tools, but also to add value to the product during the event itself.

I would suggest that the Internet has had an evolutionary not a revolutionary effect. It enables event mangers to conduct the same functions as they do offline, but typically faster, cheaper and often better. The Internet has not replaced offline communications: rather, it supplements them, meaning that the event manager has the ability to get their message across to their target audience in more ways. Digital words complement offline word of mouth to reinforce messages. As a consequence online communication is in principle no different from offline, but does require different skillsets. The trick is getting the correct combination between the right Internet modality to reach the required audience for the appropriate communication task.

Identifying the problem

We have throughout this book introduced and assessed the detail of how to use marketing and public relations for communicating information about an event. This implies understanding and applying detailed knowledge and specific techniques. We will finish by considering the bigger picture in which both a single event or a series of events sits. One central theme of this book is that all events, irrespective of size or whether they are one-offs, should be considered as strategic tools. Throughout we have identified the duality of events, and this continues with the concept of strategy. At one level it is important to identify the strategy of the event itself, which at heart means asking what its purpose is and how you will deliver this. At the other level, strategy means using events to help organisations achieve their strategic goals. As we have noted, most but not all events apply the former, but only a limited though apparently growing number of events are used for the latter. We would, therefore, logically expect more events to be used as strategic tools in the future.

In order for an event to have its own strategy, or to be used as a strategic tool, we must be able to answer one simple question: What is the problem your event is a solution to? If your event is not helping to address a problem, why are you having the event? And if you cannot provide an event's rationale it is highly unlikely that you can 'sell' it to others. Providing an event because you feel like it, or copying others, is not a recipe for success. Many event organisers internalise the reason for why they organise an event, simply because they want to do it. But I would suggest that event organisers externalise the decision making process for having an event, implying from the outset that events are part of a wider communication process. So the starting point of any event planning process should be to identify the problem it is trying to address. This helps us identify a tangible reason for organising our event.

While a simple and perfectly acceptable problem for hosting an event is an entrepreneurial desire to make money, we often have to look elsewhere to explain an event's rationale. Table 12.1 highlights potential problems that events may attempt to answer. Political actors such as politicians, pressure groups and government bodies may want to change citizen behaviour, mobilise support or maintain the status quo. Economically events might be viewed as a means of generating new jobs or raising the profile of an area. Many events are designed to bring together local communities, where perhaps there has been a limited sense of belonging.

Table 12.1 Problems events can address	

Area	Typical problems
Political	To keep the political elite in power
	To replace the political elite
	How to shape the political agenda
	How to build support for reform
	How to diffuse political ideas
Economic	Generate revenue
	Create new employment
	Defend existing employment
	Recession
	Demographic change – new population centres
	Lack of product awareness
Social	Lack of sense of belonging/identity
	High crime levels
	Creation of new communities
	Cultural diversity
	Lack of social responsibility from organisations
Environmental	Unenvironmental consumer behaviour
	Lack of public awareness of environmental problems
	The development of environmental businesses
	How to implement environmental policy change

However, this does not undermine the fact that many event practitioners simply want to make money for themselves.

The event industry does not remain static. It is constantly evolving. Allied to recognising the problem an event is designed to address is the importance for the event manager of recognising new trends. The wise event manager looks to identify new and evolving markets for events. The source of such new markets is typically driven from the possible problems, so political, economic and social change can create new markets. Table 12.2 outlines some possible new markets where events could find a home, though obviously the nature of them will differ from region to region, country to country and location to location. The successful event manager should know why people want to attend their event, and what events they might want to attend in the near future.

And finally . . .

While we have clearly covered a lot of theory, this book has been designed to apply only relevant theory to events communication. Although, inevitably, many examples are weighted towards

Table 12.2 Possible new event markets

Markets	Types of event
Green/environmental	Food festivals
	How to be green
	How to run green events
	Alternative communities
	Barter based
Luxury	Glamping
	Luxury products
	Exclusive gatherings
Sporting	Televised professional sport
	Global sporting competitions
	Quirky cultural/minority sports
Personal milestone	Divorce parties
	Anti-ageing
	Escapism
	Eco-funerals
	School proms
	Significant birthdays
Political events	Conferences
	Rallies
	Protests
	Public meetings
	Election campaigns
Urban events	Farmers' markets
	Carnivals/street parties
Rural events	Farmers' markets
	Agricultural shows
	Country sports events
	Weddings in unusual locations
Charity	Fundraising
	Coming of age celebrations
Cultural/social	Concerts
	Fairs/fetes
Corporate	Award ceremonies
	Experiential
	Sponsored
	Socially responsible

the UK situation, the wider theories, principles and trends are applicable globally. Throughout we have kept returning to three ideas which help direct event managers:

- The importance of knowing who your audience is.
- Building relationships with key audiences.
- The need ultimately to persuade these audiences, either to attend your event or to improve their perception of your event's reputation.

What I have tried to do is not just explain what happens, but also to use theory to try to explain why something happens, as it is important for you to know how communication works. Consequently, irrespective of the tool used, I have stressed throughout the importance of using both rational and emotional messages.

There is a danger as an educator in primarily using only the big obvious examples, and while these clearly help our understanding of events communication, we should not ignore smaller, lesser known events. This book was largely written during 2012, when the biggest event to visit the UK was London 2012. It would be very easy to fill the book with examples from this and previous mega-events. There are indeed some examples, such as when we look at ambush marketing and sponsorship, because they are such significant illustrations. Although London 2012 will probably act as a short-term catalyst for the UK events industry, not least because it provided a training camp for event managers to gain experience, I have tried not to mention this event too much. The main reason being that for most individual event managers, and the industry as a whole, our prime concern is with the tens of thousands of events that take place in the office, on the street, fields, in shopping centres, and venues small and large. The most important trends and developments that will affect your future career will be influenced by the myriad everyday events, not a handful of marquee happenings.

My hope is that in addition to understanding individual components of how you can use communication, the rationale behind this book helps you view communication in a different way. In short, the whole (a communications approach) is greater than the sum of the individual parts (marketing and public relations).

Appendix

Table A.1 Website coding sheet

Feature	Present (y/n)
Contact details	
Search engine	
Enmeshing	
Interactive navigation aids (online help)	
Event details/programme	
Event history/narrative	
Virtual tour	
First timer's guide	
News page	
Testimonials	
E-ticketing	
Online product of event	
Online experience during event	
Webcam	
Video of previous event	
Pictures of previous event	
Merchandising/Shop	
Corporate hospitality available	
Volunteering opportunities	
Paid work opportunities	
Sponsor's details/logo	
Link to sponsor's website	
Weblog	

Appendix

E-newsletter	
Twitter/microblog	
Social network site (Facebook, etc.)	
Online forum	
Questionnaires/polls	
Flickr	
RSS feeds	
Videos uploaded	
Visitors can upload material (photos/videos)	
Visitors can share information/views	
Links to participants' websites	
Links to other events	
Links to organiser's other events	
Links to local accommodation/hospitality	
Information/links on local tourism	
Travel information	
Weather information/links	

Type of event

Bowdin ....

Getz ....

Jackson ....

Peak ☐   Off-peak ☐

Notes

Chapter 5

1 After an absence of a year the World Nettle Eating Championships returned to the Bottle Inn in 2012, though later in the year than previously. This implies that the product life-cycle does not always apply rigidly to events, as some may take a 'sabbatical', or are revised in some form or other.

Chapter 7

1 For a review of the literature on the history of public relations see Duffy, M. (2000) 'There's No Two-way Symmetric About It: A Post-modern Examination of Public Relations Textbooks', *Critical Studies in Media Communication*, 17(3): 294–315.

Chapter 11

1 The countries selected were: UK; Australia; Samoa; Egypt; Japan; South Korea; India; USA; France; Holland; Czech Republic; Croatia; South Africa.
2 The coding sheet was adapted from Gibson and Ward 2000; Jackson and Lilleker 2009; and Lilleker and Jackson 2011.

Bibliography

Addley, E. (2007) 'Middle-class, Middle-aged Glastonbury Plans New System to Woo Younger Fans', *Guardian*, 13 July. Online. Available HTPP: <http://www.guardian.co.uk/uk/2007/jul/13/musicnews.music> (accessed on 8 December 2011).

Agrusa, J., Maples, G., Kitterlin, M. and Tanner, J. (2008) 'Sensation Seeking, Culture and the Validation of Experiential Services', *Event Management: An International Journal*, 11 (3): 121–8.

Ajzen, I. (1985) *From Intentions to Action: A Theory of Planned Behaviour*, Heidelberg: Springer.

Allen, Johhny, O'Toole, W., McDonnell, I. and Harris, R. (2005) *Festival and Special Event Management*, Milton, Qld: John Wiley.

Allen, Judy (2004) *Marketing Your Event Planning Business: A Creative Approach to Gaining the Competitive Edge*, Mississauga, Ontario: John Wiley.

Allen, M. (1998) 'Comparing the Effectiveness of One and Two Sided Messages', *In* M. Allen and R. Preiss (eds) *Persuasion: Advances through Meta-analysis*, Cresskill, NJ: Hampton Press: 87–98.

Ansoff, I. (1965) *Corporate Strategy: An Analytic Approach to Business Policy for Growth and Expansion*, New York: McGraw-Hill.

Bailey, R. (2009) 'Media Relations', *In* R. Tench and L. Yeomans (eds) *Exploring Public Relations*, Harlow: Prentice Hall: 295–315.

Baines, P., Egan, J. and Jefkins, F. (2004) *Public Relations: Contemporary Issues and Techniques*, London: Elsevier.

Ball-Rokeach, S. and DeFleur, M. (1976) 'A Dependency Model or Mass-Media Effects', *Communication Research*, 3 (1): 3–21.

Barnes, S. (2001) *Online Connections: Internet Interpersonal Relationships*, Cresskill, NJ: Hampton Press.

Bartels, R. (1976) *The History of Marketing Thought*, Columbus, OH: Grid.

Baskin, O. and Aronoff, C. (1992) *Public Relations: The Profession and the Practice*, Dubuque, IA: W. Brown.

Beaven, Z. and Laws, C. (2007) 'Never Let Me Down Again: Loyal Customer Attitudes Towards Ticket Distribution Channels for Live Music Events: A Netnographic Exploration of the US Leg of the Depeche Mode 2005–6 World Tour', *Managing Leisure*, 12 (2–3): 120–42.

Bell, D. (1998) 'The Internet and the Trajectories of Technologies', *La Revue/The Tocqueville Review*, 19 (2): 111–25.

Benoit, W. and Benoit, P. (2008) *Persuasive Messages: The Process of Influence*, Oxford: Blackwell.

Berelson, B., Lazarsfeld, P. and McPhee, W. (1954) *Voting: A Study of Opinion Formation in a Presidential Campaign*, Chicago, IL: University of Chicago Press.

Bernays, E. (1923) *Crystallizing Public Opinion,* New York: Boni and Liveright.

Bernstein, D. (1984) *Company Image & Reality: A Critique of Corporate Communications,* Eastbourne: Holt, Rinehart & Winston.

Berry, L. (1983) 'Relationship Marketing', *In* L. Berry, G. Shostack, G. Upah (eds) *Perspectives on Services Marketing,* Chicago, IL: AMA: 25–8.

Bimber, B. (1998) 'The Internet and Political Transformation: Populism, Community and Accelerated Pluralism', *Polity* 31 (1): 133–60.

Bladen, C., Kennell, J., Abson, E. and Wilde, N. (2011) *Events Management: An Introduction,* London: Routledge.

Bland, M., Theaker, A. and Wragg, D. (2005) *Effective Media Relations: How to Get Results,* London: CIPR Kogan Page.

Blood, R. (2000) 'Activism and the Internet: From Email to New Political Movement', *Journal of Communication Management,* 5 (2): 160–9.

Blumler, J. and Katz, E. (1974) *The Uses of Mass Communication,* Beverly Hills, CA: Sage Publications.

Booms, B.H. and Bitner, M.J. (1981) 'Marketing Strategies and Organization Structures for Service Firms', *In* J. Donnelly, and W. George, (eds) *Marketing of Services,* Chicago, IL: American Marketing Association: 47–51.

Borden, N. (1964) 'The Concept of the Marketing Mix', *Journal of Advertising Research,* 4 (June): 2–7.

Borkowski, M. (2000) *Improperganda: The Art of the Publicity Stunt,* London: Vision On.

Bottomore, T. (1984) *The Frankfurt School,* London: Tavistock.

Bowdin, G., Allen, J., O'Toole, W., Harris, R. and McDonnell, I. (2010) *Events Management,* London: Butterworth Heinemann.

boyd, d. and Ellison, N. (2007) 'Social Network Sites: Definition, History and Scholarship', *Journal of Computer-Mediated Communication,* 13 (1). Online. Available HTTP: <http://jcmc.indiana.edu/vol13/issue1/boyd.ellison.html> (accessed on 25 April 2008).

Braggs, S. (2006) *Extraordinary Events: Attracting and Retaining Your Most Valuable Customers,* Tempe, NSW: Power Sponsorship Publishing.

Brannan, T. (1995) *A Practical Guide to Integrated Marketing Communications,* London: Kogan Page Limited.

Brassington, F. and Pettitt, S. (2005) *Essentials of Marketing,* Harlow: Prentice Hall.

Brennan, R., Baines, P. and Garneau, P. (2003) *Contemporary Strategic Marketing,* Basingstoke: Palgrave Macmillan.

Bridges, J. and Nelson, R. (2000) 'Issues Management: A Relational Approach' *In* J. Ledingham and S. Bruning (eds) *Public Relations as Relationship Management: A Relational Approach to the Study and Practice of Public Relations,* London: Lawrence Erlbaum.

Brock, T. and Green, M. (2005) 'Domains of Persuasion', *In* T. Brock and M. Green (eds) *Persuasion: Psychological Insights and Perspectives,* London: Sage: 1–16.

Bruning, S., Dials, M. and Shirka, A. (2008) 'Using Dialogue to Build Organisation–Public Relationships, Engage Publics and Positively Affect Organisational Outcomes', *Public Relations Review,* 34 (1): 25–31.

Callaghan, J. (2002) *Inside Intranets & Extranets: Knowledge Management and the Struggle for Power,* New York: Palgrave Macmillan.

Cameron, G. and Ju-Pak, H.-K. (2000) 'Information Pollution? Labelling and Format of Advertorials', *Newspaper Research Journal,* 21 (1): 65–77.

Carlsen, J. and Andersson, T. (2011) 'Strategic SWOT Analysis of Public, Private and Not-for-Profit Festival Organisations', *International Journal of Event and Festival Management,* 2 (1): 83–97.

Center, H. and Jackson, P. (2003) *Public Relations Practices: Managerial Case Studies and Problems*, Upper Saddle River, NJ: Prentice Hall.

Chaffee, E. (1985) 'Three Models of Strategy', *Academy of Management Review*, 10 (1): 89–98.

Chaffey, D. (2003) *Total Email Marketing*, Oxford: Butterworth Heinemann.

Chaiken, S. (1980) 'Heuristic versus Systematic Information Processing and the Use of Source versus Message Cues in Persuasion', *Journal of Personality and Social Psychology*, 39 (5): 752–66.

—— (1982) 'The Heuristic/Systemic Processing Distinction in Persuasion', Paper presented at the *Symposium on Automatic Processing, Society for Experimental Social Psychology*, Nashville, IN. October.

Chaiken, S., Wood, W. and Eagly, A. H. (1996) 'Principles of Persuasion', *In* E.T. Higgins and A. Kruglanski (eds) *Social Psychology: Handbook of Basic Mechanisms and Processes*, New York: Guilford Press: 211–38.

Chaston, I. (2004) *Small Business E-commerce Management*, Basingstoke: Palgrave Macmillan.

Chen, N. and Culbertson, H. (2003) 'Public Relations in Mainland China: An Adolescent with Growing Pains', *In* K. Sriramesh and D. Vecic (eds) *The Global Public Relations Handbook: Theory, Research and Practice*, Mahwah, NJ: Lawrence Erlbaum: 23–45.

Christopher, M., Payne, A. and Ballantyne, D. (2002) *Relationship Marketing: Creating Stakeholder Value*, Oxford: Butterworth Heinemann.

Cialdini, R. (2007) 'The Science of Persuasion', *Scientific American Mind* 14 (1): 1–9.

Cialdini, R. and Goldstein, N. (2002) 'The Science and Practice of Persuasion', *Cornell Hotel and Restaurant Administration Quarterly*, April: 40–50.

CIPR 'What Is Public Relations?'. Online. Available HTTP: <http://www.cipr.co.uk/content/training-qualifications/pr-student/careers-advice/what-is-public-relations> (accessed on 1 August 2011).

Clark, J. (2001) 'Deconstructing You've Got Blog', *Fawny.org*, 24 February. Online. Available HTTP: <http://www.fawny.org/decon-blog-PR.html> (accessed on 30 May 2012).

Collins Concise Dictionary: 21st Century Edition (2001), Glasgow: HarperCollins.

Coombs, W. T. (1999) 'Crisis Management: Advantages of a Relational Perspective', *In* J.A. Ledingham and S. D. Bruning (eds) *Relationship Management: A Relational Approach to the Study and Practice of Public Relations*, Mahwah, NJ: Lawrence Erlbaum: 75–93.

Coombs, W.T. and Holladay, S.J. (2001) 'An Extended Examination of the Crisis Situation: A Fusion of the Relational, Management and Symbolic Approaches', *Journal of Public Relations Research*, 13 (4): 321–40.

Cornelissen, J. (2008) *Corporate Communication: A Guide to Theory and Practice*, London: Sage.

Cox, G. (1999) *The Digital Crowd: Some Questions on Globalization and Agency*, Cambridge, MA: MIT Press.

Cravens, D.W., Ingram, T., LaForge, R. and Young, C. (1993) 'Behavior-Based and Outcome-Based Salesforce Control System', *Journal of Marketing*, 57 (October): 47–59.

Cravens, D. and Piercy, N. (2006) *Strategic Marketing*, International Edition, London: McGraw-Hill.

Crosby, P. (1984) *Quality Without Tears*, New York: New American Library.

Crowther, P. (2010) 'Strategic Application of Events', *International Journal of Hospitality Management*, 29 (2): 227–35.

Cunningham, G. B. and Kwon, H. (2003) 'The Theory of Planned Behaviour and Intentions to Attend a Sport Event', *Sport Management Review*, 6 (2): 127–45.

Cutlip, S., Center, M. and Broom, G. (2006) *Effective Public Relations*, Upper Saddle River, NJ: Pearson.

Daft, R. and Lengel, R. (1986) 'Organisational Information Requirements, Media Richness and Structural Design', *Management Science*, 32 (5): 554–70.

de Chernatony, L. and McDonald, M. (1992) *Creating Powerful Brands*, Oxford: Butterworth Heinemann.

De Mesa, A. (2006) 'Bad Behaviour: Losing in Sports Sponsorship', *Brand Channel*. Online. Available HTTP: <http://www.brandchannel.com/features_effect.asp?pf_id=330> (accessed on 25 April 2012).

De Pelsmacker, P., Geuens, M. and Van der Bergh, J. (2004) *Foundations of Marketing Communications: A European Perspective*, Harlow: Prentice Hall.

Devine, A., Bolan, P. and Devine, F. (2010) 'Online Destination Marketing: Maximising the Tourism Potential of a Sports Event', *International Journal of Sport Management and Marketing*, 7 (1–2): 58–75.

Dixon, D. (1979) 'Prejudice v. Marketing? An Examination of Some Historical Sources', *Akron Business and Economic Review*, 2 (Fall): 37–42.

Doorley, J. and Garcia, H. (2007) *Reputation Management: The Key to Successful Public Relations and Corporate Communication*, London: Routledge.

Downes, L. and Mui, C. (2000) *Unleashing the Killer App*, Boston, MA: Harvard University Press.

Doyle, P. (2000) *Value-based Marketing: Marketing Strategies for Corporate Growth and Shareholder Value*, Chichester: Wiley.

Dozier, D. M., Grunig, L. A. and Grunig, J. E. (1995) *Manager's Guide to Excellence in Public Relations and Communication Management*, Mahwah, NJ: Lawrence Erlbaum.

Drengner, J., Jahn, S. and Zanger, C. (2011) 'Measuring Event-Brand Congruence', *Event Management*, 15 (1): 25–36.

Edgett, S. and Cooper, R. (undated) 'New Product Institute'. Online. Available HTTP: <http://www.prod-dev.com/index.php> (accessed on 1 December 2011).

—— (2005) *Lean, Rapid and Profitable New Product Development*, Product Development Institute.

Edosomwan, J. (1993) *Customer and Market-Driven Quality Management*, Milwaukee, WI: ASQC Quality Press.

Egan, J. (2008) *Relationship Marketing: Exploring Relational Strategies in Marketing*, Essex: Pearson Education Ltd.

Ehrenberg, A. S. C. (1988) *Repeat Buying*, London: Charles Griffin.

Evans, M. (2010) 'World Cup 2010: Bavaria Beer Stunt Organisers Arrested', The Daily Telegraph, 16 June. Online. Available HTTP: <http://www.telegraph.co.uk/sport/football/competitions/world-cup-2010/7832413/World-Cup-2010-Bavaria-beer-stunt-organisers-arrested.html> (accessed on 11 January 2013).

Ewen, S. (1996) *PR! A Social History of Spin*, New York: Basic Books.

Ewles, L. and Simnett, I. (1985) *Promoting Health: A Practical Guide*, Chichester: Wiley.

experient (2008) *Using Relationship Management to Optimize Attendee Marketing and Grow Event Revenue*, Twinsburg, OH: experient.

Fashion United.com (2009) 'Fashion Houses Tempt Customers with Events', 2 April. Online. Available HTTP: <http://www.fashionunited.com/news/collumns/fashion-houses-tempt-customers-with-events-200907041709> (accessed on 23 November 2011).

Fawkes, J. (2008) 'What Is Public Relations?', *In* A. Theaker *The Public Relations Handbook*, London: Routledge: 3–17.

Feigenbaum, A. V. (1990) 'Management of Quality: The Key to the Nineties', *Journal for Quality and Participation*, 13 (2): 14–19.

Ferguson, D. and Perse, E. (2000) 'The World Wide Web as a Functional Alternative to Television', *Journal of Broadcasting and Electronic Media*, 44 (2): 155–74.

Ferguson, M. (1984) 'Building Theory in Public Relations: Inter-organizational Relationship', Paper presented to the *Association for Education in Journalism & Mass Communication*, Gainesville, FL. August.

Festinger, L. (1957) *A Theory of Cognitive Dissonance*, Evanston, IL: Row and Peterson.

Fill, C. (2009) *Marketing Communication: Engagement, Strategies and Practice*, Harlow: Prentice Hall.

Fishbein, M. and Ajzen, I. (1975) *Belief, Attitude, Intention and Behaviour: An Introduction to Theory and Research*, Reading, MA: Addison-Wesley.

Foley, M., McPherson, G. and McGillivary, D. (2009a) 'Establishing Singapore as the Events and Entertainment Capital of Asia: Strategic Brand Diversification', *In* J. Ali-Knight, M. Robertson, A. Fyall and A. Ladkin, (eds) *International Perspectives of Festivals and Events: Paradigms of Analysis*, London: Butterworth Heinemann: 53–64.

Foley, M., McGillivary, D. and McPherson, G. (2009b) 'Policy, Politics and Sustainable Events', *In* R. Raj and J. Musgrave (eds) *Event Management and Sustainability*, Wallingford: CABI: 13–21.

Fombrun, C. (1995) *Reputation: Realizing Value from the Corporate Image*, Boston, MA: Harvard Business School Press.

Fombrun, C. and Van Riel, C. (2004) *Fame and Fortune: How Successful Companies Build Winning Reputations*, Upper Saddle River, NJ: Pearson Education.

Formica, S. and Uysal, M. (1995) 'A Market Segmentation of Festival Visitors: Umbria Jazz Festival in Italy', *Festival Management and Event Tourism*, 3 (4): 175–88.

Fowler, A. (1996) *Negotiation Skills and Strategies*, London: IPD.

Fruin, J. (1984) 'Crowd Dynamics and Auditorium Management', *Auditorium News*, May. International Association of Auditorium Managers. Online. Available HTTP: <www.iaam.org/CVMS/IAAMCrowdDyn.doc> (accessed on 1 June 2012).

Gabbatt, A. (2011) 'Ladies' Day Fight Bruises Ascot's Exclusive Reputation', *Guardian*, 17 June, Online. Available HHTP: <http://www.guardian.co.uk/sport/2011/jun/17/ladies-day-fight-royal-ascot> (accessed on 15 September 2011).

Gabor, A. and Granger, C.W.J. (1961) 'On the Price Consciousness of Consumers', *Journal of the Royal Statistical Society, Series C (Applied Statistics)*, 10 (3): 170–88.

Genasi, C. (2002) *Winning Reputations*, Basingstoke: Palgrave.

Getz, D. (1997) *Event Management and Event Tourism*, Elmsford, New York: Cognizant Communication.

—— (2005) *Event Management and Event Tourism*, second edition, Elmsford, New York: Cognizant Communication.

—— (2008) *Event Studies: Theory, Research and Policy for Planned Events*, London: Butterworth Heinemann.

—— (2009) 'Festivals, Events and the Community: Today and Tomorrow', Paper to the *International Conference on Festivals & Events Research*, Orlando, USA. January.

Getz, D., Andersson, T. and Larson, M. (2007) 'Festival Stakeholder Roles: Concepts and Case Studies', *Event Management*, 10 (2/3): 103–22.

Gibson, R. and Ward, S. (2000) 'A Proposed Methodology for Studying the Function and Effectiveness of Party and Candidate Websites', *Social Science Computer Review*, 18(3): 301–19.

Goffman, E. (1959) *Presentation of Self in Everyday Life*, Garden City, New York: Doubleday Anchor.

Goldblatt, J. (2000) 'A Future for Events Management', Paper to Events Evaluation, Research and Education Conference, 13–14 July, Sydney.

Goldstein, N., Cialdini, R. and Griskevicius, V. (2008) 'A Room with a Viewpoint: Using Social

Norms to Motivate Environmental Conservation in Hotels', *Journal of Consumer Research* 35 (3): 472–82.

Gordon, A. (2011) *Public Relations*, Oxford: Oxford University Press.

Gotsi, M. and Wilson, A. (2001) 'Corporate Reputation: Seeking a Definition', *Corporate Communications: An International Journal*, 6 (1): 24–30.

Gray, E. and Balmer, J. (1998) 'Managing Corporate Image and Corporate Reputation', *Long Range Planning*, 31 (5): 695–702.

Greenspan, G. (1999) 'Harvard University Commencement Address', Cambridge, MA, 10 June 1999 cited *In* T. Hannington, (2004) *How to Measure and Manage Your Corporate Reputation*, Aldershot: Gower Publishing.

Grieco, M. and Holmes, L. (1999) 'Electronic Governance and Commercial Development in Africa: The Grassroots Perspective', Paper presented to the Institute for African Development, Cornell University, 2 September.

Griffin, A. (2008) *New Strategies for Reputation Management*, London: Kogan Page.

Gronroos, C. (1997) 'From Marketing Mix to Relationship Marketing – Towards a Paradigm Shift', *Management Decision*, 35 (4): 322–39.

Gronstedt, A. (1996) 'Integrated Communications at America's Leading Total Quality Management Corporations', *Public Relations Review*, 22 (1): 25–42.

Grunig, J. E. (1966) 'The Role of Information in Economic Decision Making', *Journalism Monographs*, 3: 1–55.

—— (1989) 'Publics, Audiences and Market Segments: Models of Receivers of Campaign Messages', *In* C. T. Salmon (ed.) *Information Campaigns: Managing the Process of Social Change*, Newbury Park, CA: Sage: 197–226.

—— (1992) 'Communication, Public Relations and Effective Organisations', *In* J. Grunig, (ed.) *Excellence in Public Relations*, Hillsdale, NJ: Lawrence Erlbaum: 1–28.

—— (2005) 'Situational Theory of Publics' *In* R. Heath (ed.) *Encyclopedia of Public Relations, vol. 2*, Thousand Oakes, CA: Sage: 778–80.

Grunig, J. and Grunig, L. (1992) 'Models of Public Relations and Communication', *In* J. Grunig, (ed.) *Excellence in Public Relations*, Hillsdale, NJ: Lawrence Erlbaum: 285–326.

—— (1998) 'The Relationship between Public Relations and Marketing in Excellent Organisations: Evidence from the IABC Study', *Journal of Marketing Communications*, 4 (3): 141–62.

Grunig, L. and Huang, Y. (2000) 'From Organizational Effectiveness to Relationship Indicators: Antecedents of Relationships, Public Relations Strategies and Relationship Outcomes Approach', *In* J. Ledingham and S. Bruning *Public Relations as Relationship Management: A Relational Approach to the Study and Practice of Public Relations*, London: Lawrence Erlbaum: 23–53.

Grunig, J. and Hunt, T. (1984) *Managing Public Relations*, New York: Holt, Rinehart and Winston.

Grunig, J. and Repper, F. (1992) 'Strategic Management, Publics and Issues', *In* J. Grunig (ed.) *Excellence in Public Relations*, Hillsdale, NJ: Lawrence Erlbaum: 117–57.

Grunig, L., Grunig, J. and Dozier, D. M. (2002) *Excellent Public Relations and Effective Organizations: A Study of Communication Management in Three Countries*, Mahwah, NJ: Lawrence Erlbaum.

Guardian (2008) 'The Cost of the Beijing Olympics', 28 July. Online. Available HTTP: <http://www.guardian.co.uk/sport/2008/jul/28/olympicgames2008.china1> (accessed on 1 December 2011).

Guo, Z., Siu, W., and Wong, C. (2002) 'Full-scale Online Event Ticketing System – The Design and Implementation', *Proceeding of the 13th Chinese Process Control Conference*, Macau and ZhuHai, China, 29 July – 2 August: 688–93.

Guth, D. and Marsh, C. (2006) *Public Relations: A Values-driven Approach*, London: Pearson.

Haig, M. (2001) *E-PR: The Essential Guide to Public Relations on the Internet*, London: Kogan Page.

Hall, C. (1997) *Hallmark Tourist Events: Impacts, Management and Planning*, Chichester: John Wiley.

Hall, M. and Rusher, K. (2006) 'Politics, Public Policy and the Destination', *In* I. Yeoman, M. Robertson, J. Ali-Knight, S. Drummond, and U. McMahon-Beattie *Festival and Events Management*, Oxford: Butterworth Heinemann: 217–31.

Hampshire Constabulary (2010) 'Hampshire Constabulary Responds Following Cancellation of Glade Festival', 14 May. Online. Available HTTP: <http://www.hampshire.police.uk/Internet/news/releases/Hampshire+Constabulary+responds+following+cancellation+of+Glade+Festival.htm> (accessed on 10 January 2012).

Harlow, R. (1976) 'Building a Public Relations Definition', *Public Relations Review*, 2 (44): 34–42.

Harris, T. (1993) *The Marketer's Guide to PR*, New York: John Wiley.

Harris, T. and Whalen, P. (2006) *The Marketer's Guide to Public Relations in the 21st Century*, Mason, OH: Thomson Higher Education.

Harrison, S. (2000) *Public Relations – An Introduction*, London: International Thomson Business Press.

Harrison-Hill, T. and Chalip, L. (2005) 'Marketing Sport Tourism: Creating Synergy Between Sport and Destination', *Sport in Society: Cultures, Commerce, Media, Politics*, 8 (2): 302–20.

Hartline, J., Maxham, G. and McKee, D. (2000) 'Corridors of Influence in the Dissemination of Customer Oriented Strategy to Customer Contact Service Employees', *Journal of Marketing*, 64 (April): 35–50.

Haywood, R. (1997) *All About Public Relations: How to Build Business Success on Good Communications*, London: McGraw-Hill.

Heath, R. (ed.) (2001) *Handbook of Public Relations*, Thousand Oaks, CA: Sage.

—— (2008) 'Rhetorical Theory, Public Relations and Meaning: Giving Voice to Ideas', *In* T. Hansen-Horn, and B. Neff, *Public Relations: From Theory to Practice*, London: Pearson: 208–26.

Heitzler, C., Asbury, L. and Kusner, S. (2008) 'Bringing "Play" to Life: The Use of Experiential Marketing in the VERB™Campaign', *American Journal of Preventative Medicine*, 34 (6): 188–93.

Higham, J. (1999) 'Commentary – Sport as an Avenue of Tourism Development: An Analysis of the Positive and Negative Impacts of Sports Tourism', *Current Issues in Tourism*, 2 (1): 82–90.

Hill, E. and O'Sullivan, T. (1999) *Marketing*, Harlow: Addison Wesley Longman Inc.

Hitchins, J. (2000) Making The News, unpublished MPhil thesis, Exeter University.

—— (2008) 'Media Relations', *In* A. Theaker *The Public Relations Handbook*, London: Routledge: 205–27.

Hoffman, D. and Novak, T. (1996) 'Marketing in Hypermedia Computer-Mediated Environments: Conceptual Foundations', *Journal of Marketing*, 60 (3): 50–68.

Holbrook, M. (1999) *Consumer Value: A Framework for Analysis and Research*, Routledge: London.

Hollander, S., Rassuli, M., Jones, D. and Dix, L. (2005) 'Periodization in Marketing History', *Journal of Macromarketing*, 25 (1): 32–41.

Holtgraves, T. and Lasky, B. (1999) 'Linguistic Power and Persuasion', *Journal of Language and Social Psychology*, 18 (2): 196–205.

Hoyle, L. (2002) *Events Marketing: How to Successfully Promote Events, Festivals, Conventions and Expositions,* New York: John Wiley.

—— (2012) *Events Marketing: How to Successfully Promote Events, Festivals, Conventions and Expositions,* second edition, New York: John Wiley.

Hughes, M. (2008) 'West Ham Lose £8 million Sponsorship Deal', *Independent,* 13 September 2008. Online. Available HTTP: <http://www.independent.co.uk/sport/football/news-and-comment/west-ham-lose-1638m-sponsorship-deal-928780.html> (accessed on 14 January 2012).

Hutton, J. (1999) 'The Definition, Dimensions and Domain of Public Relations', *Public Relations Review,* 25 (2): 199–214.

Hutton, J., Goodman, M. and Genest, C. (2001) 'Reputation Management: The New Face of Corporate Public Relations?', *Public Relations Review,* 27 (3): 247–261.

'IEG Global Sponsorship Expenditure Reports'. Online. Available HTPP: <www.sponsormap.com> (accessed on 24 April 2012).

Jackson, N. (2003) 'MPs and Web Technologies: An Untapped Opportunity?', *Journal of Public Affairs,* 3 (2): 124–37.

—— (2008a) 'MPs and their E-newsletters: Winning Votes by Promoting Constituency Service', *Journal of Legislative Studies,* 14 (4): 488–99.

—— (2008b) Online Political Communication: The Impact of the Internet on MPs 1994–2005, unpublished PhD thesis, University of Bournemouth.

—— (2009) 'All the Fun of the Seaside – The British Party Conference Season', *E.Pol,* 2 (1): 8–10.

—— (2010) 'Political Public Relations: Spin, Persuasion or Reputation Building?', Paper presented at the Political Studies Association annual conference, Edinburgh, April.

Jackson, N. and Lilleker, D. (2004) 'Just Public Relations or an Attempt at Interaction? British MPs in the Press, on the Web, and "In Your Face"', *European Journal of Communication,* 19 (4): 507–34.

—— (2009) 'Building an Architecture of Participation? Political Parties and Web 2.0 in Britain', *Journal of Information Technology and Politics,* 6 (3-4): 232–50.

Jacques, T. (2008) 'Howard Chase: The Man Who Invented Issues Management', *Journal of Communication Management,* 12 (4): 336–43.

James, M.G. (1991) *PRODUSER: PROcess for developing USER interfaces,* San Diego, CA: Academic Press Professional.

Java, A., Fini, I., Song, Y. and Tseng, B. (2007) 'Why We Twitter: Understanding Microblogging Usage and Communities', *WebKDD Workshop on SNA KDD:* 56–65.

Jefkins, F. (1982) *Public Relations Made Simple,* London: Heinemann.

Johnson, C. (2008) 'Decision 08: Event Marketing or Product Sampling', *Journal of Consumer Marketing,* 25 (5): 269–71.

George P. Johnson (2009) *Global Event Report.* Online. Available HTTP: <www.gpj.com> (accessed on 19 September 2011).

—— (2010a) *Event View 2010.* Online. Available HTTP: <www.gpj.com> (accessed on 19 September 2011).

—— (2010b) *Virtual Market Outlook Report.* Online. Available HTTP: <www.gpj.com> (accessed on 19 September 2011).

Johnson, G. and Scholes, K. (2002) *Exploring Corporate Strategy,* Harlow: Pearson Education.

Joice Heth Archive. (undated). Online. Available HTTP: <http://www.lostmuseum.cuny.edu/archives/joice.htm> (accessed on 23 August 2011).

Joinson, A. (2003) *Understanding the Psychology of Internet Behaviour: Virtual Worlds, Real Lives,* Basingstoke: Palgrave Macmillan.

Jones, B. and Chase, H. (1979) 'Managing Public Policy Issues', *Public Relations Review*, 5 (2): 3–20.

Jones, C. (2001) 'Mega-events and Host-region Impacts: Determining the True Worth of the 1999 Rugby World Cup', *International Journal of Tourism Research*, 3 (3): 241–51.

Jones, D. and Shaw, E. (2002) 'A History of Marketing Thought', *In* B. Weitz and R. Wensley *Handbook of Marketing*, London: Sage: 39–65.

Jones, J. P. (1997) 'Is Advertising Still Salesmanship?', *Journal of Advertising Research*, 37 (3): 9–15.

Jowett, G. and O'Donnell, V. (2006) *Propaganda and Persuasion*, Thousand Oaks, CA: Sage.

Juran, J. (1982) *Upper Management and Quality*, New York: Juran Institute.

Katz, E. (1987) 'Communication Research Since Lazarsfeld', *Public Opinion Quarterly*, 51 (2 Supplementary 50th Anniversary): 25–45.

Kelleher, T. (2007) *Public Relations Online: Lasting Concepts for Changing Media*, London: Sage.

Kennedy, G. (2003) *Perfect Negotiation: All You Need to Get It Right First Time*, London: Random House.

Kennedy, J.F. (1956) *Congressional Record*, March 2, 1956, 102: 38023.

King, C. (2005) 'Making the Case for an Entertainment Approach to Public Relations', *Public Relations Review*, 32 (1): 74–6.

King, J. (2012) 'Ernst and Young Survey Reveals Slight Reduction in Corporate Hospitality as a Result of the Bribery Act', *Event*. Online. Available HTTP: <http://www.eventmagazine.co.uk/news/bulletin/bulletintest2/article/1128194/?DCMP=EMC-CONEventnewsbulletin> (accessed on 23 April 2012).

Kitchen, P. (ed.) (1997) *Public Relations: Principles and Practice*, London: International Thomson Business Press.

Kitchen, P. and Papasolomou, I. (1997) 'The Emergence of Marketing', *In* P. Kitchen (ed.) *Public Relations: Principles and Practice*, London: International Thomson Business Press: 239–71.

Kitchen, P. and Schultz, D. (2009) 'IMC: New Horizon/False Dawn for a Marketplace in Turmoil?', *Journal of Marketing Communication*, 15 (2–3): 197–204.

Kitson, R. (2011) 'Rugby World Cup 2011: England's Manu Tuilagi Fined Over Mouthguard', *Guardian*, 4 October 2011. Online. Available HTTP: <http://www.guardian.co.uk/sport/2011/oct/04/rugby-world-cup-manu-tuilagi-mouthguard> (accessed on 25 April 2012).

Koh, K. and Jackson, A. (2006) 'Special Events Marketing: Analysis of a County Fair', *Journal of Convention and Event Tourism*, 8 (2): 10–44.

Korstanje, M. (2009) 'Reconsidering the Roots of Event Management: Leisure in Ancient Rome', *Event Management*, 13 (3): 197–203.

Kotler, P. (2005) *Principles of Marketing*, Harlow: Financial Times, Prentice Hall.

Kotler, P. and Keller, K. (2006) *Marketing Management*, Upper Saddle River, NJ: Pearson Prentice Hall.

Kotler, P. and Levy, S. (1969) 'Broadening the Concept of Marketing', *Journal of Marketing*, 33 (1): 10–15.

Kotler, P. and Mindak, W. (1978) 'Marketing and Public Relations: Should They Be Partners or Rivals?', *Journal of Marketing*, 42 (4): 13–20.

Kotler, P. and Singh, R. (1981) 'Marketing Warfare in the 1980s', *Journal of Business Strategy*, 1 (3): 30–41.

Kotler, P., Armstrong, G., Saunders, J. and Wong, V. (1999) *Principles of Marketing*, London: Prentice-Hall.

Kotler, P., Armstrong, G., Wong, V. and Saunders, J. (2008) 'Principles of Marketing', Harlow: Pearson.

Kronin, J. (undated) 'Crisis Management Plans for Youth Sporting Events', *National Centre for Sports Safety*. Online. Available HTTP: <http://www.sportssafety.org/articles/crisis-management-plan/> (accessed 1 May 2012).

Lakhani, D. (2005) *Persuasion: The Art of Getting What You Want*, Hoboken, NJ: John Wiley.

Lasswell, H. (1927) *Propaganda Technique in the World War*, New York: Knopf.

Lazarsfeld, P., Berelson, P. and Gaudet, H. (1944) *The People's Choice*, New York, NJ: Columbia University Press.

Lazer, W. (1964) 'Lifestyle Concepts and Marketing', *In* S. Greyser (ed.) *Toward Scientific Marketing*, Chicago, IL: American Marketing Association: 130–9.

Leary, M. and Kowalski, R. (1990) 'Impression Management: A Literature Review and Two-component Model', *Psychological Bulletin*, 107 (1): 34–47.

Ledingham, J. and Bruning, S. (1998) 'Relationship Management in Public Relations: Dimensions of an Organisation–Public Relationship', *Public Relations Review*, 24 (1): 55–65.

Lee, C.-K., Lee, Y.-K. and Wicks, B. (2004) 'Segmentation of Festival Motivation by Nationality and Satisfaction', *Tourism Management*, 25 (1): 61–70.

Leighton, D. (2007) 'Step Back in Time and Live the Legend: Experiential Marketing and the Heritage Sector', *International Journal of Nonprofit and Voluntary Sector Marketing*, 12 (May): 117–25.

L'Etang, J. (2008) *Public Relations: Concepts, Practice and Critique*, London: Sage.

Levinson, J. C. (1993) *Guerrilla Marketing Excellence: The Fifty Golden Rules for Business Success*, London: Piatkus.

Lewis, D. and Bridger, D. (2001) *The Soul of the New Consumer*, London: Nicholas Brealey.

Lewis, S. (2001) 'Measuring Corporate Reputation', *Corporate Communications: An International Journal*, 6 (1): 31–5.

Lilleker, D. and Jackson, N. (2011) *Campaigning, Elections and the Internet: US, UK, Germany and France*, London: Routledge.

Lim, W.M. and Jackson, N. (2009) 'The Drivers for Event Growth', *Plymouth Business School Seminar Series*, 4 November 2009.

Lindgreen, A., Palmer, R. and Vanhamme, J. (2004) 'Contemporary Marketing Practice: Theoretical Propositions and Practical Implications', *Marketing Intelligence and Planning*, 22 (6): 673–92.

Luo, X. (2002) 'Uses and Gratifications Theory and E-consumers' Behaviour: a Structural Equation Modelling Study', *Journal of Interactive Advertising*, 2 (2). Online. Available HTTP: <*http://www.jiad.org/vol2/no2/luo*> (accessed on 13 October 2004).

Machiavelli, N. (1505) *The Prince*, translated by George Bull (1975), Penguin Classics, London: Penguin.

Mackay, S. (2003) 'Changing Vistas in Public Relations', *PRism* 1 (1). Online. Available HTTP: <www.praxis.bond.edu.au/prism/papers/refereed/paper3.pdf> (accessed on 11 November 2011).

Malvern, P. (1985) *Persuaders: Influence Peddling, Lobbying, and Political Corruption in Canada*, Toronto: Methuen.

Market Research Society (2010) *Code of Conduct*, London.

Marr, A. (2004) *My Trade*, London: Macmillan.

Marra, F. (2000) 'Crisis Communication Plans: Poor Predictors of Excellent Crisis Public Relations', *Public Relations Review*, 24 (4): 451–74.

Masterman, G. and Wood, E. (2006) *Innovative Marketing Communications: Strategies for the Events Industry*, London: Butterworth Heinemann.

McCarthy, E.J. (1960) *Basic Marketing*, Homewood, IL: Irwin.

McCarthy, E.J. and Perreault, W.D. Jr (1987) *Basic Marketing*, Homewood, IL: Irwin.

McFedries, P. (2007) 'All A-Twitter', *IEEE Spectrum*, October p. 84.

McKenna, R. (1985) *The Regis Touch*, Reading, MA: Addison-Wesley.

McMillan, S. (2002) 'A Four-Part Model of Cyber-interactivity: Some Places Are More Interactive than Others', *New Media & Society*, 14 (2): 271–91.

Meenaghan, T. (1983) 'Commercial Sponsorship', *European Journal of Marketing*, 7 (7): 5–71.

—— (1998) 'Current Developments and Future Directions in Sponsorship', *International Journal of Advertising*, 17 (1): 3–28.

Messina, A. (2007) 'Public Relations, the Public Interest and Persuasion: An Ethical Approach', *Journal of Communication Management*, 11 (1): 29–52.

Mignerat, M. and Audebrand, L. (2010) 'Towards the Adoption of e-Refereeing and e-Ticketing in Elite Soccer Championships: An Institutional Perspective', *ICIS 2010 Proceedings*, paper 114.

Miller, D. (ed.) (2003) *Tell Me Lies: Propaganda and Media Distortion in the Attack on Iraq*, London: Pluto.

Miller, G. (1989) 'Persuasion and Public Relations: Two "Ps" in a Pod', *In* C. Botan, and W. Hazelton, (eds) *Public Relations Theory*, London: Lawrence Erlbaum: 45–66.

Mintzberg, H. (1994) *The Rise and Fall of Strategic Planning*, Englewood Cliffs, NJ: Prentice Hall.

Moloney, K. (2006) *Rethinking Public Relations*, Abingdon: Routledge.

Moor, E. (2003) 'Branded Spaces: The Scope of New Marketing', *Journal of Consumer Culture*, 3 (1): 39–60.

Morgan, R. and Hunt, S. (1994) 'The Commitment–Trust Theory of Relationship Marketing', *Journal of Marketing*, 58 (3): 20–38.

Morris, S. (2000) *Wired Words: Language is the New Identity*, London: FT.com.

Morris, T. and Goldsworthy, S. (2008) *PR-A Persuasive Industry? Spin, Public Relations and the Shaping of the Modern Media*, Basingstoke, Palgrave Macmillan.

Mutz, D. (2001) 'The Future of Political Communication Research: Reflections on the Occasion of Steve Chaffee's Retirement from Stanford University', *Political Communication*, 18 (2): 231–6.

Newsom, D., Turk, J. and Kruckeberg, D. (2000) *This Is PR: The Realities of Public Relations*, London: Thomson Learning.

Norris, P. (2000) *A Virtuous Circle: Political Communications in Post-Industrialised Societies*, Cambridge: Cambridge University Press.

—— (2001) *Digital Divide – Civic Engagement, Information Poverty and the Internet Worldwide*, Cambridge: Cambridge University Press.

Nzherald (2011) 'Hip-hop Group Canned from BDO over Homophobic Lyrics', *New Zealand Herald*, 4 November 2011. Online. Available HTTP: < http://www.nzherald.co.nz/entertainment/news/article.cfm?c_id = 1501119&objectid = 10763902 > (accessed on 30 April 2012).

O'Keefe, D. (2002) *Persuasion: Theory and Research*, London: Sage.

Oliver, S. (2007) *Public Relations Strategy*, London: Kogan Page.

Ollier, A. (1998) *The Webfactory Guide to Marketing on the Internet*, London: Aurelian.

O'Malley, L., Petterson, M. and Evans, M. (1999) *Exploring Direct Marketing*, London: International Thompson Business Press.

O'Reilly, T. (2005) 'What Is Web 2.0? Design Patterns and Business Models for the Next Generation of Software'. Online. Available HTTP: <www.oreillynet.com/pub/a/oreilly/tim/news/2005/09/30/what-is-web-20.html> (accessed on 2 March 2008).

Palmer, A. and Koenig-Lewis, N. (2009) 'Social Network-Based Approach to Direct Marketing', *Direct Marketing: An International Journal*, 3 (3): 162–76.

Papachrissi, Z. and Rubin, A. (2000) 'Predictors of Internet Use', *Journal of Broadcasting and Electronic Media*, 44 (2): 175–96.

Parasuraman, A., Zeithamel, V. and Berry, L. (1988) 'SERVQUAL: A Multiple Item Scale for Measuring Consumer Perceptions of Service Quality', *Journal of Retailing*, 64 (1): 12–20.

Parry, H. (2011) 'UK Bribery Act Guidelines: Has the Lobbying Worked?'. Online. Available HTTP: <http://blogs.reuters.com/financial-regulatory-forum/2011/04/05/column-uk-bribery-act-guidelines-has-the-lobbying-worked> (accessed on 5 March 2012).

Payne, W. (2009) 'Louder, Later and Longer Boasts Festival Organisers', *Hampshire Chronicle*. Online. Available HTTP: <http://www.hampshirechronicle.co.uk/news/442 1040._Louder_later_and_longer – boasts_festival_organisers/ > (accessed on 12 January 2011).

Paxman, J. (2002) *The Political Animal: An Anatomy*, London: Penguin.

Peach, L. (1987) 'Corporate Responsibility', *In* N. Hart (ed.) *Effective Corporate Relations*, London: McGraw-Hill: 191–204.

Peppers, D. and Rogers, M. (1993) *The One to One Future: Building Relationships One Customer at a Time*, New York: Doubleday Business.

Perloff, R. (2008) *The Dynamics of Persuasion: Communication and Attitudes in the 21st Century*, New York: Lawrence Erlbaum.

Petkus, E. (2004) 'Enhancing the Application of Experiential Marketing in the Arts', *International Journal of Nonprofit and Voluntary Sector Marketing*, 9 (1): 49–56.

Petty, R. and Cacioppo, J. (1986) 'The Elaboration Likelihood Model of Persuasion', *In* L. Berkowitz (ed.) *Advances in Experimental Social Psychology*, vol. 22, Orlando, FL: Academic: 123–205.

Phillips, D. and Young, P. (2009) *Online Public Relations: A Practical Guide to Developing an Online Strategy in the World of Social Media*, London: Kogan Page.

Pickton, D. and Broderick, A. (2001) *Integrated Marketing Communications*, Harlow: Prentice Hall.

Pine, B. and Gilmore, J. (1998) 'Welcome to the Experience Economy', *Harvard Business Review*, July–August: 97–105.

Porter, M. (1980) *Competitive Strategy: Techniques for Analysing Industries*, New York: Free Press.

Powell, J. (2011) 'Don't Let Corporate Treats Leave a Sour Taste in the Mouth', *Printweek* 12 August: 22–3.

Pugh, C. and Wood, E. (2004) 'The Strategic Use of Events Within Local Government: A Study of London Borough Councils', *Event Management*, 9 (1/2): 61–71.

Rafaeli, S. (1988) 'Interactivity: From New Media to Communication', *In* R. P. Hawkins, J. M. Wiemann, and S. Pingree, (eds) *Sage Annual Review of Communication Research: Advancing Communication Science* vol. 16, Beverly Hills, CA: Sage: 110–34.

Rafiq, M. and Ahmed, P. (1995) 'Using the 7Ps as Generic Marketing Mix: An Exploratory Survey of UK and European Marketing Academics', *Marketing Intelligence and Planning*, 13 (9): 4–15.

Raj, R., Walters, P. and Rashid, T. (2009) *Events Management: An Integrated and Practical Approach*, London: Sage.

Rao, K. (2011) 'Players Can Be Thrown Out of WC for Ambush Marketing: ICC', *The Times of India*, 4 February 2011. Online. Available HTTP: <http://timesofindia.indiatimes.com/sports/cricket/news/Players-can-be-thrown-out-of-WC-for-ambush-marketing-ICC/articleshow/7425182.cms> (accessed 25 April 2012).

Rao, S. and Perry, C. (2002) 'Thinking About Relationship Marketing: Where Are We Now?' *Journal of Business and Industrial Marketing*, 17 (7): 598–614.

Regester, M. and Larkin, J. (2008) *Risk Issues and Crisis Management in Public Relations: A Casebook of Best Practice*, London: Kogan Page.

Reichheld, F. and Sasser, W. (1990) 'Zero Defects: Quantity Comes to Service', *Harvard Business Review*, 66 (5): 105–11.

Reid, S. (2011) 'Event Stakeholder Management Developing Sustainable Rural Event Practices', *International Journal of Event and Festival Management*, 2 (1): 20–36.

Rheingold, H. (1993) *The Virtual Community: Homesteading on the Electronic Frontier*, Reading, MA: Addison-Wesley.

RIAS (2011) 'RIAS Launches Its 2011 Events Programme with New "Insurance Hub"', 18 March 2011. Online. Available HTTP: <http://www.rias.co.uk/media_centre/allpress releases/rias_launches_2011_events_programme_214 > (accessed 6 June 2012).

Ries, A. and Ries, L. (2002) *The Fall of Advertising and the Rise of PR*, New York: Harper Business.

Ries, A. and Trout, J. (1982) *Positioning: The Battle for Your Mind*, New York: McGraw-Hill.
—— (1986) *Marketing Warfare*, New York: McGraw-Hill.

Rinallo, D., Borghini, S. and Golfetto, F. (2010) 'Exploring Visitor Experiences at Trade Shows', *Journal of Business and Industrial Marketing*, 25 (4): 249–58.

Robbins, S. and Coulter, M. (2009) *Management*, Upper Saddle River, NJ: Pearson Prentice Hall.

Robinson, A. (2002) Examining Advertorials: An Application of the Elaboration Likelihood Model, Unpublished thesis, Lincoln University, Auckland, New Zealand.

Robinson, J. (1976) 'Interpersonal Influence in Election Campaigns: Two Step-flow Hypotheses', *Public Opinion Quarterly*, 40 (3): 304–19.

Rogers, E. (1962) *Diffusion of Innovations*, New York: Free Press.

Rogers, T. (2006) *Conferences and Conventions: A Global Industry*, Oxford: Butterworth Heinemann.

Ruler, B. and Vercic, D. (2005) 'Reflective Communication Management: Future Ways for Public Relations Research', *In* P. Kalbfreisch, (ed.) *Communication Yearbook 29*, Mahwah, NJ: Lawrence Erlbaum: 239–73.

Russell, S. (2007) 'Experiential Joins the Marketing Party', *B &T Weekly*, 57 (2604): 8.

Sadow, J. and James, K. (2000) 'A Theory of Internet Political Campaigning: A Revolution That Isn't, Yet', Paper delivered to the Southwest Political Studies Association, Galveston: Texas, March.

Saget, A. (2006) *The Event Marketing Handbook*, Chicago, IL: Dearborn Trade.

Sale, C. (2011) One Last Scandal as England Head Home with Moody Facing Fine over Branded Mouthguard, *Daily Mail*, 11 October 2011. Online. Available HTTP: <http://www. dailymail.co.uk/sport/rugbyunion/article-2047331/RUGBY-WORLD-CUP-2011-Lewis-Moody-faces-mouthguard-probe.html>(accessed on 15 November 2012).

Schmitt, B. (1999) 'Experiential Marketing', *Journal of Marketing Management*, 15 (1): 53–67.

Schramm, W. (1954) 'How Communication Works', *In* W. Schramm (ed.) *The Process and Effects of Mass Communication*, Urbana, IL: University of Illinois Press: 3–26.

Schwaiger, M., Sarstedt, M. and Taylor, C. (2010) 'Art for the Sake of the Corporation: Audi, BMW Group, DaimlerChrysler, Montblanc, Siemens, and Volkswagen Help Explore the Effect of Sponsorship on Corporate Reputations', *Journal of Advertising Research*, 50 (1): 77–90.

Seltzer, T. and Mitrook, M. (2007) 'The Dialogic Potential of Weblogs in Relationship Building', *Public Relations Review*, 33 (2): 227–9.

Shannon, C. and Weaver, W. (1948) (eds) *The Mathematical Theory of Communication*, Urbana, IL: University of Illinois.

Shaw, E. (1979) 'Agenda Setting and Mass Communication Theory', *International Communication Gazette*, 25 (2): 96–105.

Sheth, J. and Parvatiyar, A. (1995) 'The Evolution of Relationship Marketing', *Business Review*, 4 (4): 397–418.

—— (2000) *The Handbook of Relationship Marketing*, Thousand Oaks, CA: Sage.

Shimp, T. (1993) *Promotion Management and Marketing Communications*, Philadelphia, PA: Harcourt Brace.

—— (2000) *Advertising Promotion: Supplemental Aspects of Integrated Marketing Communications*, Fort Worth, TX: Dryden Press.

—— (2010) 'Advertising Promotion, and Other Aspects of Integrated Marketing Communications', Mason, OH: South-Western Cengage Learning.

Sibun, J. (2011) 'Luminar To Go Into Administration', *Daily Telegraph*, 26 October 2011. Online. Available HTTP: <http://www.telegraph.co.uk/finance/newsbysector/retailandconsumer/8851474/Luminar-to-go-into-adminstration.html > (accessed on 15 November 2012).

Silvers, J. (2008) *Risk Management for Meetings and Events*, London: Butterworth Heinemann.

Simons, H. (2001) *Persuasion in Society*, London: Sage.

Skerlos, K. and Blythe, J. (2000), 'Ignoring the Audience: Exhibitors and Visitors at a Greek Trade Fair', *Proceedings of the Fifth Annual Conference on Corporate and Marketing Communication*, Erasmus University, Rotterdam, 22–3 May.

Slack, N. and Lewis, M. (2008) *Operations Strategy*, Harlow: Pearson Education.

Smith, S. and Shaffer, D. (1995) 'Speed of Speech and Persuasion: Evidence for Multiple Effects', *Personality and Social Psychology Bulletin*, 21 (10): 1051–60.

Sneath, J., Finney, Z. and Close, A. (2005) 'An IMC Approach to Event Marketing: The Effects of Sponsorship and Experience on Customer Attitudes', *Journal of Advertising Research*, 45 (4): 373–81.

Soloman, S., Marshall, G., Stuart, E., Barnes, B. and Mitchell, V. (2009) *Marketing: Real People, Real Decisions*, Harlow: Pearson.

Springston, J., Keyton, J., Leichty, G. and Metzger, J. (1992) 'Field Dynamics and Public Relations Theory: Toward the Management of Multiple Publics', *Journal of Public Relations Research*, 4 (2): 81–100.

Stiff, J. and Mongeau, P. (2003) *Persuasive Communication*, New York: Guildford Press.

Strinati, D. (2004) *An Introduction to Theories of Popular Cultures*, London: Routledge.

Stromer-Galley, J. (2004) 'Interactivity-as-Product and Interactivity-as-Process', *The Information Society*, 20 (5): 391–4.

Sun Tzu (2010) *The Art of War*, translated by L. Giles, Shelbyville, KY: Wasteland Press.

Swedberg, C. (2011) 'New York City Marathon Offers Enhanced RFID-enabled Apps', *RFID Journal*, 25 July 2011. Online. Available HTTP: <http://www.rfidjournal.com/article/view/8626 > (accessed on 15 November 2012).

Taylor, C. (2009) 'Hugo Boss Pulls Ambush Marketing Stunt on TV Networks', *CBS News*, 19 July 2009. Online. Available HTTP: <http://www.cbsnews.com/8301–505123_162–43743819/hugo-boss-pulls-ambush-marketing-stunt-on-tv-networks/ > (accessed on 24 April 2012).

Taylor, M. (2004) 'Media Richness Theory as a Foundation for Public Relations in Croatia', *Public Relations Review*, 30 (2): 145–60.

Taylor, M., Kent, M. and White, W. (2001) 'How Activist Organisations Are Using the Internet to Build Relationships', *Public Relations Review*, 27 (3): 263–84.

Thaler, R. and Sunstein, C. (2008) *Nudge: Improving Decisions about Health, Wealth and Happiness*, London: Penguin.

The Guardian (undated) 'London 2012 Olympic Sponsors List: Who Are They and What Have

They Paid?', *The Guardian*, Online. Available HTTP: <http://www.guardian.co.uk/sport/datablog/2012/jul/19/london-2012-olympic-sponsors-list>.

Theaker, A. (2008) 'Consumer Public Relations', *In* A. Theaker, *The Public Relations Handbook*, London: Routledge: 304–22.

Tichenor, P., Donohue, G. and Olein, C. (1970) 'Mass Media Flow and Differential Growth in Knowledge', *Public Opinion Quarterly*, 34 (2): 159–70.

Toffler, A. (1990) *Future Shock*, New York: Bantam.

Tsaur, S.-H., Chiu, Yi-Ti, Wang, C.-H. (2006) 'The Visitors Behavioural Consequences of Experiential Marketing: An Empirical Study of Taipei Zoo', *Journal of Travel and Tourism Marketing*, 2 (1): 47–62.

Unt, I. (1999) *Negotiations Without a Loser*, Copenhagen: Copenhagen Business School Press.

Van der Wagen, L. (2007) *Human Resource Management for Events: Managing the Event Workforce*, London: Butterworth Heinemann.

Varey, R. (2002) *Marketing Communication: Principles and Practice*, London: Routledge.

Veblen, T. B. (1899) *The Theory of the Leisure Class: An Economic Study of Institutions*, London: Macmillan.

Von Neumann, J. and Morgenstern, O. (1944) *Theory of Games and Economic Behavior*, Princeton, NJ: Princeton University Press.

Walliser, B. (2003) 'An International Review of Sponsorship Research: Extension and Update', *International Journal of Advertising*, 22 (1): 5–40.

Walsh, K. (1994) 'Marketing and Public Sector Management', *European Journal of Marketing*, 28 (3): 63–71.

Wang, F., Head, M. and Archer, N. (2000) 'A Relationship-building Model for the Web Retail Marketplace', *Internet Research: Electronic Networking Applications and Policy*, 10 (5): 374–84.

Ward, S. (2001) 'Political Organisations and the Internet: Towards a Theoretical Framework for Analysis', Paper delivered to ECPR, Grenoble 6–11 April.

Webster, F. (1992) 'The Changing Role of Marketing in the Corporation', *Journal of Marketing*, 56 (4): 1–17.

Weinstock, J. (2001) 'Mars Attacks! Wells, Welles and Radio Panic: Or the Story of the Century', *In* R. Browne and A. Neal (eds) *Ordinary Reactions to Extraordinary Events*, Bowling Green, OH: Bowling Green State University Popular Press: 210–21.

Wenn, S. and Martyn, S. (2006) 'Tough Love: Richard Pound, David D'Alessandro and the Salt Lake City Olympics Bid Scandal', *Sport in History*, 26 (1): 64–90.

Westen, D. (2007) *The Political Brain: The Role of Emotion in Deciding the Fate of the Nation* New York: Public Affairs.

Whalen, D. (1996) *I See What You Mean: Persuasive Business Communication*, London: Sage.

White, J. and Mazur, L. (1995) *Strategic Communications Management: Making Public Relations Work*, Harlow: Addison-Wesley.

Wightman, B. (1999) 'Integrated Communications', *Public Relations Quarterly*, 44 (2):18–22.

Williams, A. and Wells, J. (2004) 'The Role of Enforcement Programs in Increasing Seat Belt Use', *Journal of Safety Research*, 35 (2): 175–80.

Wood, E. (undated) *Event Marketing SIG*. Online. Available HTTP: <http://www.academyofmarketing.org/index.php?option=com_content&view = article&id = 125&Itemid = 92> (accessed on 10 December 2010).

—— (2009) 'Evaluating Event Marketing: Experience or Outcome?', *Journal of Promotion Management*, 15 (1–2): 247–68.

Yeoman, I., Robertson, M., Ali-Knight, J., Drummond, S. and McMahon-Beattie, U. (2006) *Festival and Events Management: An International Arts and Culture Perspective*, London: Butterworth Heinemann.

Index